D1833210

EIGHTEEN YEARS IN THE KHYBER

1879-1898

EIGHTEEN YEARS IN THE KHYBER

1879-1898

SIR ROBERT WARBURTON, K.C.I.E., C.S.I.

GYAN

Published by

GYAN

Gyan Publishing House
5, Ansari Road
Daryaganj, New Delhi-110002
Phone: 011-47034999, 9811692060
E-mail: books@gyanbooks.com

Distribution Network
gyanbooks.com
India, USA, Canada, UK, Australia, France

ISBN: 978-81-212-9324-2 (PB)
First Published, 1900

2nd Impression 2023

Printed at: Gyan Press, Delhi.

EIGHTEEN YEARS IN THE KHYBER 1879-1898

Author: SIR ROBERT WARBURTON

EIGHTEEN YEARS IN THE KHYBER

1879–1898

THIS BOOK IS

DEDICATED

BY SPECIAL PERMISSION

TO HIS ROYAL HIGHNESS

THE PRINCE OF WALES

Colonel Sir Robert Warburton, K.C.I.E., C.S.I.

EIGHTEEN YEARS IN THE KHYBER

1879–1898

BY COLONEL

SIR ROBERT WARBURTON, K.C.I.E., C.S.I.

WITH PORTRAITS, MAP, AND ILLUSTRATIONS

LONDON

JOHN MURRAY, ALBEMARLE STREET

1900

TO THE READER

Before even the manuscript of these pages could be made ready for press by the Author, the pen dropped for ever from the wearied hand which held it. Marvellous mental activity and a firm, powerful will had helped to sustain the well-knit but slender frame of Robert Warburton through nearly thirty-seven years of Indian service, the latter half of which was passed in the almost daily worry, care, and anxiety inseparable from the guardianship of the important post which had been intrusted to his charge—that of the famous and once-dreaded Khyber Pass. How well he fulfilled that trust is on official record, and will have its lasting place in the history of British rule in India. These pages give in his own simple language the modest story during years of lonely exile, of duty done under many difficulties, and often under many depressing influences. Sir Robert Warburton never thought of writing a book until the idea was aroused in his mind by a kindly hint given by His Royal Highness the Prince of Wales, who has graciously permitted this volume to be dedicated to himself. The work was then commenced with SIR ROBERT'S characteristic energy of will; but the insidious disease from which at times he had suffered in India, and which became intensified during the trying marches and labours of the Tirah campaign, had already begun its fatal inroads, and the end quickly came. Returning from the East in full hope of future employment, either in England or, as he would have preferred it, on the Frontier again, amongst the wild tribesmen who obeyed and loved him, he came home only to die.

His sad, untimely fate has brought to his widow many friends, whom she would desire to thank here for their expressions of condolence and their kindly efforts to lighten the burden of her sorrow: above all, she would humbly express her gratitude to that August Lady in whose service her husband died, the QUEEN-EMPRESS OF INDIA, who, from her own widowed heart, sent words of tenderest sympathy to hers.

INTRODUCTORY

This work is presented as the Author wrote it, retaining his own method of arrangement as regards the Chapters and the spelling of Oriental names of men and places. If the personal element has been kept much in the background and little beyond records of public or official incidents are given of the lonely and trying life led by him amongst the wild men of the Frontier, the explanation is that Sir Robert Warburton did not wish to write merely his 'reminiscences' but of his practical work as Warden of the Khyber for nearly eighteen years. He desired to give an account of that Stewardship. Before he was appointed to its charge, the Khyber Pass was the most dangerous place on the N.W. Frontier of India—dreaded by even Afghan traders and closed to all others. The state of the relations between the Government of India and the trans-frontier tribes was described in April 1877, in a Minute by Lord Lytton, then Viceroy and Governor-General, to the Secretary of State for India, as follows: 'I believe that our North-Western Frontier presents at this moment a spectacle unique in the world; at least I know of no other spot where, after twenty-five years of peaceful occupation, a great civilised Power has obtained so little influence over its semi-savage neighbours, and acquired so little knowledge of them that the country within a day's ride of its most important garrison (Peshawar) is an absolute *terra incognita* and that there is absolutely no security for British life a mile or two beyond our border.' From the date of his first appointment on the Frontier, Colonel Warburton set himself to remedy this state of things, and during the whole period of his control of the Khyber, that dreaded Pass was kept open for traffic or travel without a single European soldier or Sepoy being stationed in it beyond Jamrud, and, when he gave over charge, it was as safe a highway as any in India.

The causes which brought about the tribal rising in August 1897 and necessitated the Tirah campaign need not be referred to here beyond mentioning that it was Colonel Warburton's firm belief that no attack on the posts of the Khyber would have been successful had his services been utilised at once, immediately after he had expressed to the Government his readiness to return to duty in reply to the official telegram, to which he refers in his chapter on 'The Khyber *Débâcle*' as having been received and answered by him on August 13, 1897. He had in the month of June previous written to one of the Secretaries of Government, that a strong wave of Mahommedan fanaticism was passing over the Frontier, and he was informed in reply that 'our political success in the Malakhand, in Swat, and Dir has broken the back of Mullah fanaticism for ever'! Nevertheless, when the storm burst in August, and he was ready and most anxious to return to the Khyber to stay the evil Mullah influence which he knew would be exerted there, his services were not called for until ten days after he had tendered the offer of them. It was then too late. On August 23 the Khyber posts were attacked and taken—a day not inaptly described as one of 'shame and humiliation' for the British authorities. How bitterly the old Warden of the Khyber felt that blow may be gathered from an extract from a private letter which he then wrote to a friend in England:

'My mind is very heavy over this hideous disaster, which I feel could have been staved off even up to the day of mischief. It makes me quite sad to think how easily the labour of years—of a lifetime—can be ruined and destroyed in a few days.'

The hard work of the Tirah campaign which followed, the exposure and fatigue, coupled with unceasing attacks of dysentery, may be said to have undermined his bodily strength and finally to have caused his death—but the loss of the Khyber, after his faithful guardianship of so many years, preyed most heavily upon his mind.

It is no exaggeration to say that it broke his heart.

CONTENTS

CHAPTER IX

H.H. ABDUR RAHMAN KHAN

1885

CHAPTER X

IN THE KHYBER

1886–1888

CHAPTER XI

THE TOUR OF THE KHYBER MALIKS AND THE BLACK MOUNTAIN CAMPAIGN

1888

CHAPTER XII

THE SHILMAN ROUTE

1889

CHAPTER XIII

THE VISIT OF PRINCE ALBERT VICTOR

1890

CHAPTER XIV

THE CAUBUL RIVER SURVEY

1890-1891

CHAPTER XV

AMIN KHAN'S RISING

1892

CHAPTER XVI

ON LEAVE IN INDIA

1893-1894

CHAPTER XVII

FINAL YEARS IN THE KHYBER

1895-1897

CHAPTER XVIII

THE KHYBER DÉBÂCLE

1897

CHAPTER XIX

FRONTIER POLICY

1898

CHAPTER XX

THE TRIBES OF THE KHYBER

ILLUSTRATIONS

MAP

EIGHTEEN YEARS IN THE KHYBER

CHAPTER I

MY FATHER

1830–1863

Before going into any details of my own experiences, a brief sketch of my father's military career and its vicissitudes may not be uninteresting to the reader nor out of place here.

He was one of a family of eleven sons and four daughters, whose father, Richard Warburton, of Garryhinch, near Portarlington, was an easy-going man who permitted his boys to have rather a free hand on the paternal estate. At all events, if a strict supervision was kept over the elders, some of the younger ones managed to do much as they pleased. Of these, my father, Robert, who was the ninth son, and his brother Arthur, who was the tenth, being near to one another in age, took full advantage of the liberty allowed to them, and, according to home traditions told to me, were comrades in many mischievous pranks encouraged by the tenantry, amongst whom they used to live for days together, going from house to house, where they were always welcomed because 'full of frolic and devilry.'

After a time, however, Mr. Richard Warburton bethought himself of the necessity of some education for his children, and took his family to the south of France, placing my father and his brother at the College of Angers. Here both boys succeeded in acquiring a complete command of the French language, and they remained perfect masters of that tongue during their lifetime. But their early training, or want of it rather, and their wild Irish natures made them a terror to the French students, and much of a trouble to the kind, homely pastors and tutors who had to look after their intellectual and moral training.

Getting a nomination to Addiscombe, my father, after a course of two years' study there, was appointed to the Bengal Artillery in 1830. In those days a voyage to India was not a light undertaking, and the vessel in which my father set sail occupied 143 days on the passage from London to Calcutta.

The Bengal Artillery headquarters were then located at Dum-Dum, and my father remained there for a considerable time. But having left no record of his private life, and all his associates of those early days having long ago passed away, I know nothing of his life for several years except that he passed the Interpreter's test in Hindustani, which secured for him one or two officiating appointments and gave him an increase of pay.

When the army of the Indus was formed in 1839 for the purpose of placing Shah Shujah-ul-Mulk on the throne of Afghanistan, my father was attached to the artillery of the Shah's contingent, and took part in all the operations of the campaign, including the storming of Ghuzni, for which he received the medal and clasp.

After the evacuation of Afghanistan on the close

of the campaign, only the troops which were thought sufficient to support Shah Shujah's cause were left in that country. My father remained in charge of the Shah's artillery, and was constantly engaged with his guns in fighting rebels and keeping order in the Kohistan and other hill tracts. But all was apparently peaceful at Caubul, where the wives of the English officers and soldiers remaining in Afghanistan had arrived to join their husbands.

In November 1840 my father fell in love with and married a noble Afghan lady, a niece of the Amir Dost Muhammad, the witnesses to the marriage ceremony being Sir A. Burnes, Colonels Sturt and Jenkins. The marriage certificate containing their signatures, and which is in my possession now, is a curious document.

Matters continued seemingly quiet at Caubul, and Shah Shujah firmly placed, until September 1841, when disquieting rumours of plots and disaffection began to be circulated. Muhammad Akbar Khan, Amin-ulla Khan, Abd-ulla Khan, and other Afghan chiefs were then in fact preparing their countrymen for the outburst of that storm which in the end destroyed 4,500 of our fighting men and 12,000 followers between Caubul and Futtehabad, leaving only one solitary Englishman—Dr. Brydon—to escape to tell the story to the beleaguered garrison of Jelallabad.

On September 28 Colonel Oliver, commanding the 5th N.I., was sent with a large force from Caubul into Turmat to punish a robber chief named Akram Khan. My father with his guns accompanied this force. Akram Khan was secured and executed. But troubles breaking out in the vicinity of the capital,

Colonel Oliver and his troops were hastily recalled by Sir W. Macnaghten; and in reality it was time for them to be back to Caubul, where events were ripening with the greatest celerity. On the night of November 1, 1841, a respectable Afghan named Tàj Muhammad went in person to the house of Sir Alexander Burnes, who was living in the city of Caubul, and warned him that insurrection was about to break out; but his report was not credited, and the man went away hurt and disgusted. The next day what was considered incredible really happened. About three hundred men attacked the dwellings of Sir A. Burnes, of Captain Johnson, paymaster to the Shah's force, of Captain Troup, and the residence occupied by my father. Finding Sir A. Burnes unwilling to fire on the mob when they first appeared on the scene, the numbers soon increased and their violence also. Sir A. Burnes, his brother, Lieutenant Burnes, of the Bombay army, Lieutenant William Broadfoot, of the Bengal European Regiment, with all their escort, and every man, woman, and child found on the premises were massacred. Rs. 170,000 of the public money were plundered, and the houses mentioned were burnt to the ground. Captains Johnson and Troup, and my father happened to be in Cantonments on the morning of this insurrection, and lost everything; my mother escaped, and took refuge with her friends and people.

The story of that disastrous time need not be more than referred to here. Before General Elphinstone and his army of 4,500 soldiers and 12,000 camp followers were permitted by the Afghan chiefs to leave Cantonments, and proceed from Caubul towards Jelallabad, six hostages had to be delivered over to the Afghan Sardars for the fulfilment of certain pledges on the part of the English officials. These hostages were Captains Airey, Conolly, Drummond, Walsh, Webb, and my father.

My father's house was burnt down on November 2, 1841, and my mother had to take refuge with her friends and relations. For months the troopers of Sardar Muhammad Akbar Khan followed in pursuit of her. They searched houses and quarters where she was supposed to be sheltered, thrusting in all directions with their lances and swords, trying to find out her hiding-place. She had often to run away from one house thus treated to take shelter in another, but a merciful Providence assisted the young wife in escaping from all these dangers. If the pursuit was strong, and the animosity of Akbar Khan great, that Providence produced friends who helped and sheltered her through all her trials and vicissitudes, ranging from November 2, 1841, to September 20, 1842, when she was at length able to join her husband, with her son, myself, born in a Ghilzai fort between Jagdallak and Gandamak on July 11, 1842. Few wives and mothers have ever experienced such a terrible eleven months of dangers and sufferings.

1850–1863

On returning to India after the close of the first Afghan war my father's battery was stationed at Sipri, where he was joined by my mother with her infant son—myself. I was too young to retain any recollections of Sipri, except of two episodes: one of my being nearly killed by a fall from my pony—a scar three-quarters of an inch in length over my left eye still marks the result of that day's ride; and the other of my setting fire to our bungalow by discharging a miniature brass gun which had been presented to my father, after the battle of Maharajpore, by his old friend and brother officer the late Sir Vincent Eyre. A bit of lighted charcoal used for firing this toy weapon was blown upon the dry thatched roof, which immediately burst into flame, and in spite of all endeavours to extinguish the fire the house was burned down and hardly anything saved.

From Sipri the battery was moved to Morar (Gwalior), and there I made the acquaintance of several officers of the Bengal Artillery, only one of whom is now alive—the gallant, honoured, and popular Sir William Olpherts, V.C.

My playmates at Gwalior were the Hennessys, whose father commanded a regiment of the Contingent. The sons have all turned out splendid soldiers. One of them—George—commanded the 15th Sikhs during the Afghan war of 1878–80, and was their chief at McNeill's zareba. He is still hale and hearty, and quite fit to command a brigade or a division in any campaign.

In 1850 my father, after a great deal of opposition on my mother's part, placed me at a school at Mussoorie, which school had just been started by the Rev. Robert North Maddock, an excellent classic and a strict disciplinarian. Such a school was then greatly wanted in the Hills, and many officers gladly availed themselves of it and sent their sons to be trained under Maddock. His method of enforcing discipline was a very practical one. Near the schoolhouse there grew clumps of fine thin young bamboos, called by the natives *ringalls*, and these when properly trimmed and shortened made most excellent and flexible rattans, which when laid on a boy's person with judgment and strength (and Maddock possessed both) created a sensible impression. Our worthy master considered that a moral impression was further produced by sending out the offender, knife in hand, to cut and bring in the sample for his own flagellation. I had an experience of seven years of dear old Maddock and his impressive *ringalls*, but I can look back with affection and respect upon his memory. He was returning to England, after many years of hard and patient school work at Mussoorie, when an attack of smallpox brought his useful life to an end.

From Gwalior my father was ordered to Amritsar, to take command of a native field battery. The Panjab had been lately annexed, and it was considered desirable to locate a garrison at Amritsar. In those days 'John Company' pitched upon a cantonment, fixed its garrison, but the officers had to build their own habitations. Our house at Amritsar had just been finished at a great expense, and a large-sized garden well laid out, when an order came for the battery to march to Nussirabad. My father, who had then spent twenty-six years' continuous service in the East without a single day's leave to Europe, resolved to apply for two years' furlough and to take me with him to England to complete my education. On December 1, 1856, I bade adieu to the Rev. R. N. Maddock and his school at 'Grant Lodge,' Mussoorie, and was taken by my faithful old bearer to Ludianah to await my father's arrival after he had delivered over his battery at Nussirabad.

Ludianah was the locality where the sons of Shah Shujah-ul-Mulk, ex-Amir of Afghanistan, whose artillery contingent my father had been attached to, had taken shelter after their retreat from Caubul, subsequent to the disasters of the Afghan war of 1839–42. Whatever may have been their public failings I was not old enough to judge in those days, but the kindness of some of them to me, carried over a series of years, was always of the same uniform character. I was not debarred from going inside their *haram-serais*, and my knowledge of the Persian spoken by the Saddozai and Barakzai rulers of Afghanistan permitted me to converse with the wives of all the Shahzadas with the greatest ease and fluency. There were two brothers, Shahzada Shàhpùr and Shahzada Nadir, the youngest sons of the unfortunate Shah Shujah-ul-Mulk, who particularly took my fancy. For resignation in the midst of their troubles, for gentleness to all who were brought in contact with them, and for a lofty regard for the feelings and wishes of others, I have seldom seen finer types of the true gentleman than those two brothers. The elder was in receipt of a pension of Rs. 500 and the younger of Rs. 100 a month from the Indian Government—small sums, indeed, with which to bring up their families and support the number of ancient servitors who had been driven out of house and home at Caubul and had followed the fortunes of this royal family into the heat and plains of India.

At Agra I bade farewell to my mother and all our old retainers, and proceeded with my father in a *dâk-gharry* to Calcutta, making a halt for a couple of days at Cawnpore. There we were sheltered and entertained by Major Larkins, of the Bengal Artillery, who had his wife and two of his little girls, aged six and four, with him. My father took me to call on Sir Hugh Wheeler, commanding the station, and who was an old friend of his. Five of Sir Hugh's sons had been with me at school at Mussoorie, and Miss Wheeler, who was with her father at Cawnpore, asked me many questions about her brothers, whilst Sir Hugh was telling my father of the reasons which had induced him to give up half his furlough and return from England to India. It was then the beginning of April 1857. As we listened or conversed during that mid-day visit, we little dreamt of what was so soon to happen at Cawnpore—that we were never to see our friends, our host and hostess, and their little children again. But no one then had the least suspicion of danger, or idea of the plot which was then being hatched by the Nana and his fiendish associates, and which in a few short weeks was to bring massacre and catastrophe to all of English blood within the doomed cantonment.

Arriving at Calcutta, my father and I embarked on April 23, 1857, on board of the P. & O. steamer *Bengal*, one of the newest of that company's vessels. The journey overland was uneventful, and no rumours of the approaching storm of mutiny in the Bengal army were about. At Southampton I was asked by a gentleman who came on board, and who was scanning the faces of all the passengers, if Captain Warburton was amongst them, and, if so, would I point him out. I did so. The gentleman was my uncle Arthur, my father's favourite brother and companion in those early escapades which were the terror and sorrow of the French pastors and tutors. They now met after a separation of twenty-seven years, and were unable to recognise each other!

Within a few days after our arrival in London I was sent to the Kensington Grammar School, then under the care and charge of the Rev. G. Frost. At that time Kensington Grammar School bore a great and wide reputation amongst parents in India. It had a special class for the sons of civilians and military officers, offering a sound and technical education very suitable for the wants of both services in the country under the control of 'John Company Bahadur.' It had a splendid mathematician in the Rev. G. Frost. It had produced some fine scholars, including the gallant and brave Quintin Battye, whose young life was brought to a glorious close in the charge of the Guides before Delhi. 'Dulce et decorum est pro patria mori' has ever been the motto of the Battye family. There was a good healthy tone about the boys, who were fond of all manly sports. One of the directors of the school was Sir Henry Willock, also a director of the East India Company, who every year generously gave a cadetship to be competed for, with the object, no doubt, of making the school more attractive. Before my father returned to India, at the beginning of the year 1860, he had the satisfaction of knowing that his son had managed to secure the very last of these Willock cadetships. But, being an old Artilleryman, he was most anxious that I should join the same service as himself, and two months after my first success I tried my luck at the open competition for the R.A. and R.E. for India. My first venture was a failure in both events, in this wise: I failed to secure the proper number of marks in French for the R.A. and R.E., and Professor Cape, who had given me full marks for my mathematics at the Willock competition at Kensington, plucked me for a very easy bit in Latin when I appeared before him at Addiscombe. However, in the second attempt I was successful in both issues, but was not permitted to give away the Willock cadetship, which lapsed and was of no earthly use to anyone.

After one term at Addiscombe and two at the Royal Military Academy, Woolwich, I received my commission in the Royal Regiment of Artillery on December 18, 1861; and after five months' duty at Sheerness, three weeks of which were spent at the Armstrong gunnery course, Shoeburyness, I received orders to sail with drafts for the East Indies. My new commander was Captain Sir William Hamilton, Bart., of the late Bengal Artillery, and the first subaltern Lieutenant Mackie, just three years senior to me. There were about 150 men and three officers. We were embarked at Gravesend, on board the sailing ship *St. Lawrence*, a very fine vessel, commanded by one of the best men of the day, Commander Joseph Toynbee. In due time we anchored in Table Bay, and saw the sad havoc caused by a sou'-wester which had wrecked several large ships on the treacherous shore a short time before our arrival. Within two days we ourselves were driven out by a sou'-easter, and for the next forty-eight hours had to brave the fury of an exceedingly severe hurricane, but the *St. Lawrence* being a new vessel, with one of the most skilful of captains and a good set of officers, we were soon all right. Within 93 days of our departure from Gravesend our vessel anchored in the Hughli, facing the Eden Gardens.

My detachment was destined for the Panjab, and moving by rail and road and river I at length found myself at Amritsar, where my father was commanding, and where also, after a separation of six years, I met my mother again. I had to march my men on to Mian Mir, but, thanks to Colonel Moir, of the Royal Artillery, I was there relieved and posted to the 1st Battery 24th Brigade, stationed at Fort Govindghur, the fortress of Amritsar, getting permission at the same time to reside with my father.

My father had changed much in appearance since he had left England at the commencement of 1860. A severe illness of a painful nature had worried him for two years or more, but so reticent was he regarding all personal matters that he had never breathed a word of this in any of his letters to me. I was his only son and yet I never heard from his lips a single anecdote of his early life. The march from Ferozepore to Candahar; the assault and capture of Ghuzni; the numerous fights in the Kohistan in which he was engaged; the burning of his house and the loss of his property at Caubul; his offer of himself as a hostage in Afghanistan; the dangers which he incurred during his captivity from December 28, 1841, to September 20, 1842, when his life was hardly worth a moment's purchase; the tribulations which his young wife went through; his share in the battle of Maharajpore—of all these matters which I was so anxious to learn about he never would touch upon a single one. He never verbally complained of any man or of any circumstance. The only complaint ever made by him was a written one discovered after his death, in which he grieved that his pay during the season of his captivity had been detained for two years. Many friends whom he had assisted with loans of money, even when he was a lieutenant, testified to the help they had received, but my father's lips were as sealed on this topic as on everything connected with his life. He never made an enemy. It was hard to believe that this was the same man who as a boy had kept the holy fathers at the college of Angers 'on the hop' for several years.

A change which my father disliked came within two and a half months of our meeting. He was ordered off to command the 19th Brigade R.A., whose headquarters were at Peshawar, inclusive of the command of the R.A. in the Peshawar Division. He had no wish to approach Afghanistan again, but he never breathed a word of this to the authorities or to me. He went to Peshawar and day by day his health became weaker, yet in his letters no mention was made of the change. On November 11, 1863, two telegrams were placed in my hands at the same moment in Fort Govindghur. The first, despatched forty-eight hours in advance of the second, warned me to hasten up to Peshawar, as my father was dangerously ill. The second stated that there was no need to hurry, as all was over. The second was opened first.

CHAPTER II

ABYSSINIA—PANJAB

1863–1870

My father died on November 10, 1863, aged only fifty-one years. In his usual taciturn way he had kept even the fact of his marriage concealed from all his family at home, and, for some reasons of his own, he had declined to join the Indian Pension Funds. Possibly, he thought that his duty was to provide for his widow from his own purse, and being a man of saving habits, and well paid in his younger days for the various appointments held by him, he had left sufficient money invested in cantonment house property and in shares of a flourishing bank in India to secure in rents and dividends an income of about 1,500*l.* a year for my mother—the result of the patient economy of twenty-seven years of isolation and of thirty years of service in India. Being one of the executors to his will, I forwarded all his papers in connection with investments, and his marriage certificate, to the other executor, my uncle Arthur, and everything was soon adjusted by the lawyers in Calcutta and London.

In August 1864 I exchanged into F Battery, 19th Brigade R.A., then commanded by Major David Newall, and stationed at Mian Mir. June and July 1865 I spent at Simla, and life for me went on pleasantly and smoothly for nearly another year. The winter had passed, and the hot weather of 1866 was just setting in when I, with many others throughout India, was overwhelmed by a terrible calamity. The Agra and Masterman's Bank, in which all my father's money had been invested in shares, suspended payment. A few months previously the station of Amritsar had been broken up as a military cantonment, and our houses there were lying tenantless. The provision made for my mother was all gone! A lieutenant of four and a half years' service in the Artillery—my pay of Rs. 296 and a few annas per month was all I had on which to support my mother and myself and maintain us in separate establishments. Further, during the time of our affluence I had proposed to, and had been accepted by, a young lady in England, who knew nothing of my means, but who refused to throw me over now when she learnt that I was 'exceeding poor.' Luckily, just before the suspension of the bank I had drawn out 3,000 rupees, which would last my mother for some time, and all my ingenuity was taxed to make those 3,000 rupees go as far as possible. But it was manifestly impossible for me to remain any longer in the Royal Regiment of Artillery, and the only other service open to me was that of the Bengal Staff Corps. My first application for transfer was not successful—why, I know not; but in the second I was more fortunate. I then asked to be appointed to the Panjab Commission, a request which the Lieutenant-Governor, whose private secretary was a Gunner and friend of mine, kindly promised to support. With a joyous heart I journeyed down to Fort William, Calcutta, to pass the examination in Hindustani, which I did in my first attempt. I then studied for three months for the High Proficiency in Urdú, but before the examination came off I was posted to the 21st Panjab Infantry, then under orders for the Abyssinian campaign.

It was a great pleasure to me to find myself posted to so fine a regiment; besides, all the officers were known to me, and several were friends of mine, as we had been stationed together for some time at Mian Mir. At Calcutta the headquarters and four companies were embarked on the *Bengal*, the same P. and O. steamer which had taken my father and myself from Calcutta to Suez in April 1857, two companies were allotted to a smaller steamer, and two companies to the old sailing vessel *Alabama*. I went with these last, leaving our moorings at Calcutta in tow of the *Bengal*, on Christmas Day, 1867. Zoula was reached on January 27, but it was not until February 1 that we were safely landed and encamped with the rest of the regiment.

My first duty at Zoula was in connection with the water supply. We had to depend entirely upon the condensed water sent on shore from the different steamers, as not a drop of fresh water was obtainable from the land side for many a mile. I was put in charge of troughs from which the transport animals were daily watered, and I had to stand from 8 A.M. to 6 P.M. at this work, which was not a little trying with a burning sun overhead and neither seat nor shelter available. The tricks of the natives to obtain water for the purpose of merchandise were many and amusing. A Somali would come with the animals and, placing his mouth in the trough, would drink like one of them. If not carefully watched he would produce a large leather water bottle, which he would rapidly fill and then disappear with his loot. Reaching camp he would dispose of this for 8 annas, or a rupee—for water at Zoula was then worth its weight in silver—and he would then hurry back with some animals on the chance of being able to repeat the trick.

In the midst of my water duties I received orders to take 50,000 dollars from Zoula to Senafe, situated about sixty-six miles distant at an altitude of some 7,000 feet. It had a glorious climate, but I shall never forget the horrible, starving condition of the people. I noticed women and children digging for and eating roots of grass, picking off and eating pieces of raw fat from the hides of slaughtered oxen, and breaking bones to devour the raw marrow. The general poverty was terrible to see and think of. Journeying back to Zoula I learnt that I had been appointed to the Transport train, and whilst so serving at Dildee a turning-point I imagine occurred in my luck. Two days after my arrival our people had a disturbance with the natives, arising over some grain dispute; the Abyssinians combined against us and our men opened fire upon them, causing them to run away and leave us without carriage or carriers. The inhabitants declined to help us, and contracts and arrangements which had been made threatened to break down altogether. The matter was becoming serious, for the supply of food for the troops in front was very limited. Colonel James Grant, of Victoria Nyanza fame, had been sent down from the vicinity of Magdala to make commissariat arrangements and hurry up supplies. He made his appearance in the midst of the scrimmage and placed me in command at Dildee with the powers of Provost Marshal, but he urged me to try and make friends with the people and persuade them to furnish men and animals for carrying stores to the troops. I was fortunately successful in doing this, luckily making great friends who helped me in every way, and when Colonel Grant, who had gone to Lake Ashangi, returned, all difficulties were over. So friendly had my intercourse with the natives been that I was able to go out for five or six miles in all directions alone, or attended by only one unarmed mutineer. Supplies were brought in daily to the commissariat, and on Saturdays we had a bazaar which used to be attended by about six or seven thousand people. Sir Robert Napier, on his return after the capture of Magdala, gave handsome presents to each chief, and was kind enough to thank me for my services during the campaign.

But my health had broken down, and on reaching Zoula again a medical board invalided me to England.

Before sailing I called upon Colonel Dillon, Lord Napier's military secretary, and asked him to endeavour to get me recommended by His Excellency for the Panjab Commission, telling him the circumstances of my case. When I came away from the interview I was not very sanguine as to my petition receiving any particular attention. I had no claim to the consideration of either officer, and although my loss of fortune was a crushing blow to me, it was not a matter which would affect anybody else. But I little knew then of the greatness of heart of my Commander-in-Chief, Lord Napier, or of the kindly nature of his secretary. Lord Napier never failed to the day of his death to give me encouragement and a helping hand, and for over thirty years Sir Martin Dillon has been my friend and benefactor on innumerable occasions.

I had hardly been a week in England when I received a copy of a letter which Lord Napier of Magdala, as Commander-in-Chief of the Abyssinian Forces, had written to the Lieutenant-Governor of the Panjab on my behalf, recommending me for employment in the Panjab, particularly on the frontier, where he thought I 'might ultimately prove a very valuable officer.'

Having left India before I had completed the obligatory year's probation for the Staff Corps, I was sent back to the Royal Artillery, but on my return to India I was allowed to rejoin the Staff Corps, and was also permitted to count my former service in it towards the required twelve months' probation.

On August 29, 1868, I was married to Mary, sole surviving daughter of William Cecil, Esq., late of The Dyffrin and Llanover, in the county of Monmouth, but owing to the very delicate state of her health my wife was compelled to remain in England with her parents, and did not join me in India until 1870, after a separation of over twenty months.

Early in April 1869 I was back at Ambala. The Viceroy, the Commander-in-Chief, and all the provincial governors and high officials who could attend were there to receive the Amir Sher Ali Khan, Wali of Afghanistan, who with his son, the 'Wali Ahad,' Sardar Abdulla Jan, and certain of his great dignitaries of state, had journeyed from Caubul to Ambala for the occasion. The great fratricidal war which had waged in Afghanistan for over four years had ended in favour of Sher Ali Khan, and he had now come as the honoured guest of the Government of India.

I was attached as a probationer to the 15th Ludianah Sikhs, but before joining them at Ferozepore I hastened to wait on the Lieutenant-Governor of the Panjab, then at Ambala, armed with a copy of Lord Napier's letter, trusting that this and the hopes and promises held out to me two years previously at Lahore might ensure my speedy appointment to the Panjab Commission. But that good luck was not yet on my side, so I again made my way to Lord Napier of Magdala's camp, to solicit his good offices through my friend Colonel Dillon. I was received with the greatest kindness, and introduced to Major Owen Tudor Burne, then private secretary to the Viceroy, who told me to send in my application direct to the Government of India, which I did. In August I passed my examination for the Staff Corps, and in December accompanied the 15th Ludianah Sikhs from Ferozepore to Peshawar, where my old schoolfellow and friend, George Robertson Hennessy, who was in the same regiment, knowing my purse to be a scanty one, insisted upon my having a room under his roof at a mere nominal rental. But Hennessy would have given his last shirt off his back if he thought that a friend was in need of it.

In the month of July 1870 my anxiously-looked-for appointment to the Panjab Commission arrived. The notification came to me with a letter from the private secretary to the Viceroy, stating that His Excellency had given me the first vacancy which had arisen since Lord Mayo had become Viceroy of India. I was very glad and grateful, but I knew that I owed my good fortune to the recommendation of Lord Napier of Magdala, and to the kindly influence of Sir Martin Dillon and Sir Owen Tudor Burne.

I was immediately attached to the Peshawar Division as Assistant Commissioner.

CHAPTER III

CRIME IN THE PANJAB

1870

My duties now gave me my first experiences of a category of crimes and ways of carrying them out which would have seemed marvellous in any other locality.

These crimes were: cattle poisoning; setting fire to crops which had been reaped and heaped up for threshing purposes; murders for revenge, or on account of *zar*, *zan*, or *zamin* (wealth, woman, land).

Poisoning cattle was a cruel act, and, although one of frequent occurrence, it was very difficult to trace the crime to the real offenders. The method of poisoning was to mix arsenic and flour together, and wrap the mixture round with hay so as to attract the notice of the passing animal; or the mixture would be placed in the hollow of an ear of Indian corn and bound round with grass, and thrown on the ground where an enemy's cattle were known to be taken out to graze. The lads in charge of the animals would be seen marching in front, picking up and examining every suspicious bundle that they noticed, but even with this precaution many cattle were poisoned and died. Sometimes the poisonous mixture was introduced into a feeding-trough, but this was a dangerous experiment and more easy of detection. There were instances, however, when the crime was rather boldly executed, yet, notwithstanding the risk of detection run, the proof of guilt could not be legally brought home. On one occasion, in a crowded thoroughfare, a fruit-seller saw his enemy's buffalo coming along. The attendant, thinking that the animal was safe from harm in such a place, lagged a few yards behind his charge to talk to a stall keeper. To take a slice of melon, peel it, and plaster it with a mixture of arsenical dough, throw it in front of the buffalo, and watch it taken down with a twirl of the tongue was for the fruit-seller the work of an instant. The careless keeper of the animal, suspecting no danger, saw nothing of this; but the buffalo died, and the owner charged the fruit-seller with the offence. When I put the question to him, 'Why do you charge this fruit-seller with having poisoned your buffalo?' the immediate answer was, 'Because I have no other enemy in the world who would do me this harm.' People in the Peshawar Valley counted their enemies and knew them well.

Burning cut crops was another infamous proceeding, for at one fell stroke the season's produce belonging to one man, or to half a village, would be destroyed in a few minutes. The civil authorities used to advise the village headmen to place earthen vessels filled with water close to their ricks, and to keep men on watch and ward until the harvest grain had been gathered in; but the Pathan is a lazy individual and careless to a degree. The consequence was that great and frequent losses occurred from these incendiary fires—losses which might easily have been avoided if the owners of the ricks had only displayed a little more attention to their property and watchfulness against their known enemies. It was difficult otherwise to prevent these burnings or to detect the culprit, for an enemy determined to have his revenge had often a dust storm or the darkness of night to assist him in his nefarious design. One system of carrying out this offence which came to my notice as a magistrate deserves a passing word.

In India, away from the forest tracts, scarcity of fuel presses heavily on the poor. To meet this great want droppings of bullocks, cows, and buffaloes are carefully collected, mixed with straw, made into cakes about ten inches in diameter, dried in the sun, and used for cooking and domestic purposes. A bit of this cake when lit acts as a slow match, giving out the least modicum of smoke, which is hardly noticed even if openly carried by hand in broad daylight. To place a good pinch of gunpowder into a hollow made in a piece of this cake, to cover it over to prevent the powder from falling out, to light it at one end, creep on all fours, place it in the stacks of wheat, barley, or millet at the close of the spring, or in those of Indian corn at the close of the autumn harvest, was a very simple process. The slow match, hardly giving any smoke, burnt until it reached the powder, then there was a sudden blaze, and the whole harvest collected at that spot was destroyed. Of course the real culprit was never seen, for he is far away by the time the fire breaks out, but the complainant knows his enemy, and when the deputy inspector of police arrives to make inquiries, he is assured that no one but Din Muhammad, the complainant's enemy, could have done it. He had been seen and watched creeping towards the stacks, and on reaching them he had taken a match-box, lit a match, set fire to the crops, and then fled. Further, the blaze had revealed his features, and So-and-so could swear on the Koran that they had identified him. But Din Muhammad, on his part, is quite equal to the occasion. Was he not, at the very hour of the conflagration, at a wedding in a neighbouring village; and did not A and B meet him as he was going there? Did not C and D see him as he stood at the corner of the village guest-house; and did he not have a smoke with E and F at their well, as he was returning homewards? Din Muhammad has taken the precaution to secure his witnesses and to rehearse his defence for days before he ventures to make the attempt on his enemy's collected crops!

After many years' experience of crime in the Peshawar Valley, it is my full belief that in the carrying out of a deliberate murder the perpetrators previously rehearse the whole line of defence for days and weeks, and not until they think that they are quite perfect in their parts is the murder attempted. No wonder that some of the criminal cases which have come up for inquiry in the Peshawar Valley would have puzzled a modern Solomon.

Here is a case in point which was reported to me by the Deputy Commissioner of Kohat. A Bangash landowner had fallen in love with a neighbour's wife and taken her across the border amongst the independent tribes, who gave him shelter and food. Nothing in the world would induce them to surrender him alive, but they had no hesitation in offering to kill him, or to get him murdered whilst in their country. After some trouble, the husband and brothers of the woman induced an agent to go to the runaway couple and assure the man that if he came in and made it up in money the husband would be satisfied and divorce the woman, whom, later on, after the usual time of separation, the co-respondent could then arrange to marry. The agent was promised a large sum of money if he would bring that individual by a certain route, where the husband and his friends would be lying in ambush. This the agent succeeded in doing, but the other side, thinking it safer not to have any witnesses to their *coup d'état*, first shot the offender dead and then treated the agent in the same way, burying both bodies.

But another case which attracted great notice was the murder of Shahdad Khan, Khan of Hund. This man, assisted by a clever, unscrupulous secretary, had managed to win most of his land suits in the settlement courts. He was under the belief that he was acting on his rights. His opponents felt equally certain that these rights had for their foundation false evidence, bribery, and corrupt native settlement officials. '*Dèr tang yà*' ('We are very tang')—and when a Pathan uses this sentence he means that his cup is full, and that you must not be surprised at what he does. So the good people of Hund arranged to get rid of their Khan in their own fashion. Two hired assassins were brought from another village, and when the time came for the dastardly deed to be carried out (it was in broad daylight) the people turned in the direction of the river Indus and shouted, 'See, the river is rising and coming in,' whilst the murderers did their work in the mosque where the Khan was at prayers. They then made their escape without anyone attempting to capture them. What made the thing so strange was that the Khan's son, *munshi* (or secretary), and all his friends and supporters knew who these hired assassins were; but not a word of this did they, or would they, reveal to the authorities who came to make inquiries. Two near relations of the Khan, innocent men, who had been foremost in contesting his claim to lands in dispute, were charged with the murder and committed to sessions, but after a careful inquiry they were acquitted.

CHAPTER IV

PESHAWAR

1870–1872

AT the time of my appointment to the Panjab Commission, and of joining it at Peshawar, in the month of July 1870, Captain (afterwards Colonel) W. G. Waterfield was Deputy Commissioner of the district, Captain Macpherson was the senior assistant, the district staff, especially the European element, being rather weak owing to officers having been laid up from press of work and the unhealthiness of the place. Peshawar had at that time a very evil reputation in every way: life and property were by no means safe, the cholera season of 1869 had been an exceptionally deadly one, and the troops and residents in the entire district were being decimated by a very trying type of fever, which seemed to baffle all the efforts of the doctors and which resembled cholera in some respects. The railway from Rawal Pindi to Peshawar had not then been started, and the hundred miles of journey by dak-gharry during the months of June, July, and August managed to give the *coup-de-grâce* to more than one ailing creature trying to get away to the cool breezes of Murree. It was a station to be avoided and dreaded in 1870, and when a command came for a regiment to march from some attractive down-country cantonment to this far-away deadly hole, a pang of regret was felt by those who could not evade the order; and as for the native servants, they by some means or other frequently managed to leave their masters in the lurch, and contented themselves by keeping away from the Peshawar Valley. In spite of all this I liked Peshawar, and soon learnt that many of its evils were magnified. Therefore when a note from the Private Secretary to the Viceroy intimated that I had been selected for an appointment to the Panjab Commission, I resolved to ask permission to be allowed to join it by remaining at Peshawar. It was some time, however, before the military authorities permitted me to leave my regiment at Peshawar to join the Commission at the same place, and those days of delay appeared to me so many chances of hopes being destroyed. But at length the order for my joining arrived, and my suspense was at an end. The Commissioner of the Peshawar Division was then Colonel (now Major-General Sir Frederick Richard) Pollock.

In the early part of the spring a three days' invitation had taken me to Kohat as the guest of an old friend who had been with me throughout the Abyssinian campaign, Alfred Gaselee, formerly of the 93rd Highlanders, and at that period Quartermaster of the 4th, now Major-General Sir Alfred Gaselee, K.C.B. Whilst at Kohat I had the pleasure of being introduced to Pierre Louis Napoleon Cavagnari, Deputy Commissioner of that district, then one of the ablest and most promising officers on the North-Western Frontier of the Panjab, and with whom it was my good fortune to be afterwards associated in duty and to earn his confidence and friendship.

Peshawar could be enjoyable, in spite of its execrable climate, during the hot weather, provided your health remained good. There was a pack of hounds, and hunting the wily jackal twice a week during the cold season afforded excellent sport. Geese, duck, snipe, ubara, sand-grouse, quail, could be shot in the greatest profusion and without asking anyone's permission. Those who cared for hawking deer could enjoy that rare pleasure by going over to Hoti-Mardan, where the gallant Corps of Guides could give this sport to their friends. The hawks had to be trained in a peculiar way. They were taken young from their nests in some part of Northern Afghanistan, and when perfected they used to be sent down to the officer commanding the regiment by an old friendly Barakzai Sardar. With his death, somewhere about 1872 or 1873, the supply ceased. At least this was the explanation of the cessation of the sport given to me when I afterwards was stationed at Hoti-Mardan. Black and grey partridge, sisi, ravine deer, urial, and markhor could also be had in the surrounding hills and about their skirts. But the wild men of the hills prevented the shikarring of the last two, and the rules and prohibitions of the civil authorities barred the rest, except to a very favoured few, such as the officers of the Guides, who could arrange a week's excellent sport in the Sudum Valley towards Rustam, Baringan, Pirsai, Pallodheri; and in the Katlang quarter towards the villages of Sangao, Mia Khan, Babuzai, Shamozai. Polo was played in the centre of Cantonments, there was an excellent cricket-ground near the Residency buildings, and one of the prettiest racecourses in the world on the site of an ancient jheel below the fort, where a few years before fifteen to twenty couple of snipe could be secured by the officers on duty inside the fort, who were presumed to have the sole right of shooting on that ground. There were, further, pleasant rides in the direction of the Shahi Bagh (King's Garden), Bagh-i-Wazir (the Vizier's Garden), and in and out of the peach gardens. It was a pretty sight to go round of an early spring morning and see hundreds of acres of peach, plum, quince intermixed, all out in bloom.

In those days officers were forbidden going beyond Burj-i-Harri-Singh, which lies about four miles from Peshawar Church, towards Jamrud. Once I was permitted to go as far as Jamrud with the late Mr. W. H. Smith, when special arrangements had been made for conducting and escorting him from Peshawar to this ruined fort on his visit to the Peshawar Valley. On a later occasion I received a kindly wigging for having taken out a hawking party to the left of the Peshawar Jamrud road, under the guidance and protection of an old Khalil Arbab of Tai-Kāl Bālā. Both sides of the road from Burj-i-Harri-Singh to the Khyber (more especially that portion to the left towards the Besai spur) were well covered with jungle about this time, and I saw good-sized herds of ravine deer, ten to fourteen in number, on the occasion that I first journeyed in that direction. However, since the Afghan war of 1878 the residents of the Peshawar District, emboldened by our holding the Khyber Pass, have gradually cleared away all this wood, and with the want of cover the game has disappeared also.

As magistrates there was one duty which we were one and all bound to carry out in rotation, highly odious and objectionable as it was to us. This obligation chiefly fell on the junior magistrates, Assistant Commissioners at the headquarters of the

FORT JAMRUD.

district, and if by chance there happened to be only one official present, the unpleasant duty at times came oftener than one liked. A magistrate had to attend and be present at every execution, when the last penalty of the law had to be carried out on a prisoner in the jail. The place of execution was outside the jail walls, about 100 yards to the west in the direction of the Khyber hills. I shall never forget the first occasion I had to be present at one of these hateful exhibitions. A young lad, belonging to a well known dancing family, had been murdered under rather cruel circumstances, for the sake of the few ornaments which his foolish mother had decked the child out in. Learning the exact date on which the offender had to suffer his punishment, the mother had asked all her female acquaintances and friends to attend and see the sentence carried out on the murderer of her son. As the procession, under the direction of the Civil Surgeon, who was also Superintendent of the Jail, appeared on the ground assigned for this duty, the high mound to the south of the gallows was covered with women dressed out in their best and finest silks, a regular parterre of colours. The mother rushed towards the prisoner uttering language not complimentary to the relations of the wretched culprit, but the Superintendent directed the guard to convey her to the gateway, and so she was deprived of the satisfaction which she had anticipated of witnessing the hanging of the offender.

The forts of Michni, Shabkaddar, Abazai were then held by the military, and their commandants were Major Macdonald, Major Callander, and Colonel Soady. The last-named place was situated on the left bank of the Swat River, about five miles from the spot where it issues from the hills and about twenty-eight from Peshawar Cantonments. The officers named were often seen at Peshawar, and were much liked for their hospitality and general good fellowship to all who had to go out to these forts on pleasure or duty.

Major Macdonald was murdered in the spring of 1873 by Bahram Khan Mohmand of Lalpura, assisted by a number of his followers, a short distance out of Fort Michni, in the direction of the hills. What was the motive for this cowardly outrage I never exactly learnt, as at the time of the event I had gone to Calcutta with the object of passing the High Proficiency test in Persian. But what I heard on my return was this. Major Macdonald was the owner of a very fine bull-dog, and whilst walking out one day followed by the animal, he met Bahram Khan and some of his men, accompanied by some village curs of the commonest type. These attacked the bull-dog, and Macdonald, losing his temper, spoke in severe tones to the leader of the cavalcade, not knowing that he was related to the family of Mohmand chiefs of Lalpura. The parties after this went their way, and the British officer thought no more of the incident. Not so the Mohmand, who had the commandant of Fort Michni watched, and learnt that he was in the habit of walking to a certain quarter nearly every day quite unarmed. One day Major Macdonald and Captain Clifford, commanding the detachment from Peshawar, accompanied by the same bull-dog, were out for their usual stroll, when they were attacked by Bahram Khan and his gang. The Major was killed, and the dog, trying to save his master's body from mutilation, was badly cut about with either swords or long hill knives, whilst Captain Clifford managed with difficulty to escape. As you enter the Peshawar Church, by the door facing the Club grounds, Macdonald's monument, erected by public subscription, is on the right-hand side, and the inscription tells the reader that he was murdered by Mohmand Afridis. A strange error after twenty-four years' experience of two tribes entirely different from each other!

Colonel Soady, Governor of Fort Abazai, was an officer much feared and respected by the villagers living outside his command. To amuse himself he cultivated some of the fort lands, and in the production of his barley, wheat, mustard, and sugar-cane crops he had to indent on the water cuts for irrigating his fields. Whether he indented too freely, or whether the villagers had an idea that the fact of the commandant taking to cultivation was trespassing on their rights, an ill-feeling sprang up against him which lasted for years. They secured his English plough and threw it into the river; they used to cut down his crops at night, and he often had to stand in defensive attitude for the protection of his property, rifle in hand. He had his own ways of retaliation, however. One night, to prevent a high official from using his encamping ground, he let loose the flood-gates, and next morning, when the official's baggage and tents arrived, there were two feet of standing water on what some hours before had been dry ground. The stories of Colonel Soady's eccentric doings and sayings were many, but the people admired his frank, fearless demeanour, for he had no conception of what fear or danger meant.

A sad accident at polo lost me a very old friend

and schoolfellow, and put a stop to this game being played at Peshawar for a period. Captain Anderson, Adjutant of the 5th Bengal Cavalry, then stationed at Naushehra, was a rare good rider and an excellent exponent of the game as it used to be played in those days. He was on the ball, his pony going at the utmost stretch of speed, when another schoolfellow, mounted on a larger pony and closely following, collided with him and sent the smaller pony and rider to the ground. Anderson was picked up senseless, never rallied, and died in the house of his brother-in-law, then commanding a cavalry regiment stationed at Peshawar. He was buried in the cemetery on the Jamrud road.

A curious fatality attended three officers of this corps, the first victim being my friend and school companion, Anderson. I repeat the narrative as recounted to me by many, more especially by a native officer of high family belonging to the regiment. Captain Anderson, Lieutenant Williamson, and Dr. Palmer had lately come to be stationed at Naushehra. Houses were very scarce there in 1869–70, and these three resolved to build one suitable for their wants as a joint stock concern. A site was selected near the right bank of the Caubul River, not very far from the bridge of boats, in a tope of *shisham* trees, and about the greenest spot that could be found in the neighbourhood. Now, in all Cantonments, where land has been taken up for military purposes from a Muhammadan community, you often see an old tomb which is presumed to be a *ziarat* or shrine, the resting-place of some departed saint. Such a shrine has always a keeper attached to it, who lights the evening *chiragh*, or oil lamp of earth, about 6 P.M. every Thursday and accepts any offerings handed over by devotees, who put their faith and trust in the sacred character of the buried. Numbers of such graves are to be seen in Peshawar Cantonments, and at Naushehra, which are lit up every Thursday evening, possibly not a single keeper knowing the name of the holy man whose interests he is guarding in his own peculiar way. It is said that on the site selected for their house and enclosure at Naushehra the three officers named came across a grave of the nature described. For some reason or other the keeper of this shrine was not pleased, and prophesied that evil and misfortune would follow and overtake them and their house within a fixed period. The fate of one has already been described.

Some months afterwards the second officer, whilst hawking after ravine deer with the hawks and hounds of the Guides across the Caubul River towards Mardan, was killed in a similar manner by his horse colliding with that of another rider. The third officer was drowned in the Ganges. Lastly, an unusually heavy flood in the Caubul stream swept away every trace of the house and of the servants' buildings within the compound area. Whether the story of the devotee's curse be true or not, the other facts are. Time after time have I passed by and walked round the site where those buildings once stood, without noticing any remains that had been saved from the flood. And no one has attempted to build another house on the same site.

The work with the tribes living beyond our boundary used to be arranged and managed through certain native Khans and middlemen of the Peshawar District, who happened to be living in close proximity to that particular border, or whose families had been in friendly intercourse with men of note belonging to the border tribe concerned. Our representative generally was a man of good family, whom our system wished to make much of. The jirga, or council of the tribe, invariably consisted of men each of whom by some deed of daring, or some act of savage, treacherous murder, had brought himself to the front in his own proper section of the tribe to which the whole Council belonged. Our middleman had to see the independent jirga, and bring them up before the Deputy Commissioner of the district to settle all disputes that might spring up between British subjects and the tribesmen beyond the border. In fact, he acted as an envoy or ambassador on behalf of the Deputy Commissioner to the particular tribe he was in touch with, and every other British subject in the district was barred from interfering in any way with his charge. In those years Ibrahim Khan, of Zaida, was in charge of the Gadun and Khudu Khel tribes; Amir Khan of Shewa looked to Narinji and Chamla; Ajab Khan had control of arrangements with all the sections of the powerful Bunerwals, mustering about 13,000 fighting men. The Khans of Hoti and Mardan were rival candidates for Swat and lower Ranizai. Mir Hassan Khan of Tangi and the Miahs of Abaazi had their eyes on the Utman Khels. The Mohmands were managed through the Khan of Matta Mughul Khel and the Tehsildar of Daodzai. Arbab Abdul Majid Khan, Khalil of Jaikàl Bala, threw his influential mantle over the Mullagoris and the six Afridi tribes of the Khyber Range; whilst Arbab Sarfaraz Khan, Mohmand of Landi Yarghajo, chaperoned the Aka Khel and the Adam Khel Afridis.

This system, which was a most pernicious one, was in existence from the confines of Agror in the Hazara District, right through to the extreme southern limits of the North-Western Frontier, under the control of the Panjab Government. After spending about twenty-nine years of my service on the Peshawar Frontier, including eighteen years in charge of the Khyber Pass—where, by living amongst Afridis, Shinwaris, Mohmands, &c., for several months at a time, I had opportunities of learning personally from men who had come to place confidence in me—my firm and solemn conviction is that the majority of the wars and fights between the British Government and the independent tribes of the Panjab Border were due entirely to the evil intrigues and machinations of the Arbabs and middlemen, who had been employed by us to do our work with the tribesmen. I shall refer to this subject again further on.

Every Englishman who pays a visit to Peshawar Cantonments should stop and examine a small monument which stands on the Mall, a short distance west of the Civil buildings, and facing what used to be known as the Royal Artillery Hospital. It is impossible to miss it. The ground and surroundings are extremely pretty and nicely kept. The tablet reads thus:

HERE LIES THE BODY

OF

FREDERICK MACKESON

LIEUTENANT-COLONEL OF THE BOMBAY ARMY, COMPANION OF

THE BATH, AND COMMISSIONER OF PESHAWUR

WHO WAS BORN SEPTEMBER 2ND 1807

AND DIED SEPTEMBER 14TH 1853

OF A WOUND INFLICTED BY A RELIGIOUS FANATIC.

'The reputation of Lieutenant-Colonel Mackeson as a soldier is known to and honoured by all. His value as a political servant of the State is known to none better than the Governor-General himself, who in a difficult and eventful time had cause to mark his great ability, and the admirable prudence, discretion, and temper which added tenfold value to the soldierlike qualities of his character. The loss of Colonel Mackeson would have dimmed a victory. To lose him thus by the hand of a foul assassin is a misfortune of the heaviest gloom for the Government, which counted him among its bravest and best.'

This grand tribute to the dead appeared in the orders of the Marquis of Dalhousie, then Viceroy and Governor-General of India, who knew how to appreciate and value services rendered to the State. The monument was erected by private subscription, and a few yards away from it a well was excavated which was to provide pure drinking water for rich and poor. 'Take care you fetch my drinking water from Mackeson Sahib's well,' was a command invariably given to your water-carrier in Peshawar thirty years ago.

Mackeson's name first appears in notice when as a political assistant he is found collecting supplies for the army of the Indus, then about to march from Ferozepore to Bhawalpur in the first Afghan war of 1838–42. When his task was completed, and the army had passed Bhawalpur towards the Bolan Pass, he came back to Ferozepore and moved to Peshawar to take up his duties in the Khyber and keep the pass open. The difficulties he had to face for years, and the indomitable pluck he displayed in carrying out his work single-handed in such a place and amongst such people, few can understand who have not had the experience of working single-handed with

Afridis and Shinwaris. With a large Sikh army, semi-hostile at that period, holding Peshawar, and a powerful Sikh State intervening between Afghanistan and our then boundary on the river Sutlej, Colonel Mackeson, after the breakdown of the Sikh power, was made Commissioner of the Peshawar Division. One evening in the month of September 1853 he had completed his day's work, and as he was seated outside his house receiving and hearing petitions, a man came up and handed to him what appeared to be a petition. As Mackeson was examining it, the miscreant drew a dagger, either from his sleeve or from beneath his shirt, and stabbed him. He lingered some days, but the wound was fatal, and he died on September 14, 1853. The assassin was a Talib-ul-Ilm (a searcher after knowledge, *i.e.* a religious student), a resident of the Kuner Valley. Mackeson's house, which was built on a mound adjoining the residence now tenanted by the Commissioner of Peshawar, was in 1869 in the hands of the Commissariat Department, but it has now been levelled with the ground. It was my good fortune to have been associated with the Peshawar Valley first in 1863, and after that continuously from 1869 to the month of April 1898, and wherever I have been, in every part of the Peshawar District, in the Khyber Range, in the Shinwari country, in Shilman or the Mullagori hills, or Jelallabad, the name of Mackeson (known as Kishin Kàka or Uncle Kishin by the elders) has been honoured and respected by all the residents of those lands above that of any other Englishman who has been on the Peshawar Border. Let it be remembered that as Mackeson's control of the Khyber ceased in 1842, and his untimely death occurred over 45 years ago, there must have been something in the character, deeds, and life of this man to have kept his memory still fresh and dear to the savages of the Khyber Range.

In Peshawar during 1870, as now, necessity forced every officer to have a watchman to keep guard over his horses, goods, and chattels from about 5 P.M. to say 7 A.M. the next morning. This gentleman, who was generally a thief himself, came to the house as the sun was setting, and cleared out the next morning, when he went away to his own home and kept to his own business until evening again approached, when he re-appeared at his master's house. He had no hesitation in getting his master's neighbour robbed, or if two officers lived in the same house and only one kept a night watchman, the other officer was almost certain to be robbed, unless he consented to pay blackmail to the tune of Rs. 5 a month by entertaining another scamp of a *chowkidar* or watchman. When I was living with my friend Colonel Hennessy, the Kotwal of the Cantonment Police supplied me with a ragged ruffian wearing shoes made from the dwarf palm, with a useless pistol stuck in his waist-band, as my guardian. He was a Bassi Khel Afridi, a sub-division of the Aka Khel, numbering about 300 armed men, every one of whom was a thief by birth, instinct, and profession; but in those days I was ignorant of these matters. My guardian took fair care of me, until one night he had a portion of my tent removed from my verandah. The police, however, having traced his footsteps, my watchman's security, amounting to Rs. 30, was handed over to make good my loss, and the Bassi Khel made himself scarce. When I went to live with the Head of the Police in the month of July 1870 my old rooms at Colonel Hennessy's were given over to a brother officer who had returned from leave in Kashmir. He refused to keep a watchman, and so one evening after mess, on returning to his quarters, he found his rooms entirely cleared out. Poor fellow, he was an officer always neat and exceedingly particular about his appearance and dress, and his loss was close upon 300*l*. sterling in value, hardly any of which was ever recouped to him.

The audacity with which thieves in the Peshawar Valley broke into houses and barracks in Cantonments, and carried off property, chiefly rifles, baffles all description. This applies not only to the old days of our occupation, but to very recent dates. In the spring of 1897 a thief shot a Dogra sentry of the 20th Panjab Infantry dead not far from their main guard, and managed to escape with his rifle. During March 1898, as the Headquarter camp of the Tirah Expeditionary Force was encamped at Peshawar on the parade ground of the 35th Sikhs, a sentry of this regiment was shot dead and his Martini taken away. The more valuable the arm is, the more daring and the more venturesome will the thief be to get hold of the weapon. But the boldness of these thieves is not only practised in the Cantonments of Peshawar and Naushehra; it is exemplified at Taru, Naushehra, Akora, Khyrabad, the four marching stages between Peshawar and Attock. I do not know which of these stages has the worst reputation, but from my experience of it Taru would be hard to beat. A regiment of the Panjab Frontier Force, marching from Kohat through the Kohat Pass to the Rawal Pindi darbar in the spring of 1885, had all their night sentries' rifles loaded with buckshot cartridges. Nothing was lost on the journey, and Rawal Pindi was reached in safety. Here, thinking that they were out of the region of rifle thieves, an order was issued to discontinue the use of buckshot cartridges by sentries placed on duty round the camp between sunset and sunrise. The very first night of the discontinuance two Martini-Henry rifles were carried off. Rifle thieves had followed the regiment over every inch of their march from Kohat, and had accepted the very first opportunity and chance given them of carrying away the weapons, which weapons I recovered for the regiment some years afterwards. Instances have occurred in which professional thieves have followed a regiment on the march from Peshawar to some down-country station for a month or more, waiting for the chance of getting a good loot, and they seldom returned empty handed. I believe there is hardly a station or encamping ground in Northern India and the Panjab where these men have not one or more friends and allies, who house and feed the thieves, and help them in secreting and removing arms and rifles stolen, receiving in turn a share from the sale and disposal of the same. Honour amongst thieves is exemplified in the way in which the above custom is always respected and thoroughly carried out, whatever be the nationality or religion of the thief and his helper.

One morning in the seventies it was whispered about Peshawar Cantonments that the bandmaster of a distinguished regiment had disappeared. The secret of his whereabouts was well kept for two or three days, and then it leaked out that he had been carried off, and was a prisoner amongst the Zakha

Khel Afridis of the Khyber Pass, by whom he was well fed and kindly treated. The civil authorities called upon Arbab Majid Khan, Khalil of Taikal Bala, to recover the bandmaster, and within a week or ten days he was brought back safe and sound to his regiment at Peshawar. Some years afterwards, when I had been for a long period in charge of the Khyber Pass and had become well acquainted with the Zakha Khel, I remembered the anecdote of the bandmaster, and asked his captors to tell me what had occurred on that occasion. They said that a band of Nikki Khel Zakha Khels of the Khyber started on an expedition towards Peshawar, and passing the cemetery on the Jamrud road, they descended into the ravine, which commences at the Brigade parade ground and goes round the whole of the Cantonments on that side, past the second cemetery by the road that leads from Peshawar to Michni, where it joins the Sheikh-ka-Katha and the Budni stream, through the Military Works Department brickfields. On the night in question they had not gone far, had not even reached the lower cemetery, when they noticed a lighted lantern in the ravine and a European lying on the ground close beside it. They scattered at once, thinking it was some trap laid by Mr. Nyx, at that period Inspector of Cantonment Police; but, crawling round and round the light, they gradually approached it until they came upon the figure of a European fast asleep. Extinguishing the lantern, they raised the sleeper on their shoulders, and carried him for a distance of four miles, until they had passed the police station of Burj-Harri Singh, where they placed him on his feet and, supporting him, made him walk towards Jamrud Fort and the Khyber. It must have been a powerful narcotic that had been administered to him that evening, for he walked eight miles and had reached the entrance to the pass before the dawn began to appear and the cool morning breeze brought him to his senses. Making use of a friendly expression he attempted to break away from his captors, but they immediately drew their long Afridi knives, called *chāras*, and gave him to understand by visible signs that they had no intention of being trifled with. After this he went quietly with them to their Zakha Khel settlements, and remained there until brought back to Peshawar. The Zakha Khel spoke well of the behaviour of the bandmaster, to the effect that during the week or ten days he was under their charge he displayed no fear.

One other incident to illustrate the boldness of Afghan thieves. One morning the men of the Corps of Guides, whilst at their target-practice at Mardan, were astonished to see a Pathan mounted on a horse with a military saddle going away at full speed towards Gujar-Garlie (a village two miles from the cantonment of Hoti-Mardan) followed by a police sowar with a drawn sword mounted on a horse with a hunting saddle. Coming up to the runaway the sowar fetched him down with a cut, and pursuer and pursued moved on to the civil lines, where the matter was thus explained. The Sessions Judge of Peshawar Division, followed by his police orderly sowar, had ridden into the compound of Mr. Beckett, Assistant Commissioner, and, dismounting, made a sign to his orderly to hold his animal pending the arrival of his syce or groom. The orderly, seeing a Pathan seated in the compound, called to him to hold *his* horse whilst he took charge of the animal ridden by the Sessions Judge. The Pathan did so, and, getting into the saddle, made off as hard as his mount could go; the sowar, seeing how the land lay, jumped on to the judge's horse, gave chase, and managed to cut down the thief and secure his own horse. It appears that this same Pathan had previously played a similar trick on a groom in the service of the Executive Engineer, who was taking his master's horse from Mardan to Katlang. Meeting the Pathan on the road, he asked him to hold the animal for a moment whilst he dismounted. The Pathan did so, but immediately went off with his prize, which he produced before the Akhund of Swat, Sayad Abdul Ghaffur, at Saidù in Swat. But the Akhund—or Babaji, as he was reverentially called by his followers—sent the animal back to the Assistant Commissioner at Mardan. The Pathan, who was committed for trial to the sessions court, endeavoured to make himself out insane. At that stage I was sent to officiate for Mr. Beckett, and had to record the medical evidence, which substantiated the fact that the culprit was entirely free from any symptoms of insanity.

CHAPTER V

MARDAN

1872–1879

About the end of September 1872 orders came that I was to officiate for one month in charge of the sub-district of Yusufzai in place of Mr. Beckett, proceeding on short leave, and on the 30th of that month I found myself at the small station of Hoti-Mardan, the headquarters of that grand regiment the Corps of Guides. This was my first meeting with a regiment with which I had the honour and pleasure of being associated off and on for the seven years that I was in charge of the sub-district. With them I took part in the expeditions against Iskhàkot, and the Utman Khels of Nawedand, Bucha, and Rang-Miana, and we were together in the Afghan war of 1879–81, subsequent to the death of my much lamented friend Cavagnari. From the period of my first meeting this regiment on October 1, 1872, to the date of my leaving India in 1898 I was treated by the officers with a kindness which could not have been exceeded had I really belonged to the corps itself. In all respects and in all matters they looked upon me as one of their own body. The names of Sir J. McQueen, Sir Francis H. Jenkins, Campbell, Charlie Hunter, George Stewart, Wigram Battye, Hutchinson, Fred. Battye, Walter Hamilton,

Ambrose Kelly, Hughes-Buller, and others recall to my memory that happy past.

My fellow lieutenant of the 24th R.A., M. J. King-Harman, who had been with me at Fort Govindghur in 1863–64, was now with the Guides, and he received me most kindly, helping me in many ways. Mr. Beckett, who was anxious to be off at once, introduced me to my work, and also to a gentleman of the district who had been a thorn in the side of every Civil officer who had the misfortune of having to deal with him, and who later on made my life a torment for five years. This was Ajab Khan of Chargullai, a village in the Sudum Valley about two miles west of the police station of Rustam. He had just been brought in with all his sons, family, and servitors from the Buner country, where they had taken shelter after being implicated in a cruel murder, presumed to have been instigated and carried out by orders of the old head of the family. When I first saw this remarkable man, standing about six feet high, of spare body, fairly good features, long black beard, and with the silver toothpick suspended from his neck, and heard his words softly delivered, I had no knowledge of his past history and little idea of what his future would be. I had heard that the authorities were not pleased with him, as they had had to send Subadar Major Habib Khan of Khunda and the head of the police to bring him in from the Buner country; but he had come in with some 400 men of the Buner jirga forming his retinue, all of whom were to be fed by the civil authorities, so that his journey looked like the march of a victorious general rather than that of a penitent offender returning to ask for pardon.

Ajab did not seem to mind whether he was under a cloud or not. At that time my chief anxiety was that he should not, during my short tenure of thirty-one days' office, do any act or commit any offence which I could not dispose of myself but have to leave to my successor to settle.

I have used the words 'remarkable man' in conjunction with Ajab Khan's name, and the following brief history of his career, made out by me many years ago, will show that the words are not out of place. Mir Babu, the father of this family, was a strong landowner in the Sudum Valley at the time that Futteh Khan of Panjtar, and Sayad Ahmad Shah, Chief of the Hindustani fanatics, were at the zenith of their power, about the year 1827. Mir Babu joined their combination, but did not fall with them when the Pathans rose up and massacred Sayad Ahmad's Hindustani followers. When the Sikhs became the rulers, Mir Babu was appointed a farmer of revenue on their behalf, but the date of his death has not been rightly noted. He left several sons, all of whom I knew, except Aziz Khan, who died before I took charge of Yusufzai. Just before the commencement of the Ambeyla campaign in October 1863 the two brothers, Aziz Khan and Ajab Khan, were all powerful in the Sudum Valley, and what added to their influence was that they were connected by marriage with Nawab Khan of Bagra and Zaidulla Khan of Daggar, the two families which gave hereditary Khans to the whole of Buner. Through them all Buner could be induced to side with or against the British. For some reason the military strategic movement on our side of October 19, 1863, from Nowa Killa to Surkhawi, and through the Ambeyla Pass into the Chamla Valley was not revealed to the brothers Ajab and Aziz. They considered that they had been deceived, and the same idea came into the minds of the chiefs and people of Buner, strongly agitated as they already were by the letters and exhortations of the heads of the Hindustani colony at Malka. 'If you do not do something now, your Buner *parda* has gone for ever' was the message sent by Ajab Khan by the mouth of his most trusted henchman to his friend and ally Nasir Khan of Barkilli, then at Kanga, a village in the Chamla Valley. Nasir Khan, although he had but a small contingent of fourteen to fifteen men with him, commenced his attack, well knowing that the first few shots fired by him and the Chamlawals would bring the whole of Buner down on the left flank of the invading force. And it happened exactly as he had anticipated. This fact and Ajab Khan's message were told to me in 1877 by the very same henchman in whom he had reposed so much trust fourteen years before; but in 1877 cruelty had turned the faithful servant into a deadly enemy, and it was his aid and evidence which brought Ajab Khan to execution in the spring of 1878.

After the termination of the Ambeyla campaign Ajab Khan was not punished. A few years later the small hamlet of Pirsai was burnt by the Bunerwals, and the two brothers Aziz and Ajab, being suspected of having a hand in the business, were brought into Peshawar pending inquiry. As usual, no action was taken against them, possibly on the grounds that sufficient evidence could not be produced to warrant a conviction. Aziz Khan died between 1869 and 1872, when Ajab fled with all his family into Buner, leaving several sons, the eldest being Ibrahim Khan of Hamzakòt.

During the same October 1872 I had a visit from Hukmat Khan, son of that fine old Buner chief, Zaidulla Khan of Daggar. After the battle of Lalu on December 15, 1863, when the combined forces of the confederate tribesmen were defeated by our troops operating in the Chamla Valley, it was agreed with the Buner chiefs that they should go and destroy Malka, the Hindustani outpost in the Amazai country on the Mahaban Range; and that Colonel R. Taylor and several other officers, escorted by the Guide Infantry, commanded by Captain Jenkins, and local levies under Aziz Khan of Sudum, should accompany to see the compact carried out. It was a ticklish undertaking, and looked as if the Guides were being sent to their destruction, for the surrounding hills and the Chamla Valley swarmed with portions of the 12,000 to 15,000 men that had just been defeated at Lalu, and more were coming from distant hills. But there was no fear or hesitation in a single man of that splendid regiment. What I am relating here was told to me by officers of the Guides who shared in this undertaking. As they moved into the Chamla Valley (December 19, 1863) the tribesmen gathered round them, occupying posts of advantage and ready to attack the regiment. But out rushed an old Buner chief, having only one arm and deprived of the sight of one eye, who shouted to the tribesmen that the Buner jirga had given their word to destroy Malka, and to take the English party there and bring them back safe and sound, and they meant to carry out their compact, and if any wished to interfere they must first of all fight the united strength of Buner. This scene was acted and reacted time after time, even with the Amazais, and in every instance the one armed chief was successful, until Malka was destroyed, and the English officers with the Guides Infantry conducted back to Ambeyla (December 23). The one eyed and one armed chief was Zaidulla Khan of Daggar.

At the commencement of 1868 a large band of the Hindustani fanatics had come to Bajkatha in the Daulatzai section of the Buner country. They had been invited to strengthen the party opposed to the Akhund of Swat, headed by Zaidulla Khan and others. Zaidulla made the first move by seizing some Swat traders passing through his lands. The Akhund replied by mustering his followers and directing the Buner chiefs to kill the refractory Khans and turn the Hindustanis out of Buner. The Salarzai and Ashazai sections at once attacked Daggar, and Zaidulla Khan was cut down by an individual named Zabta Khan, Aya Khel of the Ashazais, who was introduced to me at Mardan during 1875. I have dwelt on the fate of Zaidulla Khan in remembrance of his action five years before, and on his account a warm welcome was given by me to his son Hukmat Khan.

In 1873 I officiated for several months at Mardan, and with each experience my admiration of Ajab Khan's strategy increased, as well as my dislike. Pirsai, Pallodheri, Hamzakòt, Beroch were the property of his brother, Aziz Khan, now replaced by his son Ibrahim. The first commanded the Pirsai Pass leading to the Salarzai Bunerwals, which Ajab had secured through the medium of the civil authorities on the ground that his nephew was not strong enough to hold it. He was trying hard to get a footing into Beroch, which had two outlets into Buner and a safe passage to the Malandri Pass. His manœuvres had frightened his nephew, Ibrahim Khan, out of his wits. He tried to oust another brother of his, Pir Muhammad, from Baringan, as it lay directly on the road to the Malandri Pass half a mile from the Buner Border and a mile south of Beroch. Nyamat Khan of Surkhawi, a village commanding the western outlet of the Ambeyla Pass, was not in his good books. He particularly objected to the Deputy Inspector of Police at Rustam. He wished to get complete control of the Pirsai, Malandri, and Ambeyla Passes. Besides, some thirty outlaws under feigned names were sheltered in his village and hamlets, and when a warrant was served for the arrest of any individual the usual reply was, 'There is no man of that name living here.' However, knowing that for the time being I was only a bird of passage, Ajab Khan did not attempt to crush me entirely till the year 1877.

Mukarrab Khan of Panjtar, ex-chief of the Khudu Khels, styled by the officials at Lahore as that 'stormy petrel of the frontier,' was another pleasing character connected with Yusufzai politics. The Khudu Khel jirga, wearied out by twenty years of incessant trouble at his hands, invited him to a meeting, trusting to get rid of him in some way. Mukarrab Khan, however, was not to be caught napping, and managed to massacre more than half the Council at this very interview.

Having officiated five times during three years at Mardan, I was in hopes of getting the post permanently when it became vacant; but this was not to be. Every year the tension with Ajab Khan had become worse, but the climax had not been reached, and luck had enabled me to smooth over all the troubles raised by him. In December 1876 I was appointed permanently to the charge of the Sub-district of Yusufzai, but before I could start from Peshawar to take up the berth an event happened at Abazai with which I had nothing to do in any way. Works had been commenced on the Swat River canal a short distance above the fort (three miles), and one night, whilst the coolies were resting after their labours and were sound asleep, a band of raiders came down and killed some thirty or more of these poor creatures. A short time previous to this Lord Lytton, Viceroy and Governor-General of India, had paid a visit to the Peshawar Valley.

Returning to the Mardan, it seemed apparent that Ajab Khan had playod his last trump card since my incumbency to ruin his nephew, Ibrahim Khan. He had induced Ibrahim's stepmother to run away from his keeping, and with her two sons take shelter with her brother, Hukmat Khan at Daggar. No greater disgrace could have been offered by one Pathan to another. Remembering my kindness to him on former occasions, Hukmat Khan sent his private scribe and placed his sister's case entirely in my hands. By the beginning of July 1877 the case had been settled to her entire satisfaction, and she had been located at Pallodheri at her own request, and her brother's agent had been sent back to report the result to Hukmat. The settlement was duly notified to Major Cavagnari, who fortunately for all had come from Kohat to take up the duties of Deputy Commissioner of Peshawar, and he wrote on

July 12: 'I fully approve of all that you have done in effecting the return of Aziz Khan's widow, and consider that you have managed the affair with great tact and judgment.' I was rejoicing over this settlement and, trusting for quieter times, was having *chota haziri* with the officers of the Guides in their garden, when a trooper galloped in from Rustam with the report that the Bunerwals had attacked the Sudum villages. Handing the report to the officer commanding the Guides and asking his aid, a detachment of cavalry under the gallant Wigram Battye were soon on their way to Rustam, followed by a wing of the infantry. It was a day to be remembered, for the overpowering heat of July and not a particle of shade in the eighteen-mile ride to Rustam. But what made it more trying was that our own subjects should be allowed to play these pranks without any punishment ever overtaking them. As we rode up the incline to the police station at Rustam, Ajab Khan, standing with a long staff in his hands, closely scanned our faces. I must have revealed by mine what was passing in my mind, for the District Superintendent of Police, coming up almost immediately after us, learnt from one of his police officials 'that Ajab was preparing for a flight, as the Sahib had looked badly at him.' It was true. He had placed three of his sons in the towers at Pirsai, seven miles away, where they could not be touched. He and another son were at Rustam, and orders had gone to get the family at Chargullai ready for a speedy flight into Buner. It was a time to disguise one's intentions, so, sending for Ajab, I did my best to solicit his advice and to ascertain the reason of this raid, and who could possibly have carried it out. He said he would send a trusty agent to Buner, and have careful inquiries made there. Our own people were going to do the same. In the meanwhile it was necessary to examine what had happened and what was the damage caused by the raid.

A band of 2,000 Bunerwals, headed by Ajab Khan's best friends, had been launched against the Sudum villages, 700 coming through the Ambeyla Pass against Surkhawi, whilst the larger unit issued by the Malandri Pass and made direct for Rustam. There had been no quarrel between the Buner people and our villagers, and in consequence no preparations had been made for defence, as the secret was so well kept of the coming irruption that not a single Sudumite was aware of the pending calamity until it actually came upon them that morning of July 1877. Surkhawi was capable of defence, so Nyamat Khan manned his three towers and kept at bay the 700 Bunerwals, who made no serious attempts to capture the place. It was different in the other direction. Baringan was entirely destroyed, Ali and Bazar were partially sacked, and it was just as the Buner hordes were about to enter Rustam that our people, headed by a brave man named Malik Mansur Khan, one of the headmen of that village, made a resolute attack on them, and, once in retreat, the Bunerwals never stopped till they got back to Malandri. They left fifteen dead and thirteen prisoners, and carried away some thirty wounded. Our villagers lost about ten killed and twenty-two wounded, the greatest damage falling on Malik Tar Muhammad Khan of Ali, who was hated by Ajab Khan.

There were thus three pleasant complications on hand in the north-west, north, and north-east corners of the Peshawar Valley—(1) the murder and wounding of the coolies at Abazai; (2) just before my taking permanent charge of Hoti-Mardan, the strong Ranizai village of Iskhàkot had some of its men implicated in a murder carried out in rather a high-handed manner in a border village close to Landkhwar (*landa*, wet, *khwar*, ravine, implying a ravine with running water in it); (3) this Buner raid. Luckily we had Cavagnari as Deputy Commissioner of Peshawar at this period.

Within two days we had ample evidence to prove that the raid was the sole handiwork of Ajab Khan, and a telegraphic report was made of this to Peshawar, and Cavagnari came out to Mardan and desired to interview the Khan of Chargullai. Ajab by this time was happy in the belief that any suspicions that had been originally created in our minds regarding his complicity in this affair had long been removed, and he was now charging every impossible man as being the primary mover and cause of 2,000 Bunerwals pouring down for the destruction of our peaceful villagers. When he was called up and told that Cavagnari wished to see him at Hoti-Mardan his face fell at once, and he made every possible excuse to evade obeying the order. However, it was getting late in the day, and as night would fall in about three hours and it was hopeless to keep him in safety at Rustam, he was sent in with Ibrahim Khan, of Mardan, Inspector of Peshawar Police, and a sufficient escort to prevent his being rescued by his retainers of Chargullai, and fortunately Mardan was reached without any mishap. His son Akram at Rustam was secured, and the Deputy Inspector of Police was sent to bring in Karam, Aslam, and a third son, who were holding Pirsai. Karam was met on the road and gave himself up, and was sent into Rustam. Aslam, from the towers of Pirsai, fired on the police and drove them back, and that same night he set fire to Pirsai and fled to Chorbanda in the Buner country. Next morning he came down and burnt another small hamlet, went back to Chorbanda, and retired into the heart of the Buner country. Karam and Akram, sons of Ajab Khan, were escorted into Hoti-Mardan, and the whole valley, wearied out by the annoyances they had received at the hands of this family, turned out to see the spectacle.

Being directed to make a full inquiry into the case, I was fortunate enough to secure the services of that trusted follower who, in October 1863, had been sent by Ajab Khan with a message to Nasir Khan of Barkilli asking him to attack our troops for the sake of the Buner *parda*. All his former services had been forgotten, and a long period of persecution had turned him into a bitter enemy of Ajab Khan's, and from hints given by him evidence was forthcoming which left no doubt of Ajab's guilt. After a long and careful inquiry for the prosecution and defence recorded in presence of the accused, Ajab Khan was committed to take his trial before the Court of Session, and he was brought before Mr. (now Sir Donald) Macnabb, Commissioner of the Rawal Pindi division, who was specially deputed to Peshawar to undertake the trial. It lasted twenty-two days, and Ajab was sentenced to suffer the extreme penalty of the law, subject to the confirmation of the order by the Chief Court of the Panjab. In a judgment of 150 pages, Mr. (now Sir H. M.) Justice Plowden confirmed the order of the Sessions Court, and in spite of the utmost efforts of the barrister who took up the appeal, not a flaw could be discovered in the evidence given in proof of the guilt of the accused. When the result of his appeal was explained to Ajab in his solitary cell in the Peshawar Jail, and he was told that on a certain morning he was to be taken out and hanged, he admitted that he had brought the raid down, hoping to head it at the border, stop and force the Bunerwals to return to their country, and in this way regain the favour of the British officials which he had lost by his conduct. He suffered the extreme penalty of the law in presence of a very large assembly of headmen of the Peshawar District, to whom, in a few short, impressive words, he admitted the justice of his punishment and warned them to avoid the ways which had brought him into trouble.

The expedition into the country of the Jawaki Afridis during the winter of 1877–78 had kept Cavagnari fully occupied, but he never left out of his mind that the Abazai outrage had to be punished, and that Iskhàkot and Buner had to be dealt with for their misdeeds. The General Officer commanding at Peshawar required 5,000 men and the assistance of the heavy battery at that station to punish the Utman Khels, but it was difficult to assemble so large a force just then. Cavagnari proposed another plan of campaign. There was a holy man, named Rukn-ud-din Mia (generally known as Mia Rukn), who had his home at a place called Sapri, consisting of two or three hamlets of twenty to thirty houses each, located in the hills about four to five miles in the interior and about the same distance from the works on the new canal. This tract, lying between the Mohmands and Utman Khels, was inhabited by Mullagori hamsayahs (*ham-sayah* means a person or persons living under the shadow or protection of someone else). Mia Rukn was supposed to have brought down the raid which caused such fatal execution amongst the coolies. He had an evil reputation, because he had several unholy sons who were hand-and-glove with all the cattle thieves associated with the Peshawar District, and every animal stolen from certain quarters was brought to Sapri and either sold or ransomed through their means, they securing a certain share in each and every transaction. It was thought that by capturing Mia Rukn the settlement of the Utman Khel question would be rendered much easier. But how was this to be done? Cavagnari planned out the daring scheme himself, and received sanction to carry it out. He appeared at Hoti-Mardan one morning in February 1878, accompanied by Gholam Muhayuddin Khan, Tehsildar of Daudzai, Mahbub Khan, of Matta Moghal Khel, and a Mia of Abazai, own cousin to that of Sapri, but a great enemy of his, the last two being told that they were required to assist me in disposing of a local dispute. Mahbub and the Abazai Mia came to see me before I could get an interview with Cavagnari, and I nearly let the cat out of the bag, not knowing at that time that they were not in the secret. One look at the Mia's face warned me of my danger in time, and I was enabled to turn the conversation and obtain the reason of their coming to Hoti-Mardan. The secret was well kept, and at sunset about 200 of the Guides cavalry and 30 infantry mounted on grass-cutters' ponies started from Hoti-Mardan and took the road through the desolate *maira* for the hills north of Abazai, some thirty-seven miles off in a bead-line. Here they dismounted from their animals, and, leaving them in charge of some thirty men, clambered up the difficult mountain-side, and by 3 A.M. were on the hill above Sapri. The difficulty was to find out the house occupied by Mia Rukn. First one village was tried, then another, and at last came the certain news that he occupied a house near the mosque in the first hamlet. Everything depended on his capture, alive or dead. Cavagnari, Wigram Battye, the Tehsildar, and a small party got to the house and desired Mia Rukn to come out. By this time the alarm had spread and the firing was very brisk, whilst friendlies came pouring in to the aid of the residents of Sapri. Mia Rukn, finding that there was no escape, asked for the Tehsildar to come near him, as he had a request to make. When Gholam Muhayuddin Khan got quite close to him the holy man suddenly whipped out a small dagger and struck hard and straight at the waist of the Tehsildar, but the point of the dagger glanced off a pocket-book of Major Cavagnari's which he had asked him to carry for him. It was a lucky escape. As the Mia moved to further action he was shot down by Duffadar Torrabaz Khan, Kuki Khel Afridi, of the Guides cavalry. Killing some five or six of the enemy, which now numbered some 300 persons, the gallant Guides fought their way leisurely to the level country, removing their wounded, got to their horses, and went into Fort Abazai for that day, the officer commanding the fort having received orders from the Brigadier-General commanding the Peshawar District to give them every aid and help in his power.

Cavagnari would not let me take part in this affair, as Sapri was too far from my charge. He received great and deserved praise from the authorities for his little campaign, carried out with the greatest dash and bravery; but it did not bring the Utman Khel to their senses, and it required another little brush to bring them down on their knees.

By the close of February 1878 the Jawaki war was over and the Guides infantry were back at Hoti-Mardan, and on account of the moral effect it would produce a battery of mountain guns was located with us for a period. Cavagnari, being too busy at Peshawar, directed me to arrange for the surprise of Iskhàkot, in consultation with the Commandant of the Guides. Many were the consultations we held secretly as to how this was to be done, and above all it was necessary that not a breath of our intentions should be revealed to anyone, since Ranizai spies swarmed in numbers at Mardan and in every village to the Swat Border. It was a hard nut to crack for the following reasons. It was a strong village, numbering 500 armed men. It was situated on a ravine with perpendicular banks fifty to sixty feet in height, with only two passages through it. The villages near to Iskhàkot could supply some 3,000 men, irrespective of any aid that might come from Swat. A short time previous this village had defied the Khan of Dir and thousands of his gathering, who had been compelled to retire in disgrace. In May 1852 a force of 3,265 rank and file, with eight guns, under command of Sir Colin Campbell, had defeated these Ranizais and Swatis at this very spot, burnt Iskhàkot to the ground, with a loss of eleven killed and twenty-nine wounded on our side.

We went to the Takht-i-Bahi hill one day, nominally to inspect the ruins and have a picnic, but in reality to examine the Iskhàkot position with our telescopes and field-glasses. We came to the conclusion that the venture was risky with our small force of Guides infantry and cavalry, about 700 strong, but possible of success if we could only get, without alarming the residents, to a hill on the opposite side of the village, which hill commanded Iskhàkot. At last the eventful day arrived, and Cavagnari came over from Peshawar. At sunset the Guides infantry, cavalry, and guns of the mountain battery started from Hoti-Mardan on this expedition, the secret of which had been carefully kept, so much so that even the guides to direct us through that tremendous ravine at night time had to be secured at the last moment. Luckily, one of them, a Malik of Shergarh, knew every inch of the country, and besides was an enemy of the Iskhàkot Maliks. The plan of campaign was as follows.

Major (now Major-General) G. Stewart, with two companies of the Guides infantry and led by the Malik of Shergarh, was to go on in advance and get to the top of the hill on the other side without attracting attention. The remaining six companies were to cross the ravine by the same ford, and move in a north-easterly direction on the village. The guns, under a suitable escort, were to remain on our side of the ravine, about three-quarters of a mile above our ford, and help us with their fire when the time came. Major Wigram Battye was to remain with the guns until dawn, and then trot up by the northern ford and take up his position on the north of the village to prevent the residents from escaping in that direction. As we rode along Cavagnari made two remarks to me. The first was, 'I hope we are not going to have a running campaign all this spring and summer.' The second was a question as to the amount of fine to be imposed on the residents if our attack was successful; I replied, 'Three rupees per house, or 1,500 in all, there being some 500 houses in Iskhàkot.' On we went, hoping that our advance would not be noticed, for in the still night the fiendish neighing of the grass-cutters' tats could be heard for miles. Cavagnari and I went with the six companies, but our advance was delayed for some time by the guide proving false. At last, however, the ravine was crossed, and we were advancing in skirmishing order on the village, and were about three-quarters of a mile from it, when it became dawn, and the drums in Iskhàkot began sounding the alarm. They had noticed the Guides cavalry moving to the position assigned to them. Old men, women, and children were streaming in our direction and ascending their hill of refuge, which had been secured by the two companies under Stewart. Without firing a shot we occupied Iskhàkot, and, having remained a couple of hours there and seen the headmen of the neighbouring villages, we took twenty of the headmen as hostages to Hoti-Mardan, and wended our way back, reaching our quarters the same evening, the troops having done fifty miles in twenty-four hours.

Some time later on, several days having elapsed, I happened to call on Major Cavagnari at Peshawar, and he suddenly turned to me and said, 'Do you remember the *hujrà* or guest-place we were in at Iskhàkot, where we had our milk? Well, I have heard, on information which I believe, that at the very moment we were there the *hujrà* contained 2,000 rupees, being a tax of four rupees per house, collected for the Khans of Aladand and Thanah.' It was a kind way of showing to me that my estimated fine of three rupees per house was not an excessive one.

The Utman Khels having failed to surrender, the same force which had operated against Iskhàkot was moved up to Zam, near Tangi, some three miles north-east of Abazai, and encamped there for the night. No one expected a fight, for reports had been brought in that on our appearance the people would at once give in. The bugles sounded at 3 A.M. on a March morning, and we advanced inside the zone of low hills leading into the southern Utman Khel country. Bundles of dwarf palm, dry wood, and grass lying about here and there showed that the men of the hills had taken the alarm and meant fighting. Nawedand lay on our left, but not a sign of man, woman, child, or village cattle. One company, under Hammond, was sent to the right, and I was deputed to go with it. We came across more loads recently thrown down, then to the village of Rang-Maina and two Bucha hamlets; still not a sign of any human being or animals. The third Bucha lay close to an incline that led up gradually to high lofty hills, and here all the able-bodied males, some 300 in number, were collected. Even then we did not expect an attack, although circumstances all looked the other way. Suddenly three men started from the group and came rapidly in our direction, calling out 'Come! come!' in Pashtu. Mahbub, Khan of Matta Mughul Khel, again happened to be with me, and had evidently been employed by the Tehsildar in negotiations with the Utman Khels, for he never expected any opposition, and replied to the opposite side, in Pashtu also, 'Come on; don't be afraid.' We were standing on a hillock, scattered about but not under shelter, when Hammond, putting up his field-glass to examine the advancing party, called, 'Look out! They are going to fire.' By this time the leading man had approached to within eighty yards or less, when he raised his rifle and fired at a Sikh soldier standing near me, the bullet entering at one ear and passing out at the other, the rifles of the other two men cracking almost simultaneously. Then the three turned and fled, whilst the Sikh company opened fire on them. The first man attracted attention most, and as he ran the bullets cast up the dust in front of him and below his legs, and his escape was marvellous. Just, however, as he was reaching the door leading into the village, and when another two steps would have brought him into a place of safety, a bullet caught him in the middle of the back and knocked him over. The main body then advanced, the guns opened fire, and at last the Utman Khels, having lost sixteen killed and fearing that their villages would be burnt down, gave in. We marched back to Zam, encamped there for the night, and the next morning reached our quarters at Hoti-Mardan. We had only one man killed, the Sikh aforesaid, who died within twenty-four hours of his being wounded.

Nothing would or could induce the Panjab Government to take active measures by force against the Bunerwals. The Ambeyla campaign was still remembered, and twenty years more were to pass away before the hollowness of the Buner bubble was to be exposed by the events of 1898. When at last the Hindus of Buner, tired of a blockade that was ruining them and was not touching the Pathan element, forced the whole Buner jirga to come in and make terms, the Ashazai Maliks (the strongest section in Buner), Saadat, Nawab, and Kadir, old men who had fought against us at Ambeyla, came before me with the jirga and said: 'Sahib, up to and after the fight at Lalu, every combination that we had formed against you had been defeated and routed. There was nothing to stop your troops entering the Buner country. Why did you not go there?'

This was a question to which I could give no answer.

Thanks to my kind chief, Major Cavagnari, who never failed to remember my small services, I was five times complimented by the Government of the Panjab, on three occasions by the Secretary of State for India, and the accompanying telegram, dated March 27, 1878, was received from the Commissioner: 'The Lieutenant-Governor telegraphs that his Excellency the Viceroy desires congratulations and warmest thanks to be conveyed to you and all concerned for the successful issue of concluding Utman Khel affair.' Cavagnari was the beau-ideal of a chief, and it was a treat and honour to serve under such a man. 'Do your best, and I will back you through thick and thin.' 'Never mind reporting, but act; when a man gets into difficulties he generally takes to reporting,' were phrases that Cavagnari in his genial way implanted in my mind. He never forgot a junior who had once served him well, but would do all in his power to push him on whenever the chance came in his way. In this wise he made himself loved by his subordinates, and his memory is dearly cherished by those who had the privilege of being connected in official life with him. He was, in addition to other matters, gifted with one quality which I have never seen or met with in any other official. He would gallop off forty miles or so, go through some such expedition three of which I have described, hurry back to head-quarters; then, without having taken or made any notes, he would sit down and write his report of ten, fifteen, twenty pages of foolscap, all in the best English, in a most beautiful clear hand, without a single blot or erasure, then post it off himself, and the thing was done. The morning after our fifty-mile trip to Iskhàkot about seven of us were in Wigram Battye's room, talking and making a hideous noise, whilst seated at a table in the same room was Cavagnari, writing out his report, clear, full, and in the most beautiful penmanship, utterly indifferent to the din going on round about him. Had his precious life been spared for another year or two he would have asked the Government of India to bestow the frontier medal on those troops which had served with him in these three expeditions, and they richly deserved it.

CHAPTER VI

KHYBER AND JELALLABAD

1879–1882

Faiz Muhammad Khan, Ababakkar Khel Ghilzai, son of that Muhammad Shah Khan who had custody of Lady Macnaghten, Lady Sale, General Elphinstone, and all our hostages at Badiabad given on the occasion of the disastrous retreat from Caubul in 1842, had stopped General Sir Neville Chamberlain's mission advancing beyond Ali Masjid towards Dakka *en route* to Caubul. At this period he had been made Civil Governor of Ali Masjid by Amir Sher Ali Khan, and the interview between him and Cavagnari, when the progress of the mission was barred, took place on September 21, 1878, at a small watermill on the right bank of the stream between Lala Chena and Ali Masjid. When war had been declared against Amir Sher Ali Khan in the beginning of November, Cavagnari was encamped at Jamrud with the cavalry and infantry of the Guides, 1st Sikhs Panjab Field Force, a battery of mountain guns, while other troops were collecting. I journeyed from Hoti-Mardan to see him. 'I have worked well for you,' I said, 'on the Yusufzai Frontier; take me with you as your assistant in this coming campaign.' Cavagnari reflected, and then asked, 'In what way could I utilise your services?' My answer was, 'Persian and Pashtu are as familiar to me as English. I could be useful at Dakka, Jelall-

LALA CHENA—THE PLACE OF INTERVIEW BETWEEN SIR L. CAVAGNARI AND FAIZ MUHAMMAD KHAN, GOVERNOR OF ALI MASJID, ON SEPTEMBER 21, 1878.

abad—in fact, at any place where these two languages are spoken.' 'I shall do my best for you,' Cavagnari replied, 'but I am not sure of the Panjab Government.' I went back to Hoti-Mardan and made no further application, knowing that a promise once made by Cavagnari was sacred. That he had not forgotten me I afterwards knew, because one of the District Staff had applied for the berth that I had asked for and was told that it had been promised to me; and this same officer asked me to exchange with him, but my answer was, 'Not for your weight in gold.' Time slipped on quickly to November 21, 1878, when the advance into Afghanistan was to be commenced from three different points. About three days of grace remained when Major Hutchinson, of the Guides, riding over to Mardan to bid good-bye to his wife, brought me a letter from Cavagnari, saying that he had telegraphed to the Government of the Panjab for my services, and he desired me to join him within twenty-four hours after receipt of his orders. The answer from the Panjab Government was, 'We cannot spare Warburton, but we will give you Cunningham (Panjab Secretariat), and also Tucker' (District Superintendent Police, Peshawar, and nephew of the then Lieutenant-Governor of the Panjab).

The advance commenced on November 21, and Ali Masjid, attacked the same afternoon, remained in the hands of the enemy at nightfall. By this time, or a little later, the Afghan Commandant was informed that the British were holding the Khyber Pass at Katta Kushtia, about three miles west of Ali Masjid, and that therefore his line of retreat by the Khyber Pass and Landi Kotal back to Afghanistan was cut off. A few words will explain how this body of British troops got behind the enemy's position at Ali Masjid. The main road from Peshawar to Caubul passes through Jamrud, going almost due east to west. After leaving Jamrud it passes through an easy country, having low hills on the left hand side, and about the third mile it enters the hills at an opening called Shadi Bagiar. A ridge from the lofty Ghund-ghar on the left runs down to the road, and faces a similar ridge coming down from a prolongation of the Rhotas Range. The highway runs for a short distance through the bed of a ravine, and then joins the road made by Colonel Mackeson in 1839–42, until it ascends to the Shagai plateau on the left hand side, and here Ali Masjid is seen for the first time. Still going westward the road turns to the right, and by an easy zigzag descends to the stream (Ali Masjid) and runs along its side, and below Ali Masjid goes up the waterway. The new road along the cliff was made by us in 1879–80, and here is the narrowest pass of the Khyber, not more than 15 feet broad, with the Rhotas hill on the right hand fully 2,000 feet overhead. Still progressing, at about 400 yards from Ali Masjid, on the left hand side, three or four large springs issuing from the rock give the whole water supply to this quarter. Between two and three miles comes the Malikdin Khel hamlet of Katta Kushtia; soon after Gurgurra is reached, and then we are in Zakha Khel limits in the real 'Khyber proper,' until we come to the Shinwaris of Landi Kotal, or more properly Loargi. The valley now widens out, and on either side lie the hamlets and some sixty forts of the Zakha Khel Afridis. Here there is no stream, and the residents have to

VIEW TOWARDS PESHAWAR, SHOWING MACKESON'S ROAD AND NEW CART ROAD.

depend on rainwater collected in tanks. The Loargi Shinwari plateau is some seven miles in length, and three in its widest part. Just here, above Landi Khana, the old road was a very nasty bit. After Landi Khana the great Caubul highway passes between low hills, until it debouches on the Caubul River and leads to Dakka. From Shadi Bagiar to Landi Khana the pass cannot be more than twenty miles in a direct line. When the first detachment of our troops returned from Caubul they marched from Ali Masjid along the bed of the stream, by Lala Chena, Jabbagai, Gagri, Kaddam, and Jam, villages of the Kuki Khel Afridis, to Jamrud; but Colonel Mackeson, finding this way extremely difficult and unsuitable for guns and wheeled traffic, made an excellent road from Ali Masjid to Fort Jamrud through the hills, the same that we now use. Starting from Fort Jamrud a footpath over the stony country goes in a north-west direction to Gudar, a small hamlet, the birthplace and home of that grand old soldier Subadar Major Mauladad Khan, C.I.E., of the 20th Panjab Infantry, and passing round the eastern bend of the hamlet crosses a fairly good perennial stream, winds through the Lashora Valley and Saprai belonging to the Kuki Khel Afridis, passes between Rhotas and the highest peak of the Tartarra range, Lakka Sar, and descends into the Khyber road at Katta Kushtia. It was a most difficult road to traverse in those days, especially at night time.

At 4 p.m. on the evening of November 20, General Macpherson's brigade commenced a turning movement, and about 4 p.m. on the 21st, after a march of twenty-four hours, the Guides infantry and 1st Sikhs found themselves at Katta Kushtia, and prepared to close the Pass against the retreat of the Afghan troops in Ali Masjid. This arrival at Katta Kushtia was soon communicated to Faiz Muhammad Khan. The Afridis had not then thrown in their lot with the Afghans, and in reality never did, but there was one good man with them in Ali Masjid with a few of his clansmen, namely Malik Walli Muhammad Khan, Zakha Khel. During the night of November 21 he removed the whole garrison by a road known to him and every Afridi, leading due South of Ali Masjid, thence to the Bazàr Valley, and by the Sassobai Pass into Jelallabad. The rascally Zakha Khel deprived the Afghan troops of about 800 of their rifles, and on the morning of November 22, 1878, Ali Masjid was found vacated, and was occupied by our troops.

Reaching Dakka and requiring another assistant to go on with him, as Cunningham and Tucker were posted between Jamrud and Dakka, Cavagnari made a second application for my services. The reply was couched in similar terms to the first telegram, 'We cannot spare Warburton, but you can have Jenkyns.' At that time Jenkyns was officiating as Deputy Commissioner of Peshawar, and to enable him to go on this new duty he was relieved by Major Hastings, then carrying out the Kohat Settlement. A short time after this Cunningham went back to the Panjab Secretariat, and, a vacancy arising, Cavagnari made a third application on my behalf; but the result was the same as before so far as I was concerned, but Major Conolly, Judicial Assistant from distant Dera Ismail Khan, was sent up by the Panjab Government.

The division under command of General Sir Sam Browne advanced, secured Jelallabad, and there it had a short rest. Cavagnari wrote to me, stating that he had made several attempts to get me employed under him, all of which had failed, but that he intended continuing to apply whenever any further chance occurred. I also heard from the gallant Wigram Battye—the only letter I ever received from him, and which has been treasured ever since—to the same effect, regretting that I had been stopped from going up, but saying that Cavagnari had one other idea, which he meant to carry out, with a view to get me.

Going in to see Mr. (now Sir Donald) Macnabb, Commissioner of the Division at Peshawar, I accidentally came upon Cavagnari, who had just ridden down from Jelallabad, and was proceeding to interview his Excellency Lord Lytton, Viceroy and Governor-General of India, then shortly expected at Lahore. Cavagnari assured me that he had not forgotten me. Bad news, however, now came pouring in: gallant Wigram Battye had been killed at Futtehabad, charging at the head of his cavalry, and so beloved was he by his men that his troopers carried the dooly that contained his body all the way to Jelallabad, about fourteen miles. A squadron of the 10th Hussars in crossing the Caubul River had some forty-six men and one officer drowned.

Living with Wigram Battye, and sharing his quarters during the winter of 1877–78, I had a good opportunity of seeing the way he treated and was beloved by his men. The most troublesome troop in the Guides cavalry was the 'Farsiwan' troop: troublesome in this way only—that they were a very smart and peppery lot, and on any grievance which they felt individuals would come forward and ask to have their names removed from the regiment, *i.e.* they wanted their discharge. A few words from Wigram and the most discontented man went away thoroughly happy. One night, as we were at dinner, news was brought to mess that a Sikh rissaldar, who was dying from a long and lingering illness, wished to see Battye, who went, and we followed him to the dying man's bedside. He was one of the old school, who had fought for the Khalsa against the British between 1845 and 1848, and, having taken service with us on the break up of the Sikh power, had fought equally gallantly for the Queen Empress of India. With his long white beard falling over his chest, the dying soldier seized Wigram's hands and said, 'Sahib, if at any time that I have been serving under you I have committed any fault or made any mistake, please forgive me now.'

A telegram came from Major Cavagnari at Lahore, directing me to meet him at Naushehra that same evening, as he had at last obtained sanction to my being employed under him. So, riding to Naushehra, I had my dinner and retired to rest, as I knew Cavagnari could not possibly be there before 3 or 4 A.M. He arrived about the first hour, and, rousing me, gave me instructions regarding my new duties under him, and told me to hurry up from Hoti-Mardan as soon as possible. He then said, 'I must start now, as I have to reach Peshawar and go off at once to Gandamak, where I am shortly expecting the Amir Yakub Khan.' Going up to his dak-gharry to see him make his start, I found Ibrahim Khan of Zaida perched on the seat by the coachman. After breakfast I went back to Hoti-Mardan, packed up my things, and received the usual Panjab notification order that my services had been placed at the disposal of the Government of India Foreign Department for employment under Major L. N. Cavagnari, C.S.I. After waiting, however, two or three more days, and receiving no further orders regarding my movements, I was constrained to telegraph to Major Hastings, Deputy Commissioner at Peshawar, who informed me in reply that after Cavagnari left Lahore all had been changed. Mr. Macnabb, the kind-hearted Commissioner, sent me a copy of the accompanying letter, adding the words that are given at the end.

Extract paragraph 3 *of a letter, No.* 7 . 96 . 2, *dated April* 4, 1879, *from Secretary to Government Panjab to Secretary to Government of India Foreign Department.*

3. The Honourable the Lieutenant-Governor, however, desires me to place distinctly on record his opinion that the deputation of this officer on special duty is injurious to the interests of the public service.

Captain Warburton is an officer of intelligence and industry, and he has been in charge of Yusufzai in the Peshawar District for so considerable a period as to have obtained great local knowledge and valuable influence with the tribes and headmen on the northern border of the Peshawar District, and has an intimate acquaintance with the politics and intrigues of Swat and Buner, territories lying immediately beyond his jurisdiction. The Government of India is well aware that the Yusufzai border is always a difficult one to manage, and the more especially at the present time when the independent tribes along the whole of the North-West Frontier are in a state of excitement, and, under the guidance, or instigated by, the preaching of fanatical Mullahs, may at any time make incursions on British territory.

The troops stationed at Mardan are new to the district,

and the officers in command of them have no local experience. The removal of Captain Warburton will therefore leave Yusufzai without any officer—civil or military—who knows and is known by the headmen of the trans-border tribes.

This being the case, the withdrawal of the only officer available with competent local knowledge is to be seriously deprecated.

My dear Warburton,—I send you this extract from a letter sent to me by Government, as I think it will satisfy you that it is not from any want of appreciation of your merits, or from any intention of hindering your success in your professional career that the Panjab Government have prevented your going to Cavagnari. Now that the hot weather is coming on you should be more reconciled to staying at Mardan.

Yours, (Signed) D. C. MACNABB.

Major Cavagnari then urged that the control of the Khyber Pass portion, from Fort Jamrud to Landi Khana, should be managed by the Government of the Panjab, and in this wise the Khyber Pass was transferred from the Government of India to that of the Panjab in April 1879. Major Hastings was sent up to Landi Kotal as Political Officer of the Khyber, Mr. W. R. Merk going as his assistant to Ali Masjid, whilst Mr. H. B. Beckett, Deputy Commissioner Dera Ghazi Khan, was transferred in the same capacity to take Hastings's place at Peshawar. The Afridis, urged on by mullahs and agents of Amir Sher Ali Khan, had brought down a *lashkar*, or army, as they called it, on Ali Masjid, about three days after it had fallen into our hands (about November 25, 1878). They attacked our troops one night, fired into our camp, and then went back to their homes, as they had no heart for fighting against us. All the mischief that was being done was the work of the Zakha Khel marauders living at Ilacha, Karamna, Barg, and in the Bazàr Valley. This will be dealt with later on, when I come to my management of the Khyber charge.

The Treaty of Gandamak was signed towards the end of May 1879, and all the troops—British and native—were hurried back out of the Jelallabad Valley towards Peshawar. Cholera followed in their footsteps, and tainted every encampment from Jelallabad to Abbotabad, to Murree, and past Rawal Pindi towards Lahore. The Guides cavalry and infantry returned to Hoti-Mardan.

Jenkyns, who, as Senior Assistant to Sir L. Cavagnari, had come to make arrangements for the march of the mission to Caubul from Hoti-Mardan *viâ* Peshawar, Kohat, and Kurram, said to me in the kindest manner, 'I have got the berth Cavagnari meant for you; as I served under him, and you were not allowed to come, he could not throw me over.' It was impossible to resist thanking him, and I wished him every good fortune. Besides, a friend had written to me from Simla, and imparted to me as a secret that Cavagnari had asked for me to go with him to Caubul as his private secretary. I had, therefore, still hope of joining their party—a hope which, now recalled in the light of after events, was fortunately, perhaps, not fulfilled.

The month of July came round, and Mr. Macnabb, our Commissioner, had gone away to Rawal Pindi, and his place had been taken by Colonel W. G. Waterfield, C.S.I., just returned from Kurram. I received a letter from the latter asking me into Peshawar, and when I appeared before him he said, 'The

Lieutenant-Governor of the Panjab offers you the post of Political Officer Khyber. Will you accept it?' I, of course, said, 'Yes.' I then learnt that Mr. Merk had left Ali Masjid, and had gone away stricken down by a bad attack of fever, and that Major Hastings was anxious to take furlough to Europe, and hence the chance of my taking over his work and duties. On July 31, 1879, I reached Fort Jamrud in the evening, and met Major Hastings, who had come down from Landi Kotal early that morning. I had not been inside the fort since my one visit some years before with Mr. W. H. Smith, M.P. But what a change was now going on! In every direction officers' quarters and barracks were being put up with lightning rapidity. We were entertained by the officers of the 10th Bengal Lancers, and the heat in the verandah as we had our evening meal was something to be remembered, but I felt it more as it was my first day of initiation. Early next morning we rode to Ali Masjid, had lunch, and in the afternoon journeyed on to Landi Kotal, which was reached about 6 P.M. August 1, 1879. At that time there were two British and three Native Infantry regiments, three mountain batteries, two companies of Sappers and Miners, a troop of the 10th Bengal Lancers, two companies of Khyber Jezailchies, and a goodly staff, with officers of the Commissariat and Ordnance Departments, located at the plateau. The dreaded cholera was in camp, and every morning and evening one or two victims were consigned to the cemetery; and the funeral procession, from the time it left the hospital mortuary to the time the body was consigned to earth, was clearly visible to all. But what had made the place so unhealthy? Irrespective of other evils of our system, over a thousand dead camels, bullocks, donkeys, etc., had been buried at Landi Kotal, and every now and then one came on a mound which on inquiry was found to be a dead camel, left on the ground and covered over with only some dust and stones.

Here I met for the first time Malik Walli Muhammad Khan, Zakha Khel, the same individual who had conducted the Afghan troops from Ali Masjid on the night of November 22, 1878, through the Bazàr Valley. Like a loyal man he had gone to Caubul and presented himself before Amir Yakub Khan and asked if he had any further commands for him. The Amir replied that he had acted like a true man, but must now go and make friends with the English, as he could do no more for him. So he had journeyed down to Gandamak, and interviewed Sir L. Cavagnari, who asked him if he intended running away at any time? Malik Walli Muhammad said: 'Here is my hand that I will remain true to you for the future.' Cavagnari directed him to proceed to Landi Kotal, and to wait there for instructions. Not only for his own sake, but also for that of Sir L. Cavagnari, I was drawn to this loyal old man, the only one of the Khyber Afridi Maliks who, having fought for Yakub Khan, and when he had done all that he could for his old master had desisted from embroiling himself further solely on the advice given to him by the ex-Amir. Later on I shall note how this man swore on the Koran to carry out my orders and wishes, and for upwards of fifteen years, through good luck and bad luck, helped me to break up every combination of the Khyber Maliks directed against the British Government.

In spite of the large garrison at Landi Kotal, and the abundance of picquets and sentries thrown out every night, nothing was safe from the depredations of Shinwari, Shilmani, and Zakha Khel thieves. Nearly every night some tent was entered and property carried off. Firing, as might be expected, was brisk, but the bullets seemed to cause more annoyance to the sleeping garrison than to the sneaking thief, who escaped in the darkness. The Government of the Panjab urged on us to hasten down all the Maliks who had thrown in their lot with the British Government, as well as those who had shared the fortunes of the Amir of Afghanistan, together with full complete jirgas from every tribe sharing in the allowances of the Khyber Range, and, having brought them down to Peshawar, to see whether some arrangement could not be made with them by which peace could be assured throughout the Khyber from one end to the other at all seasons of the year.

Four of the most important Maliks—Ahmad Khan, Sipah, Sarfaraz Khan, Malikdin Khel, Abdulla Nur, Kuki Khel, and Walli Muhammad Khan, Zakha Khel—had thrown in their lot from the very beginning with the Amir's party, because it was from that quarter that they had been getting their Khyber allowances whenever these, at rare intervals, were doled out to the tribesmen, and because they had no faith in the continuance of any British policy. The Caubul allowances were certainly small, but the tribesmen got something in the end; on the other hand, they did not know how long the war would last, and whether at its close the British Sarkar would not throw them over if it suited the Government to do so. The lessons of the first and second Afghan wars were firmly implanted in their minds and memories. After a good deal of needful pushing and urging, every Malik or chief and every tribal jirga, fully represented, marched down to Peshawar; and by September 6, 1879, Hastings first, and then I, joined them, and the work of arrangement commenced.

Just then came the terrible news from Ali Khel in the form of a telegram telling us that on September 3, 1879, the Residency at Caubul had been attacked, and that Sir L. Cavagnari, Jenkyns, Walter Hamilton, Ambrose Kelly, with all the escort of Guides cavalry and infantry, servants, etc., had been massacred, and the buildings destroyed by fire, after being plundered by Yakub Khan's soldiery and the Caubul mob.

This crushing calamity fell like a thunderbolt on the Indian world, and every one deplored the death of our brave and gifted Envoy, of gallant Walter Hamilton (just aged twenty-one), and of those companions who had made a defence against overwhelming numbers—a defence never to be forgotten so long as Englishmen know how to admire and reverence such feats as the Guides performed on that sadly to be remembered day. To me, personally, Cavagnari's loss was irreparable. I had the greatest admiration for the man and his splendid abilities as a public servant of the State; but on personal grounds I had every reason to deplore the death of one who had always stood my friend and had helped me whenever opportunity offered in his way.

Hastings had been appointed to the Political Staff of General Roberts, commanding the troops in Kurram, and as they were to move as early as possible in advance of the Jelallabad Field Force he left at once for Kohat, *en route* to Kurram, to join there. For twenty-two days after his departure the arrangements with the Afridis were left in my hands, and on September 28, 1879, I sent up my final report to the Commissioner for the information of Government. My friend Malik Walli Muhammad Khan, Zakha Khel, had got what he wanted, and what was his right, viz., the Maliki (or chieftainship) of half the Zakha Khel Afridis, the most important tribe in the Khyber Range, mustering some 5,000 armed men, every individual being a thief, raider, and robber by birth, inclination, and habit carried down for many centuries. The rival chief was Malik Khwas Khan. Years after this arrangement with the Khyber Afridis, which was the best that could be made under the circumstances, Walli Muhammad Khan, whenever charged by me with any neglect of my orders, would say, 'When I was in want and trying to get my Maliki, did you not bring out a bag of rupees and say, "Here is money for you to spend and strengthen your party if you are in want of cash"? And did you not secure for me my Maliki? And am I going to work against you after what you have done for me?' After an experience of this individual extending over eighteen years I can say he was always a good and staunch friend to me.

I was appointed Chief Political Officer with General Sir R. O. Bright, commanding the Jelallabad Field Force; but as we were not expected to advance until carriage and transport had been secured, we were not much hurried in our movements. Having completed my work at Peshawar, I went up to Landi Kotal, Mr. Merk having been sent to me as assistant at Dakka. Just about this period there occurred one of those cases which one seldom comes across in the career of British soldiers serving in India. An old man—a Zakha Khel of Garli, Lala Beg—having sold his wood in the bazaar, was returning to his home one evening, accompanied by a young relative some ten or twelve years of age. A soldier, meeting him in a lonely part, knocked him down, kicked him violently in the ribs, then went at the lad, who escaped. He then moved rapidly towards his regimental tents, his appearance and the bloodstains on his clothes exciting remark amongst his comrades. When the report of what had occurred reached headquarters, this soldier was at once arrested on suspicion, and as he was being conducted to the guard-tent, he picked up a tent-peg and felled a tent-pitcher for no cause or reason. His defaulter's sheet afterwards explained that he was a man of violent temper, and addicted to assaulting natives of India. His victim died, and the Colonel of the regiment, being anxious to see the man punished, asked me to get the Afridi lad who was with the deceased when he was felled and kicked, to see whether he could identify the soldier. On my summons, the lad and two of his uncles came up to regimental headquarters; but all our endeavours to induce them to give evidence failed. Nothing would persuade the uncles to permit the lad to look at the soldiers paraded for his inspection, as they declared 'that the British soldier must have been the worse for liquor when he committed the act, and a drunkard was not answerable for his actions.' The Commissioner was good enough to support a recommendation that 300 rupees should be given to the heirs of the Afridi who had died from the effects of the kicking, and, the sanction being received, the money was made over to them, and this made them happy.

Mr. Cunningham, from the Panjab Secretariat—the same who had been appointed under Sir L. Cavagnari in November 1878—having arrived at Landi Kotal to take my place, I gave over charge about October 10, 1879, and joined General Bright's camp, then pitched at the same locality. A telegram from the Foreign Secretary hastened my departure in advance to Jelallabad, for the purpose of making an inquiry into the revenue returns of that district, and when I reached Jelallabad, I found General (now Sir Charles) Gough, with portions of his command, including the Guides cavalry and infantry, encamped there. I pitched my tent near the camp of the Guides, and was made at home at their mess. Colonel (now Sir Francis H.) Jenkins introduced me to Sardar Abdul Khalik Khan, Barakzai, of Besud (brother of Sardar Maddat Khan, of the same place), who just at that moment happened to be in his camp. Both these brothers had done good service for Sir L. Cavagnari in the previous spring, and to each a written acknowledgment had been given, recommending him to the good graces of all Englishmen. The Besud family consisted of four brothers; of these Sardar Maddat Khan was the senior, then came Sardar Abdul Khalik (Khalo) Khan, both these being extremely handsome men, about six feet high, and of splendid appearance. Next day, the General, with the Guides and other troops then present at Jelallabad, moved away towards Gandamak, their places being taken by other troops from the rear.

My work about ascertaining the revenues of the

district was lightened by discovering that a good-sized volume had already been lately written by Jenkyns, who was killed at Caubul, giving a complete list of everything that one could wish for. This work had been printed at the Foreign Office Press, and all that I had to do was to draw the attention of the Foreign Secretary to it, and to ask that several copies should be sent down for our use. In a few days General Bright and his Staff appeared at Jelallabad, a large camp was formed there, and we were looking forward to a merry Christmas, and dreaming of happy times, little thinking of what would actually take place before December 25 came round.

Sardar Muhammad Hassan Khan (the same who came to England with Shahzada Nasrulla Khan in 1895), grandson of Sardar Futteh Khan, was then Governor of Jelallabad on behalf of Amir Yakub Khan, to whom he was deeply and devotedly attached. And with some reason. They had been brought up together in their childhood at Herat. When Amir Yakub Khan, trusting to his father's word, came from Herat to Caubul, and was thrown into a cell to undergo nearly six years' imprisonment, the cell adjoining his had been allotted to Muhammad Hassan Khan, who was sent in chains from Mashad to Herat, and thence to Caubul. Amir Sher Ali Khan's flight to Mazar-i-Sherif in 1878 was the immediate cause of the release of Amir Yakub Khan and of Sardar Muhammad Hassan Khan, who was then appointed Governor of Ghuzni. After the signature of the treaty of Gandamak, Amir Yakub Khan transferred him in the same capacity to Jelallabad, and he rode on one horse from Ghuzni to Caubul, interviewed his master, remaining some days there, and then rode the same animal in twenty-four hours to Jelallabad. Feeling assured that if Amir Yakub Khan was to remain Amir of Afghanistan, his Governor of Jelallabad would be a better man and far more useful than any nominee that we could appoint, it was urged on the General to accept him as Governor, and receive him under a guard of honour at a public durbar—which was done. But Sardar Muhammad Hassan Khan's feelings were too much tied up in his master's cause, in which he had fought and suffered so much for many years; and, although he became exceedingly friendly with me, and opened his mind freely to me on every subject, he still watched closely every move that was going on at Caubul with feverish anxiety. He worked hard for us in every way, hoping that Amir Yakub Khan might yet remain as Amir of Afghanistan, and he would thus have pleased both his master and us. I will quote one special instance where his services were extremely useful to us. A large caravan of camels belonging to the Kaka Khels of the Ziarat Kaka Sahib, near Naushehra, were carrying warm clothing from Peshawar for Lord Roberts's troops at Caubul; the winter was coming on, and the clothing was urgently required there. The caravan reaching Dakka would not take shelter inside our fort under the guard of our soldiery, but went on to Girdi Sarkani, a small hamlet on the right bank of the Caubul River, and three miles further west. The Kaka Khels, being looked upon as holy men, deeply reverenced by all Mussulmans, felt they would be quite safe anywhere, especially at Girdi Sarkani. That same night, however, a band of Sangu Khel Shinwari raiders came down, secured the camels, laden with the clothing, took the property away to their own hills, and then returned the camels to the owners. The Kaka Khels presented a petition to Mr. Merk at Dakka, asking for the clothing to be recovered; but as the offence had not been committed in his limits, and the Sangu Khel were not in his charge, he recorded this fact on the back of the petition, and referred the Kaka Khels to the authorities at Jelallabad. On my representation, Sardar Muhammad Hassan Khan sent for the entire Sangu Khel jirga to Jelallabad, and gave them a severe reprimand, warning them that if the clothing was not recovered and brought back, he would go into their country with a force, as he had done some two months before, and destroy every village and fort he could lay hands upon. He then sent the jirga back to their hills to carry out his orders, letting them have a few of his men (Khasadars) to assist them, and directed Ali Khan, Dehgan of Pesh-Bolak, a man of great character, to superintend the business and see it rapidly carried out. In a few days news came that the clothing had all been collected, and the jirga asked that carriage might be supplied them to bring the things into Jelallabad. They were told that as they had stolen the clothing from Girdi Sarkani, they must carry the property so far on their own animals, and deliver it over to the Jelallabad authorities at that village. They then appealed secretly to the Political Officer at Dakka, who was under the Panjab Government. Mr. Merk let them have transport, and the clothing was conveyed on our animals, and delivered over at Dakka. I have noticed this incident because it explains that it was no easy matter to force the Sangu Khel Shinwaris to collect such a large quantity of stolen clothing in their far-away hills merely on the mandate of the Governor of Jelallabad.

At the request of the General, the Governor and I went away from Jelallabad to see where and in what quarters forage could be procured. As we left the city by the gate that faces Caubul, the head priest of the Hindu community met us, and presented me with three to four cardamums. For three days and three nights I was the guest of Sardar Muhammad Hassan Khan in a Ghilzai fort, near Rosabad, and entirely in his power. I went one evening to see the General who had just come to Rosabad, and the next day we purposed returning to Jelallabad. As the Governor and I rode into our fort, the messenger from Caubul followed in behind us. The Sardar was in daily communication with Caubul, and it is very strange that he was not apprised of Amir Yakub Khan's coming down to Jelallabad, which actually happened the next day. More curious still was it that, knowing I was in Sardar Muhammad Hassan's power, without a single man to protect me, I was not told of what was going to happen on the morrow. If, on the other hand, Sardar Muhammad Hassan Khan knew the evening before, when we went together to Rosabad, that his master and friend was being brought down as a prisoner, he certainly dissembled his feelings in a wonderful way. After dinner we played chess, and when I retired to rest his manners never showed the agony that must have been gnawing at his heart. He might have had me carried off or killed whilst in this lone Ghilzai fort surrounded by his followers, but he trusted and treated me as an honoured guest, whose safety must be assured.

The next morning Sardar Muhammad Hassan Khan and I, with a few of his followers, rode up to the battlefield of Futtehabad, and examined the spot where Wigram Battye had charged at the head of his squadron to save the guns. Coming back, I saw an escort of the Carabiniers and 24th Panjab Infantry out, and learnt that they were waiting for Amir Yakub Khan, who was being brought down from Caubul under an escort. This forced me to hurry our movements, and the Governor, wanting to return to Jelallabad by Sultanpur, turned off the road to Cantonments, whilst I kept to the main route, and got in advance of the cavalcade escorting the ex-Amir. Turner, of the 2nd Panjab Infantry, was in charge of the party, and sundry demands had to be made for the comfort of the royal captive, and, curious to relate, the Governor of Jelallabad had it in his power to let him have a whiff from a 'kalian' that once belonged to him in the old days, when he was ruler over the Herat province. After being introduced to Amir Yakub Khan, and seeing that all his wants were satisfied, I ventured to ask a question harking back to the time when Arminius Vambery, after having seen Khiva and Bokhara, arrived at Herat, and appeared in Sardar Muhammad Yakub Khan's presence. Mr. Vambery in his book states that, having given the benediction, he sat down next to the Sardar, and pushed his wazir to one side with a good deal of violence. The young Sardar, peering into his face, said, '*Walla au billa, Faringhi hasti.*' This Vambery denied, and the conversation was then changed. Having reminded Amir Yakub Khan of the above circumstance, I asked him if he had identified Mr. Vambery as a European, and on what grounds. The ex-Amir said, 'I was seated in an upper chamber, watching a parade of my troops, and the band was playing on the open ground in front of my window. I noticed a man beating time to the music of the band with his foot. I knew at once that he must be a European, as Asiatics are not in the habit of doing this. Later on, when this man came into my darbar, I charged him with being a Feringhi, which he denied. However, I did not press the matter, being afraid that if suspicions had been roused against him, his life might not have been safe.' The same circumstances had been told to me by Sardar Muhammad Hassan Khan six weeks before Amir Yakub Khan's arrival at Jelallabad. It may be noted that Sardar Muhammad Yakub Khan and he were both at Herat when Mr. A. Vambery journeyed there after his wonderful adventures and vicissitudes in Central Asia. Strange it must seem to have associated hourly for months throughout his dangerous travels in Khiva and Bokhara with his darwesh companions, to have shared in all their meals, and joined in all their prayers, and yet to have defied all detection; and then to have been discovered by one keen-eyed observer for beating time with his foot to the music of an improvised European band playing on the glacis of the fortress of Herat!

Amir Yakub Khan went away the next morning towards Peshawar, and after this it seemed certain that nothing would keep Sardar Muhammad Hassan Khan with us. He swore on the holy book that he was going to remain true, but this was only to gain time. In a friendly way he was told that if he found his duties irksome and intolerable, I would represent his case to the General, and ask him to let the Sardar depart with honour and dignity. However, he preferred running away one night in the month of December 1879, and suffered for this afterwards, for many, many years. Things were looking dark in the direction of Caubul, but no one in or about Jelallabad had the least idea what a serious combination Mushki Alam and Muhammad Jan Khan were raising against us. The Jelallabad garrison was weak, because every man that could be spared was pushed on to the front, and communications with Caubul became interrupted. Having to act promptly, the General obtained sanction for appointing Sardar Maddat Khan as Governor of Jelallabad, his deputy being his brother Sardar Abdul Khalik Khan, whom I shall hereafter style Sardar Khalo Khan, the name he was best known by to the people and to us. This gave us the support of their strong party in the Jelallabad Valley.

The eve of Christmas 1879 fell particularly dark and gloomy, and a very unlucky and unlooked-for event occurred that night which did not tend to make the morrow any brighter for us in camp at Jelallabad. A party of ailing and sick doolie-bearers were started for Barikab, a long stage sixteen miles towards Peshawar, in carts under the usual escort. The last two or three carts lingered on the way, the doolie-bearers halting whenever a chance offered of having a smoke, so that by sunset of the 24th they had made but seven miles, and were at a road-post in Chor-Galli (the Thief's Alley), a most dangerous spot, always avoided at night time. The guardians of the post warned the bearers that they must clear out at once, as the place was not safe for any one, and they themselves dared not remain there during the hours of darkness. Nothing could or would move the *kahars*, and there they remained. As bad luck would have it, a band of Mandezai Shinwari raiders came down that very night and cut up these unfortunate men, the tidings of the sad event reaching us about 9 A.M. on Christmas morning. A party of cavalry was sent out to make inquiries, and the information brought back was that the Mandezai raiders from the hills had passed the night of the 23rd at a village called Banda-Kaddi-Roghani, the residents of which had fed and sheltered the gang, knowing the purpose for which they had left their homes at the base of the Safed-Koh mountains. This was the village to punish, for there were no troops available to go against the Mandezais in the hills, who mustered 3,000 fighting men. I was called up, and in my presence the reporting officer told General Bright that the offending village was some seven to eight miles away, and had no defences. I was then asked my opinion as to the force necessary to surround and take the village, and I said, 'If the place is situated as has just been reported, a couple of guns, 200 infantry and some cavalry would be enough.' I had not been out myself, so knew nothing about the village or its capabilities. It was deemed necessary to strike at once for offence or defence. With considerable difficulty, 100 Europeans and 100 Native infantry, with two guns and a troop of Carabiniers, under command of Colonel Mackenzie, commandant of the 3rd Bengal Cavalry, were collected at Barikab in about two days. We took Sardar Khalo Khan with us, and disclosed to him that we were ordered to go to Banda-Kaddi-Roghani that night, surround it, and bring so many of the headmen away prisoners, because they had fed and sheltered a band of Shinwari raiders who had cut up our doolie-bearers. The old gentleman was very angry, said our force was far too weak, and that we were going on a fool's business. We replied that orders had to be carried out.

At 1 A.M., with a troop of Carabiniers, two guns of Maginnis's battery, 200 infantry, and a troop of 17th Bengal Cavalry, we commenced our march from Barikab, and just before sunrise our small force was drawn up on the rounded plateau to the west of and commanding the valley where the village was presumed to be. A thick impenetrable fog hid every hamlet in the Rud-i-Hissarak Valley. As the sun's rays gradually dispelled the mist, and portions of the valley in our neighbourhood became visible, the troop of Native cavalry was sent to get behind the village, and prevent the residents from escaping to the hills. Soon the whole valley lay exposed to our view, and my heart made a great jump at seeing the trap we had got into. Banda-Kaddi-Roghani consisted of three villages, each with high thick walls and two towers, and as far as the eye could see towards the Safed-Koh, the whole valley was closely packed with strong, defensible forts. By the route we had come from Barikab lay three or four large open villages with no towers or high walls, but in case of a retreat before the enemy the residents could have made it very hot for us in such a broken country, full of ravines and water-channels. Sardar Khalo Khan sent his special agent with a few of his men to tell the villagers that we had come with 5,000 men, and if ten of the headmen did not come in to us at once, their villages would be levelled with the ground.

They found the residents in their houses, mostly in their beds, and pointing to our array on the hillside, the guns brought into action, levelled at their towers, and the cavalry in their rear, they delivered our message and demanded a speedy answer. With my field-glass I carefully watched the proceedings. First of all there was intense excitement amongst the community, one or two swords were drawn, a few rifles handled, then they all sat down near the fire for a conference, and one man brought a 'hookah,' which was passed round, and every one took a whiff in turn. I closed my glasses with a sigh of intense relief; for I then knew that the game was up. The ten captives soon appeared, and we started on the return journey to Barikab.

Gradually the district became more peaceful, and the influence of Sardar Maddat Khan and his friends in the valley began to be exercised in the right direction. The Barakzai Sardar was a well-meaning man, entirely in the hands of his more able and cleverer brother, who knew as well as any man in the world how to look after number one. It was Sardar Khalo Khan's own folly that in the end ruined himself and all his brothers.

Orders now came from Caubul for a brigade to move into the Laghman Valley, and see what could be done with the residents of that turbulent district, and our march commenced early in the beginning of 1880. General Bright and some of his Staff came on as spectators, and I was directed to open up communications with the people of the country, and see what supplies and forage could be obtained for our troops and transports. We crossed from the right to the left bank of the Caubul River by the Daronta ford, and after going for about half a mile, recrossed to the right bank, and encamped by the very large fort of Azmatulla Khan, Jabbar Khel Ghilzai. A portion of the troops kept entirely to the right-hand side of the treacherous stream, and went by a zigzag road made by us up the hillside, which descended in like fashion into the plains of Laghman, and by this route I also journeyed. The Jabbar Khel Ghilzais had certainly some very fine forts about here, and very useful they proved to be for locating our troops within their houses and walled enclosures. Sardar Asaf Khan was governor of this district, and he soon came in to see the General; but for many days the Maliks and chiefs would not venture near us, and our commissariat prospects began to look very gloomy so far as Laghman was concerned. One by one a few chiefs came in, were spoken to kindly and treated in a very friendly manner; then a large gathering were received by the General in open darbar, a few presents made to them, and the ice was broken. After this we had no trouble: the chiefs of the different villages in the Alishang and Aliangar valleys had hundreds of their retainers out every day, bringing in forage and supplies. Part of the brigade went out for three days and encamped near Tigri, at the junction of the two rivers; from here we visited Badiabad and saw the fort—then levelled with the ground—where Lady Macnaghten, Lady Sale, and the unfortunate prisoners secured during the dreadful retreat in the winter of 1842 had passed many cruel days of captivity. The brigade marched from Tigri to Mandrawar, whilst Sardar Asaf Khan and I went to see the ziarat, or shrine, of Mehter Lamech (Noah's father), which lies in the sandy desert about two miles due south of Tigri. I also saw the tomb of Muhammad Shah Khan, at one time lord of Badiabad, who had treated our ladies and other prisoners with great harshness. Badiabad had been destroyed by order of Amir Dost Muhammad Khan; and when the great Ghilzai chief died, and was buried in this ziarat, so hated was his name, and so powerful were the enemies that he had made, that twice his body was exhumed out of the precincts of the most sacred shrine in Afghanistan, and thrown into the open. He was buried for the third time, and a guard placed over the tomb night and day to protect his remains from further insult. On my representations, the General had spared Faiz Muhammad Khan's villages which lie near Badiabad (Muhammad Shah Khan was father to Faiz Muhammad Khan, who had the interview with Cavagnari néar Ali Masjid in the Khyber on September 21, 1878), and later Faiz Muhammad sent in a verbal message to me that he would never after this raise his hands against the British Government. As Sardar Asaf Khan and I were leaving the shrine, the head keeper rushed up to us in great alarm and said, 'Here is a Sahib taking a picture of the ziarat, and he has only two men with him. This is Thursday, and hundreds of Talibs will come and say their prayers here this day; they may mob the gentleman, and then you will come and hang me. Please take him away.' We found the intruder to be Mr. McNair, of the Survey Department, quietly sketching, with two troopers of the 17th Bengal Cavalry behind him, but we persuaded him to come away with us. Some days afterwards I sent a few men with Mr. McNair to conduct him over the Adrak Badrak Pass, and having effected this with safety, he appeared before the General commanding the Gandamak Brigade, then on tour near Seh-Baba, much to that officer's astonishment, who would hardly credit that he had accomplished such a dangerous trip without a large escort. Mr. McNair, some few years later, disguised himself as a native doctor, and went with Hussain Shah, Mia Kaka Khel, through Swat to Dir and the confines of Kafiristan, and came back after many hairbreadth escapes. A rascally Kaka Khel enemy of Hussain's disclosed to the people who he really was, and it required all 'Shu Baba's' influence to shelter his life. When I saw him last at Peshawar, having escaped all dangers in Swat and Dir, he was trying to induce the Panjab Government to punish Rahat Shah Mia, the Kaka Khel referred to; but before he could succeed in his object I think he died from a severe attack of fever.

Our expedition into Laghman was presumed to have been a great success, insomuch that it had attracted all the chiefs and Sardars to us, and certainly they and the people became very friendly towards our Government. When the troops came back to Jelallabad and were withdrawn from Laghman, most of the headmen followed us, and we tried to repay them in a measure for their attention to us. In May 1885, when I went down to Landi Khana, to hand over the heavy guns presented to Amir Abdur Rahman Khan by the Government, I was brought face to face with Sartip Muhammad Hassan Khan, the commandant of the *Khasadars* at Dakka. This man's home was in a village just above Tigri in the Laghman Valley, and he was one of the few men who kept aloof from us when we went up there in 1880. This he revealed to me in a bold, offensive way; then after a pause he said, 'The Amirs of Afghanistan never could get their revenues from Laghman without sending a large force to overawe its residents; how was it, then, that you managed to go all over that district, and secure all that you required, without any opposition?' I left the Sartip to answer the question himself.

A severe attack of dysentery and breakdown of system compelled me to go before a medical board, which sent me back to Peshawar in the month of April 1880. But before this happened, most of the notables in the Jelallabad Valley, more especially Ali Khan, Dehgan of Pesh-Bolak, had opened their minds to me on the subject of our policy in Afghanistan in general and at Jelallabad in particular. The language used by one and all was of this nature: 'Sahib, when Major Cavagnari first came here we joined him and threw in our lot with the British Government, thinking you were going to remain here for good. But you cleared out on the first opportunity, and left us to our fate. For six months we lived with rifles in our hands, dreading every moment that our last day had come—not that Amir Yakub Khan oppressed us, but that our real enemies, our cousins, heirs to our landed property, were hounding on the Mullahs to attack and kill us because we had been friends to the Feringhi, so that our cousins might get hold of our houses, lands, and possessions. You have come again, and we have once more joined our fortunes to yours. Tell us now what your Government intends to do in the future. Are you going to forsake us once more, and leave us in the hands of our enemies?'

My reply was—and I could give no other—that I

was only a servant of the British Government, and that I had no power over its policy, my duty being only to obey its orders.

In a letter dated October 29, 1879, from the Government of the Panjab to the Secretary to the Government of India Foreign Department, Sir Robert Egerton expressed his opinion that Lieut.-Col. Waterfield, C.S.I., Major Hastings, Deputy Commissioner, and Captain Warburton, Political Officer in charge of the Khyber, with the native officers who had served under them, had accomplished a difficult task creditably and satisfactorily. Later on, in April 1880, General (afterwards Sir R. O.) Bright, commanding the Khyber Line Force, writing to me from Safed Sang, said:

> I cannot let you leave without telling you how valuable your services have been to me during the six months we have been associated in working the difficult problem of Jelallabad politics. Your labours were incessant, and the clearness and tact with which you managed the affairs left nothing to be desired. I am particularly indebted to you for your exertions in providing forage and supplies, in which you were entirely successful and so prevented what at one time threatened to be a very serious difficulty. Our success in the Laghman expedition in establishing friendly relations with so many of the Khans and head maliks was entirely due to your tact in managing them, and it was not the least of the services for which I am indebted to you.

I was carried in a doolie stage by stage to Peshawar, and kept to my room ten days before I was permitted to undertake the journey to Bombay. From there I sailed for England in the Peninsular and Oriental Company's steamer to Venice, and made my way to London by Turin, Paris, and

Folkestone. The day after my arrival in London, I was taken before the late Sir Richard Quain, who carefully examined me for nearly an hour. On my offering a fee, Sir Richard accepted one guinea and refused to take a penny more, on the ground that I had been fighting the battles of my country. Next day he came to see me as I was laid up with a touch of Peshawar fever, and on my wife offering a fee he shook his head and passed downstairs. It is right that such acts should be remembered and noted down. Extreme hard work and exposure in Jelallabad and Laghman brought on an illness which kept me ten months in the hands of various medical advisers, and confined me for eleven weeks to my bed in the home hospital at Fitzroy House, Fitzroy Square. Time after time news came from the direction of Jelallabad that after my departure troubles had recommenced in that quarter of Afghanistan, proving once more that to deal with Afghans officers must be employed who have knowledge of their languages, customs, and ways.

CHAPTER VII

RETURN TO THE KHYBER

1882–1884

On February 16, 1882, I was back again in charge of the Khyber Pass arrangements. But what a change it was from the old days, when the Pass was occupied by 5,000 British and native troops, when small local convoys went up and down at stated periods under a regular guard, and no *armed* Afridi not in our service was permitted to be seen in the defile! Kafilas or caravans worked regularly between Peshawar and Caubul, the *modus operandi* in entering and going out of the Khyber Pass limits being as follows. The caravans from the direction of Caubul were escorted by the Amir's *khasadars* from Dakka to Landi Khana every Monday and Thursday morning in the week, and were met there by a party of our Khyber Rifles, who brought them to Landi Kotal by the evening, and they there passed two nights. H.H. the Amir's limits ended at Tor-Kham, about 2,000 yards from Landi Khana on the road to Dakka; but as there was no water to be had at Tor-Kham, and there were 200,000 gallons available every twenty-four hours at Landi Khana, the Amir's levies had been allowed to exchange the caravans at Landi Khana before they went back to Dakka. The convoys proceeding to Caubul left the city of Peshawar every Monday and Thursday, and by sunset collected at Jamrud, paid their tolls, and passed those nights there. Every Tuesday and Friday the caravan collected at Landi Kotal, came down with its guard to Ali Masjid, and halted there until the caravan from Jamrud came up with its escort; then the caravans changed hands, and the Landi Kotal escort taking charge of the Jamrud lot took them up to Landi Kotal, kept them there during the nights of Tuesday and Friday, and on the mornings of Wednesday and Saturday took them down to Landi Khana, and delivered them over to the safe custody of the Amir's levies, who marched them away to Dakka. In a similar way the Caubul caravan was brought down to Jamrud on Tuesdays and Fridays, and went on to Peshawar City on the mornings of Wednesday and Saturday. These arrangements were the best that could have been organised and the safest. One thing, however, seemed to me to be highly objectionable, and that was that after the troops were withdrawn from the Khyber in 1881 no Europeans were permitted to go beyond Jamrud in the direction of the Pass.

A few words are necessary regarding the Khyber staff and some of the most notorious maliks or chiefs of the tribes of the Khyber Range. An Orakzai gentleman named Akbar Khan, scion of a good family, who had formerly been in the Peshawar Police and in 1879 had been sent up to aid Major Hastings, was Assistant-Political in the Khyber. Sardar M. Aslam Khan (now Lieut.-Col. Aslam Khan, C.I.E.) was in command of the Khyber Jezailchis. When he took charge they were an untidy, unkempt band of excellent men, very good material for warfare in any country, but without any discipline or *esprit-*

LOOKING DOWN THE KHYBER PASS FROM THE WALLS OF FORT ALI MASJID.

de-corps. The tribesmen called them Sùr-Lakkais, or red-tails, from a piece of red tag stuck in their turbans to distinguish them from the rest of their brethren. By dint of patience, and contrary to the advice of certain people who objected to seeing the Khyber levies either properly dressed or fairly drilled, we persevered in the course we had adopted, knowing for certain from long experience that the Afridi recruit was just as proud of a good, well-disciplined corps as either Goorkha, Pathan, or Sikh, all that he objected to being interference with his ancestral tribal customs.

We were rewarded in the end, when the Khyber Rifles behaved splendidly in the Black Mountain expeditions of 1888, 1891, and when they fought against their own kith and kin, brother against brother, in that fatal month of August 1897, killing and wounding 180 of the Afridi lashkar, until, having no head to look to or to guide them, treachery and discord ensued, and the Landi Kotal serai was delivered over to the Mullah gathering.

Abdulla Nur, Kuki Khel, was the oldest malik amongst the Afridi chiefs, and about this period he was close upon eighty-four years of age. In 1861 he had paid a thousand rupees to have Malik Gholam Kadir killed in his fort about two miles east of Ali Masjid, and in this way not only did he secure the chieftainship of the whole tribe, but he married at the same time the mother and the widow of the murdered man. By the first he had his eldest son Hyder; and from the second were born to him three or four lads, the senior being Amin Khan, the next Zaman Khan, whose names will appear further on in one or two troublesome episodes. Abdulla Nur had always been hostile to the British Government. He was the only Afridi senior who was or tried to be rude to Sir L. Cavagnari when he had his interview with Faiz Muhammad Khan at Lala Chena on September 21, 1878; and he was the last malik to come in to us in September 1879, and then only did so when he was distinctly and emphatically told by Amir Yakub Khan at Caubul that he must expect nothing from him or from Afghanistan in the future. He worshipped rupees, and was in the full belief that the Indian Government could be squeezed at all times and on all occasions. He was always accompanied by his favourite son Amin Khan, whom he had trained according to his own principles. The most clever chief was Malik Khwas Khan, Zakha Khel. The most honest and most true was my friend Walli Muhammad Khan, and for years part of my work was to prevent him from falling into the clutches of Khwas and ruining himself—the fate which actually happened to him within five weeks of my giving up charge of the Khyber on July 11, 1897.

Just at this period Peshawar was swarming with Afghan refugees, who had cast their lot with us when our troops entered Afghanistan, and who had been compelled to clear out of their country, leaving homes and ancestral property, when our forces retraced their steps towards India. Many things came back to my mind when I remembered Jelallabad in the years 1879 and 1880, and thought of what the chiefs and sardars had then said to me. One morning at Jelallabad I happened to be watching work in the commissariat yard in company with Sardar Khalo Khan. An energetic Cashmiri contractor, by name Habbo, was working like a slave, seeing his grain duly weighed in. He was reputed to have made three lacs—say about 20,000*l.*—by his contracts with us. Hearing Sardar Khalo Khan make a remark about his wonderful activity, Habbo called out in an insolent manner, 'I do not trust the Barakzais, and when the English leave Jelallabad I shall go with them, and take my money with me.' But he remained just a little too late, and lost every penny he had made. Sardar Maddat Khan and all his brothers, with their sons and families, cleared out of Jelallabad when our troops came away in 1880, but, arriving at Peshawar, the old gentleman and his young son fell victims to cholera. Sardar Khalo Khan and his brothers tried very hard to secure a pension from the Government of India, through the medium of the Panjab Government. In every direction one met residents of Caubul, of Laghman, and of Jelallabad, who, when asked what they were doing in Peshawar, rightly or wrongly declared the cause to be that they had befriended the English during their invasion of Afghanistan; and hundreds of these men were to be found at Rawal Pindi, Lahore, Amritsar, Dera-Dun, Karachi, Quetta, and various places on the Panjab Frontier.

Hardly had I taken over charge when my native assistant, Akbar Khan, commenced playing tricks. He prepared a letter, which was to have been copied out by the Khyber maliks, signed by them all and submitted with a petition, that Sardar Aslam Khan should be sent back to his regiment, the 5th Bengal Cavalry. Only Abdulla Nur and one other Afridi malik were in this secret; the rest were told that when they went before the Commissioner they were to beg that the lands of Regi-Lallam should be bestowed on Malik Abdulla Nur. When the whole gang appeared before Mr. Cordery, the Commissioner, they, unfortunately for themselves, produced in original the letter written by the Assistant Political; but, on its being read out, they declared that they had come to ask about the Regi lands, and knew nothing of the plot against Sardar Aslam Khan!

Just before February 22, 1882, information was received at Jamrud that the Annai Zakha Khels intended raiding into the Khyber Pass because their Malik, Khwas Khan, would not give them their proper share of the Khyber allowances. We received timely warning of what was going to happen, and the raiders, caught in a trap, lost five killed and about nine wounded. Four other sections of the Zakhas, who could not be managed by their chiefs, had their allowances taken away from their maliks, and paid direct to them by me. In this manner a very serious trouble was removed, because these men respected neither malik nor chief, nor any human being outside their own community. If any individual thought that he was wrongfully deprived of his rights by malik or chief, he at once committed some outrage on the residents of the Peshawar District, and in this way drew the attention of the authorities to his grievance and expected us to right him. However, they took the precaution of selecting a very weak set of elders to receive their allowances from me, on the grounds that the weak men would be unable to deprive the others of their lawful rights in the proper share of the Khyber allowances.

The Malikdin Khel freebooter, Kamal, was another gentleman who continually kept Peshawar and Kohat on the *qui vive.* Having once upon a time served in one of our native regiments located in Peshawar, he was well acquainted with all the rules by which sentries challenged strangers approaching their posts at night and the replies that should be given. He was further well aware of the condition of the various roads and regimental lines in Cantonments. One night, without any warning, he stole out and cut up the cavalry picquet of the 19th Bengal Lancers stationed on the Circular Road, just by the highway that leads from Peshawar Cantonments to Jamrud. All were killed or wounded, except one man who was saying his prayers on the Circular Road some twenty yards away from the picquet building. Some nights later he made a swoop on a cavalry picquet at Kohat, where he was not so successful. One of his gang was killed, and the rest were chased to the frontier by the cavalry scouts and escaped with difficulty. For these two outrages the Malikdin and Kambar Khel Afridis were called upon to pay a fine of Rs. 8,000 and to turn Kamal out of their limits. After considerable pressure, the headmen and tribal jirga went to Tirah, burnt his house, and did so. When they came back, Kamal returned to his own, and, by the aid of the Mullahs, rebuilt his house. Twice again was his place destroyed, and twice again rebuilt. But he had some more adventures in hand, and enjoyed a joke in his own fashion. The Commissioner was proceeding to Kohat on duty, and his horses, under escort of a police trooper, were sent off to Matanni, to remain there one night, and then to journey through the Pass to Kohat on the following morning. This news was conveyed to Kamal by some friend, and he and several of his companions, armed to the teeth, sat down a short way from the side of the road leading from Peshawar to Matanni, at a spot from which no human habitation was visible for miles, and awaited events. Soon the escort, and horses with the grooms, and mules carrying loads appeared; and, noticing a fire and the friendly pipe going round, the men were attracted to the spot without knowing the quality of the party they were about to join. Kamal removed every animal and took them away to Tirah. The Malikdin and Kambar Khel Afridis were again fined for not controlling Kamal, but that individual did not mind this in the least, as he had numerous quarters where he could be sheltered when his tribesmen turned against him. In this instance he received Rs. 900 from Muhammad Sarfaraz Khan, Arbab of the Mohmands, who was most anxious to recover the Commissioner's horses and readily paid this sum to get them back.

One morning, about 2 A.M., I was called up by the Deputy Commissioner of Peshawar, who had driven over to my house to tell me that a report had just been brought to him that Kamal had attacked and cut up the whole of the picquet stations on the road leading to Fort Bara, and he asked me to come out and investigate the matter. Away we went, but learnt that affairs were not so bad as had been reported; only a sentry of the Sappers and Miners had been wounded and his rifle carried off. As we moved in the direction of the Sapper and Miner lines, we met an Afghan Kuchi driving about fifty to sixty camels through the centre of the Peshawar Cantonments in the dead of night, with no one to interfere with him!

For six years Kamal—whose name means Perfection—kept us alive in that quarter of the Panjab; and not only he, but a lot of lesser ruffians, committed deeds which were all put down in the records of the greater rogue, whose training in the ranks of our native army enabled him to pass any sentry with the greatest ease. He was killed at last, and in this way.

A reward of Rs. 2,000 had been offered for the capture and surrender of Kamal alive, and something less if he was slain whilst resisting capture. It was difficult to explain this clearly to the Afridis who came before me for their allowances or on some other business. The first clause was easily understood by all: 'Bring Kamal here alive, deliver him over, and Rs. 2,000 shall be handed to the party bringing him in.' 'But what is this other clause of the provision?' they asked. 'Something less if he is slain whilst resisting capture? How much less—five, ten, fifty, one hundred rupees? Can you not tell us what the exact sum is which will be given, instead of leaving it in this way?' This question we were never allowed to answer; but on every occasion, not once but many times, it was explained to all that no reward would be given if Kamal was deliberately murdered and his body then brought in. One tall Afridi, cousin to Kamal, who limped from the effects of a rifle bullet lodged in his right thigh by Kamal, was a keen inquirer into this reward question. He could not understand our objection to, and horror of, paying to get a man murdered. He argued in his own savage way: 'See how much easier and better it is to kill Kamal than to do what you want. First of all, I am to catch and deliver him alive—a most difficult matter, to begin with. Then you will try him with all the intricacies of your law, and if he is sentenced to death, and the judgment upheld, Kamal will be hanged. My way and yours both mean death to the man, but mine is the simpler, and surer in the end. Why not reward me for working in my own fashion?'

After several interviews, he went away to hatch his own scheme of revenge, for he was very anxious to kill Kamal on his own account, and at length he succeeded in his object, after some years of patient waiting. Kamal and his cousin lived in the Bairami section of the Malikdin Khel country in Tirah, the forts of the two families being near to one another. Kamal, finding that he was supported by the priesthood, became a little careless in looking after his own safety, his precautions lessened, and he was in the habit of taking walks behind the village mosque, feeling assured, in his own mind, that no spot was so safe as one in close proximity to the holy place. But he had a vigilant enemy, who watched him and his movements very closely. One day in February 1888 this cousin, concealing his rifle, entered the mosque, remained there for hours without letting people know what object he had in view. With an iron spike he made a good-sized hole in the back mud wall of the building, and kept his eye on the ground in front of it. Kamal, according to his habit, came out for a stroll, and the cousin, putting his rifle through the hole, took careful aim and shot his kinsman dead. He then hurried down to Peshawar to claim the reward. Of course no reward was given for the murder, and the cousin's own end came soon. Akbar, brother of Kamal, a young man known amongst the Afridis as a *chaubak sarai*—i.e. an extremely active and smart fellow—managed to kill him, and in this way revenged Kamal's death. No more was heard of Akbar after this; he may have been killed in a feud, or he may have taken to a useful life and given up his thievish raiding habits, but so far as we were concerned he disappeared entirely.

No cantonment or station that I have seen in India is so open to attack from thieves and robbers as Peshawar, and none so difficult to protect by means of guards or sentinels. The station is in the form of a large ellipse, the western end touching the road that comes from the Bara Valley, by Fort Bara, and joins the Mall by the cavalry lines, the eastern end adjoining the Peshawar Jail, whilst further east, on the Grand Trunk Road, lies the fort of Peshawar almost touching the city. A road, called the Circular Road, goes round the station. From the Bara Road there is a succession of small hamlets and large peach gardens; to the south of the Cantonments, quite close to this Circular Road, is the Saddar Bazar, right up to the city. Three or four villainous villages, full of thieves, face the station in the direction of the Khyber. All Afridis coming from the direction of the Bara Valley, or the Khyber Hills, or Mohmands journeying by the Michni Road, must enter and pass through the heart of the Cantonments. But the worst evil of all is the location of the Civil Courts in the very centre of the station, close to the cricket ground. Here thousands of the best and worst characters of the district assembled for hours every day and watched the nakedness of the land, making their arrangements by day for visiting the houses at night. It is impossible to alter these circumstances now, but the evils are observable even to the casual visitor to Peshawar to-day, and the number of sentries that have to be placed in Cantonments at night time make night duty heavy on the garrison, and on this account Peshawar is not beloved by the soldiery.

Owing to the recommendation of my predecessor between 1880 and 1881, a sum of 6,000 rupees had been sanctioned for the repair of the old Tartarra Road, but no one had made any attempt to carry out these repairs. To those who are not acquainted with this highway, I may explain that formerly the Khyber Pass, thanks to the quarrels and exactions of the Afridis, was always closed to caravans, trade, and travellers except when some strong man forced them to keep it open for the time being, and when he passed away, or the whim left him, the Pass was closed again. On this account the rulers of Caubul preferred to negotiate for the opening out of the Tartarra route, which was a much more difficult road, but far easier to arrange with the tribesmen there than with those of the historical Pass. Leaving Fort Dakka, this route goes through Loe Dakka (Larger or Greater Dakka), Kam (Lesser) Dakka, and ascending the Shilman Ghakha (Pass or Fork) passes through the country of Loe (Greater) Shilman, ascends and descends the Dabrai Hill, passes through the Mullagori country, and descends into the plains of the Peshawar Valley close to the police station of Mathra, the first halting stage in the Peshawar Valley. The Shilmanis were about 700 armed men, all Mohmands under the Khan of Lalpura, who was able to keep them in thorough order by means of the large Mohmand clans to the north of the Caubul River. The Mullagoris were a small tribe of some 600 men, having Mohmands on the north and west, their enemies the Afridis on the south, and the Peshawaris to the east. It was a far easier task to bend these two petty tribes than to coerce 20,000 to 25,000 armed Afridis. And it therefore happened that from 1848 to 1878 the Khyber Pass was always kept closed, except on rare occasions, such as when Amir Sher Ali Khan came down to the Ambala darbar in 1869 and returned by the same way; but the Tartarra route was always kept open for traffic. Even now H.H. Amir Abdur Rahman's Caubul post never goes by the Khyber Pass, but travels by the Tartarra route, which is now, however, closed to traffic. If the repair of this road was not taken in hand during the running year, the grant would lapse, and as there was a fear of its not being renewed I determined to undertake the trip, although the month was May and the heat fairly great in the low hills. Taking Malik Afridi Khan, second in command of the Khyber Jezailchies, now named Rifles, with an escort of 50 men, we went up to Lwara Miana in the Mullagori hills, where the weather was cool, the height of this place being nearly 2,500 feet. The second stage was at Shahid Miana, in a ravine about the level of the Caubul River, and the heat unbearable. Ascending the trying Dabrai Hill, we descended into Kam Shilman Valley, and made our third stage at Malik Kamran's village. The heat was not so trying, but the biting of the midges and mosquitoes intolerable. The fourth day we got to Landi Kotal, clouds were overhead, and a warm overcoat was welcome. Malik Khwas Khan and his rival Malik Walli Muhammad

Khan, with the nine Shinwari headmen, met me, and the first said, 'Welcome, Sahib, we thought you had forgotten us for ever.'

A day was spent here to examine a few localities. It was painful to see all the quarters for the General, his staff, and the lines for the British and native regiments ruined and roofless, our own handiwork, the result of our own policy. The look-out post at Pizgah and others were all in ruins, their timbers and rafters having been given over to the Shinwaris. The masonry ducts and drinking-places all wanted repairs. The caravan inclosure, an open piece of ground, was ankle deep in filth and manure. The two company barracks at Landi Kotal, every building down the Khyber Pass, and the road all required mending, nothing having been spent on repairs for upwards of a year. After this I went down the Pass to Peshawar, arriving there on May 21, 1882.

The four troublesome sections of the Zakha Khels had been settled with, but this summer proved a trying one. To protect the Peshawar villagers and their cattle, which would insist on straying into independent limits, a guard of one company of the Khyber Rifles was placed day and night on the Besai Hill to keep watch in the Kajourie plain. This company was changed monthly, its food and water being sent out from Jamrud, and a big drum and rockets, &c., supplied to it to give alarm in case of any attack by raiders. Twice a week our men patrolled the Kajourie Valley, and in this way, by taking these precautions, we avoided giving the Afridi robbers a single chance. Sardar Afzab Khan, C.S.I., brother to Sardar Aslam Khan, being appointed British Agent at the Court of Amir Abdur

Rahman Khan, left for Caubul along with his suite, and we saw him safely through the Khyber Pass and in the plains of Jelallabad, *en route* for his new and troublesome post.

A sharp attack of illness in the month of September 1882 forced me to proceed to the hills near Murree on ten days' leave. This event would not be mentioned except for a curious incident that occurred on the journey when the train stopped at Naushehra. I happened to notice on the platform a man dressed in the garb of a fakir, who recognised me without my thinking or dreaming of his identity. This man was Sardar Muhammad Hassan Khan, Governor of Jelallabad, who had fled from us in December 1879. Dressed in the garments of a beggar, he had got so far, when, seeing me at Naushehra, he thought that he was recognised, and so turned off to Hoti-Mardan, journeyed through Hashtnagar into the Mohmand country, and then made his way to Kuner with the object of raising the country against Amir Abdur Rahman Khan. In the spring of 1883 the Shinwaris of the Jelallabad District revolted against Amir Abdur Rahman Khan, and on this Sardar Muhammad Hassan Khan slipped one night from Kuner into the Shinwari hills, and helped the insurgents to damage the cause of their lawful ruler. I shall refer to him again, when relating the vicissitudes of his extraordinary career.

A sad case of Ghazi outrage occurred in the Peshawar Mall, in which the victim was an old friend of mine. Captain Fulford, who had been appointed Assistant Quartermaster-General to the Peshawar Brigade, arrived and took up his residence in a house adjoining the Royal Artillery mess, and almost touching the 'nine-yard' shrine facing the Mission House. Every Thursday evening a cloth is placed along the whole length of this tomb, which in the earlier days of our rule in the Peshawar Valley used to increase in length every year until a clever Feringhi stopped its further growth by building a mud wall round it. Flowers are placed and scattered all over the cloth, and a few earthen lamps or *chiraghs* lighted. One or more sweetmeat sellers come and sit on the ground, and display their saleable articles ready to do a good business. A crowd of children take their stand on either side of the tomb. Then come the devotees, not Mussulman but Hindu women, who spend a few pice in the purchase of sweets which are distributed amongst the children, a pice or two given to the shrine, and in an hour or so the crowd disperses. Few fanatics as a rule visit the place, but on this fatal Thursday evening, a few days after Fulford's arrival, one did so, and, seeing Fulford passing by the shrine, followed him. Turning back homewards, Fulford had reached the empty space behind the Royal Artillery bazaar, when the fanatic crept up quietly behind and shot him in the back with a pistol which he had kept concealed in his garments. Captain Fulford lingered for a few days, and then succumbed to his injuries.

My own troubles in the Khyber were plentiful enough in those early days. From the month of October 1878 to the spring of 1881 the troops stationed at Jamrud had daily appropriated twelve hours of the entire Kuki Khel water supply out of the twenty-four. After four years' delay the Panjab Government had awarded Rs. 5,000 compensation to the tribesmen for the losses incurred by them on account of their water supply having been forcibly taken from them for a period of three years. They were to get Rs. 150 a month from a certain fixed date for giving twenty-four hours of their entire supply one day in the week for the use of the garrison and all inside and outside Fort Jamrud. If this decision had been arrived at when our troops were holding the Khyber, Abdulla Nur would never have dared to utter a word against our award; but now, thinking that we could be squeezed and that we would rather pay anything than interrupt the Khyber arrangements, he held a consultation with his elders, and, acting on his advice, they refused to take a penny of the money. The coin was deposited in the treasure chest of the Khyber Rifles, and I waited to see what would be done next. For two years the case remained pending, until at last, learning that Malik Abdulla Nur and his son, Amin Khan, had sent to me asking that the money should be paid over to them only, so that they might distribute it, the whole tribe with their elders turned up and took over the full amount of cash in my hands, and agreed to the terms settled by the Panjab Government.

Another little trouble was started by this old man, Abdulla Nur, in the autumn of 1882. Below the fort of Ali Masjid, and to the east of the mosque which gives the name to the place, is a little bit of ground, about a tenth of an acre in extent, known as *shaddal* lands—i.e. ground left untilled. It was claimed by and belonged to the Kambar Khel Afridis. Its intrinsic value may have been fifteen to twenty rupees. Abdulla Nur, knowing to whom the land belonged, sent a message to Malik Nurulla at Jam, and asked him to take up all the Kuki Khels with their ploughs and yokes of oxen to plough this *shaddal* plot. Nurulla came and asked me what he was to do, and was directed to remain quietly at home, but to communicate to Abdulla Nur the orders he had received from me. The Malikdin and Kambai Khel Afridis are descended from one stock, and between them can turn out 9,000 excellent fighting men, and in this quarrel they had combined against the Kuki Khel. The Malikdin chiefs lived at Chora, some ten miles due south of Ali Masjid, and at this juncture the Malikdin Khel company of the Khyber Rifles happened to be stationed in Fort Ali Masjid. Both the native officers were near relations of the chiefs. Both went round with Korans in their hands, urging their men not to vacate the fort whatever orders came from Jamrud. However, when the hour of trial came the two havildars or sergeants brought the company down to Jamrud, leaving the Subadar and Jemadar to their own devices. Both these havildars were promoted. In this way a very troublesome question was disposed of for the time being, and when all the Afridi jirgas appeared at Peshawar in November 1882, it was settled for good by the aid of the Maliks of the Zakha Khel Afridis. There is an old Persian saying,

> The Jackal that haunts the wilds of Mazindaran
> Can only be caught by the hounds of Mazindaran.

Certainly the Zakha chiefs caught Abdulla Nur firmly in their clutches this time, and for sixteen years the *shaddal* land dispute has not been opened up again.

In the spring of 1883, on the recommendation of

the Commissioner, my salary was reduced. This was done in the face of a promise made to me in July 1879 before I took up the Khyber appointment, and of a letter sent by Sir R. Egerton's Government in October 1879, fixing my pay. This was my reward for serving the Government of the Panjab for thirteen years during a fairly troublesome period.

Improvements were being made in the Khyber gradually but surely. A small conservancy establishment was sanctioned for Landi Kotal, and the caravan inclosure cleansed of the filth which had been allowed to accumulate there for ages. The road was being repaired and put in order, under great opposition at first, but gradually by patient waiting we had our own way. One or two of the maliks, especially Khwas Khan, Zakha Khel, were opponents to the bitter end, and did their utmost to prevent the Khyber road being improved or any work taken in hand; but the tribesmen happily would not accept that view. The following procedure was therefore adopted. From Jamrud to Ali Masjid the road was worked by men supplied by the Kuki Khels. Ali Masjid to near Gurgurra belonged to the Malikdin Khel. Gurgurra to Malik Khwas Khan's house to his section of the Zakhas. From Khwas Khan's fort to the Shinwari limits was the share of Malik Walli Muhammad Khan's party amongst the Zakha Khels. The last bit to Landi Khana and Tor-Kham was allotted to the Shinwaris. Some man able to manage his particular tribe was selected, and asked to bring men to work on the road at four annas a day; and as this meant money put into the hands of the tribesmen direct, they were quite willing to set aside the wishes of their chiefs where their private interests were concerned. The same difficulty had to be encountered when repairing the military posts between Fort Jamrud and Landi Khana, but once a move was made the friction year by year decreased in intensity.

Malik Abdulla Nur had feathered his nest pretty well, in spite of having been in constant opposition to the British Government all his life. He had received something like Rs. 13,000 in value for injury to crops and damage to water mills at Ali Masjid during its occupation by our troops. He was granted a special pension of Rs. 150 a month for life, on account of some claims to lands at Ragi Lallam. He had robbed his tribesmen of their share of the Khyber allowances during 1880, 1881, 1882, and in one way or another he had accumulated between 30,000 or 40,000 rupees, which he had carried off secretly to his fort at the western limit of the Bara Valley. This hoard was of great use to his son in troubling me for the space of eight years. The incident will be related in its proper place. Abdulla Nur, in the spring of 1883, had secured all his own and the tribal allowances, and wanted to fly secretly to his summer home in the Bara Valley, where, with the support of the Tirah or Rajgal Kuki Khels, he could defy his brethren who lived in the villages between Jamrud and Ali Masjid. But these last were quite equal to the occasion, and, surrounding his fort, they had it out with him for several hours in rifle practice, and made him pay up a fair proportion of their share of allowances, but not the full portion, before they permitted him to take his departure.

The Shinwaris of the Jelallabad District claimed certain posts on the road between Tor-Kham and

Dakka on the Landi-Khana-Dakka road, and they felt they had a claim to certain allowances on this account from H.H. the Amir of Afghanistan, who was running this highway by means of *khasadars* with great profit to his treasury. And so, in the fashion of wild hillmen, they came in large numbers and tried to stop the traffic; but Amir Abdur Rahman Khan was not the ruler to permit this infringement of his rights. He had been informed by spies of what was about to happen, and hurried up his troops to meet the storm, who inflicted severe defeat on the tribesmen when they commenced their mischief. In one fight some 200 hillmen were driven to take shelter in a fort, which was breached down with guns, and nearly every man was killed. In this way the petty Shinwari war commenced which has raged at intervals for fifteen years, is going on now, and will only end with the complete subjugation of those sections whose valleys lie far up in the hills and cannot be touched easily by the Amir's soldiery. After the victory noted, the commandant of the troops, in accordance with an ancient Asiatic custom, had a small pyramid made with the heads of the enemy killed in battle. A story came down from Jelallabad that a widow who had a son in the Amir's army, not receiving news of her lad, went to the Shinwari country to make inquiries herself. She failed to gain any information or find any trace of her son until, going over the battlefield, she came to the pyramid, and was horrified to see his head fixed on one of the tiers. The section that had suffered so terribly were brethren, kith and kin of our Shinwaris of Landi Kotal, who often told me of the difficulties that were experienced in getting husbands for the daughters, sisters, and widows of the tribesmen killed in the spring of 1883.

In September 1883 Captain Nixon, of the Peshawar police, Sardar Aslam Khan, and I undertook a trip from Jamrud Fort to the top of Lakka Sar, the highest peak of the Tartarra Range. We started from Jamrud, as our route went by Gudar, through the Lashora Valley, up the Saprai Hill, and so far we went by the road taken by General Macpherson's turning column on the evening and night of November 20, 1878. After this we had to wheel a bit to the right, and go up a very steep ascent which our tired animals could not manage. The journey was both long and trying, the road very bad, and the transport extremely indifferent, so we made for Kambela, the summer quarters of the Mullagori tribe, and halted here for the night. The ridge to the east in the direction of Peshawar, and the hills to the west, would have made excellent summer quarters for troops. It was quite cool at Kambela, and the Mullagoris had scattered for their winter settlements; but, hearing of our arrival, many of their headmen hurried up to render any aid they could give. The journey to Lakka Sar being impossible now, we turned to Lwara Miana the next morning, halted for the day, and went to Peshawar the following morning.

The year 1884 promised badly, as I thought, at the beginning, but in the end matters improved, and I look upon that year as the one when our trips to the Khyber Hills really took a tangible form, and gradually in course of time produced that good fellowship with the tribes which made us heartily welcomed at every place we went to. Abdulla Nur and his son, owing to some cause or other, did not come down to his winter quarters at Jam till the month of January 1884. He went at once to see Sardar Aslam Khan, whose quarters were then in the barracks of the Khyber Rifles, and the two had a very cordial meeting. The next day father and son went into Peshawar, and had an interview with the Native Assistant Political Officer, Akbar Khan, living at Bhana Mari, a suburb of the city of Peshawar. What actually transpired at this meeting was never clearly revealed, but Abdulla Nur and his son turned back to Jam, and the following morning Amin Khan went to old Malik Nurulla's house, accompanied by a few of the bad lot that always were with him, and murdered Nurulla and two of his sons without any warning or apparent cause. At the funeral of these men Abdulla Nur declared that he was guiltless of the deed, but everyone knew that his son and his own retainers would never have committed so dark and treacherous an act without his orders. Within forty-eight hours of the murder of Nurulla he himself was shot in his own guest chamber, seated in the midst of his relations and retainers, and died instantaneously. The murderer, fired upon repeatedly as he ran, had a wonderful escape, and took shelter in the house of Akbar, a leading man of Jam, living at the western limit of the village. I was called upon to make a long inquiry into this matter, which was futile in the end, as the events occurred across the border and necessitated no interference on our part. But the result went far to show that the Native Assistant Political was at the bottom of the business.

In the month of July 1884 Sardar Aslam Khan and I went up to Landi Kotal, and lived in large tents taken up from Jamrud. The mornings, evenings, and nights were cool, but the great force of the sun's rays made the tents very warm between midday and 3 P.M.; still, it was a great improvement on the Peshawar Valley. During the mornings we took our walk, discussed matters with all the headmen and visitors till breakfast, when the tribesmen went away for their morning meal. From 10 A.M. to 5 P.M. was reserved for work; in the evenings the people assembled once more, and we again had a walk and a talk. Often whilst we were out the time came round for prayers, when the hillmen would spread their cloths, turn their faces towards the supposed correct quarter, and proceed with their devotions, whilst I waited seated on a rock near at hand. We then walked back to camp, and separated for the night. In this way two weeks were spent at Landi Kotal, when we moved to Kurre-Nao, a small valley in the Tartarra Range about 5,700 feet in height. The weather here was glorious, the only objection to the place being that the valley was rather narrow, being open towards the west, and the fierce wind at times very annoying. To the east rose the spur of the Tartarra Range which ends in Lakka Sar, a huge barrier towering 1,000 feet above us. Its eastern and southern faces form huge precipices with sheer drops in places of 2,000 feet; but on the western quarter where we were the ascent to Lakka Sar, though steep, had gentle slopes down to the ravine where our camp was. In this amphitheatre were about two hundred deep snow wells, and the system of filling them in was as follows: When the snow fell, commencing generally in November and continuing till February, the Shinwaris came up, collected it, and beat it into the wells. If the drainage was good and the season a prosperous one, this snow would keep well into the month of October following. It was conveyed on mules into the city of Peshawar, commencing with the month of February, when the price was two rupees a load, and lasting through the hot season into October, when a mule load would fetch sometimes eight rupees. There is a great demand for *sharbat*, *faluda*, and ices amongst the Mussulman residents of Peshawar.

One morning Sardar Aslam Khan and I started at 4 A.M. to ascend Lakka Sar. By fair good luck the Peshawar Valley was free from a dust storm as we reached the crest of the peak, a small place not more than ten or twelve feet in diameter. A ridge ran westwards, not quite so high as the spot we were on. In the centre was a small inclosure three to four feet in diameter, said to be a very holy shrine, and he or she who wished his or her desires to be fulfilled had to cut a small stick from the branch of the nearest tree, point it at one end, limit the length to four or five inches, and then peg it down close to the shrine. I conformed to the rule fourteen years ago and more, but somehow my wishes have not yet been fulfilled. The panorama from here was grand to a degree. Just below us nestled Fort Jamrud. Peshawar, with its church and double-storeyed barracks and its mass of trees, occupied the foreground. To the left lay the Caubul River, and further north could be seen the Swat stream, with the plains of Yusufzai, the Mora and Illam Ranges, with the Indus in full flood running due south at the eastern extremity of the Peshawar Valley. I went up again to helio with certain stations from Lakka Sar a few days later, but the west wind was blowing and a storm raged over the Peshawar Valley, leaving nothing visible. I remained the whole night there, wanting to try if a message could not be delivered by lamp; but the dust storm made it hopeless, and it continued thus for a whole week.

Having spent two weeks here we broke up camp and moved to Tor-Sappar, due north of Landi Kotal, its highest altitude being 5,600 feet. This was the best place we had yet discovered, and later on it was the plateau where we spent many happy months in certain seasons during the years we went up to the Khyber Hills.

As the Afghan Boundary Commission was about to move down to Quetta, and as Sardar Aslam Khan had been selected as one of its members, we had to return to Peshawar, and in this way our first seven weeks' trip to the Khyber Hills came to an end.

Before concluding this chapter I may note that it was understood by the tribesmen that wherever my camp was in their hills, the greatest enemies might resort to it with perfect safety. No private, public, or tribal feuds were to be carried out on any condition. Hence for six or seven weeks my camp was full of men having deadly blood feuds with one another, armed to the teeth, each man having his loaded rifle, yet no outrage was ever committed; and I may say that this rule was implicitly carried out by me for more than fifteen years. During all that time there never was an attempt made to steal a farthing's worth of property from our tents or camp, except on one occasion when a few trifling items belonging to one of our Khyber cavalry sowars were carried off from the lines at Landi Kotal.

Two months later a man knocked at Malik Walli Muhammad Khan's fort in the Khyber during dark. He having many enemies, the gate was opened only after due precautions had been taken, and outside placed on the ground were found all the sowar's property which had been taken from Landi Kotal.

I found that the people were better pleased when they felt assured that I trusted them entirely with my safety. I therefore always went about with only a stick in my hand.

CHAPTER VIII

THE DUKE AND DUCHESS OF CONNAUGHT'S AND THE AMIR'S VISITS

1884–1885

EARLY in September 1884 it was notified that their Royal Highnesses the Duke and Duchess of Connaught would pay a visit to Peshawar, and it was thought that possibly they might extend their tour to the Khyber Pass as far as Ali Masjid. This was the first occasion of Peshawar being honoured with a royal visit, for when H.R.H. the Prince of Wales was in India his journey to the North-West Frontier was limited to a trip to Jammu, and afterwards to the Chenab River to open the great Alexandra railway bridge. Peshawar had not an opportunity of showing its welcome to the Prince in 1875–76, and therefore the present visit of the Duke and Duchess of Connaught was doubly welcome. A bountiful programme was arranged, which accounted for nearly every hour of their stay in the Peshawar Valley. It was shown to me, and I was asked if I could suggest anything to fill in a two hours' gap, which appeared to be the only blank in time left. I suggested that a two hours' rest might possibly be needful and appreciated! But the ceremonial programme was very strictly carried out. The royal visitors arrived on the morning of September 30, and were received at the railway

VIEW FROM CENTRE TOWER SOUTH OF ALI MASJID LOOKING TOWARDS PESHAWAR AND SHOWING RIDGE.

station by the General Officer commanding the Peshawar District, the Commissioner of the division, and the heads of departments. My wife and I had to journey out at once to Fort Jamrud, to arrange for the reception of the Duke and Duchess, who had expressed their wish to visit the fort on the morning of October 1, and to ride up the Pass as far as Ali Masjid. Very early that morning the royal visitors drove to Jamrud, where, mounting their horses, the whole party with escort moved along the road leading into the Khyber Pass. The Khyber Rifles had manned the heights the whole way as far as Fort Ali Masjid, but the Duke and Duchess only caught a glimpse of the fort from near the Shagai ridge, when the order was given to turn back. The morning had not been a cool one, and as the sun rose higher the heat began to tell. The return to Jamrud was made, therefore, at a sharp trot. On the way an incident occurred which gave a momentary alarm. Two Kuki Khel women suddenly appeared, and, rushing up to the horse the Duke was on, caught the reins. They turned out to be the mother and sister of a man who was then undergoing a sentence of imprisonment in Peshawar for burglary; and the object of the ladies in thus stopping his Royal Highness was to implore pardon for their kinsman. They were, of course, quickly removed, but were told that their petition would be looked into at Peshawar.

At Jamrud the Khyber maliks and headmen were presented, and, after a look at the structure of the fort and a view of the surrounding country from its highest point, the Duke and Duchess with their party went back to Peshawar. I was very sorry that they had not gone to Ali Masjid and seen the narrowest and grandest part of the Khyber after journeying so far, and I had made every preparation for such a visit. The Commissioner, however, did not like visits to the Khyber, and was apprehensive that by going beyond Fort Jamrud some danger might be incurred, and therefore he directed that, as far as possible, visitors should not be permitted to journey much to the west of Jamrud. My own opinion was that the most dangerous spot on the whole road was the ground in the vicinity of that fort, because the near Kuki Khel villages had living amongst them a number of murderers, thieves, and housebreakers who had run away from the Peshawar District, and taken shelter with the Kuki Khel. These outlaws, many of them with rewards on their heads—and who, if captured, might be executed—were the individuals who were to be dreaded and guarded against. The further you got away from Fort Jamrud the safer the road and locality and the more pleased the people were to see Europeans. I always on this account encouraged such trips, and in time Ali Masjid on Tuesdays was turned into a pleasant picnic-ground. There were several cases of Ghazi outrages in Peshawar Cantonments during 1882 to July 11, 1897, and not a house was actually safe from the prowling thieves during the dark nights of every month, but the lives and property of European visitors to the Khyber were as safe as in the streets of London.

The name Fort Jamrud, which we had given to this Sikh fortress built by Harri Singh in the year 1836–37, has always been a puzzle to me. *Jam* is the name of the Kuki Khel village which lies nearest to the fort on the left bank of the ravine which forms the eastern entrance of the Khyber Pass. *Rud* in

Persian means stream or rivulet. The stream that flows down by Ali Masjid, and is joined at Jabbagai by the waters of the Chora rivulet, irrigates after this meeting the lands of several Kuki Khel villages, the largest of which is named Kaddam. The correct name for this very tiny river might be Rud-i-Khyber, Rud-i-Ali Masjid, Rud-i-Kuki Khel, but no Oriental would style it Jamrud. However, once upon a time someone gave this name to the fort, and Fort Jamrud it will now remain.

Early in the year 1885 Amin Khan, Kuki Khel, commenced to play pranks, which, after seven and a half years of constant and incessant trouble on his part, ultimately ended in bringing him to grief. He had a fairly full treasury, if one could apply such a term to the thirty to forty thousand rupees collected by his father during his four years of maliki; but this sum was a very large amount in the eyes of Afridis. The young lad had a number of evil advisers, but his training under his father's eyes and according to his father's principles was his greatest misfortune. He had been brought up to believe that we could be squeezed to any extent, and that, to prevent rupture, the authorities would give in to any demand as much as it was possible to surrender, and this mistake on his part he did not discover until it was too late to rectify it. He wrote an angry letter (his father had had him taught to read and write Persian) asking that the special allowance of Rs. 150 a month bestowed on his father should be continued to him. It was pointed out to him in reply that the condition under which the grant was made to Malik Abdulla Nur was that it was only for his life. The Lieut.-Governor of the Panjab, Sir C. Aitcheson, had arrived at Peshawar, and being about to hold a darbar, had expressed a wish to see the Khyber road as far as Ali Masjid. Sardar Aslam Khan having gone away on the Afghan Boundary Commission, his place was temporarily filled by Sayad Badshah, Banuri of Germa in the Kohat District, a gentleman well known on the frontier and who had done good service under me at Hoti-Mardan and Jelallabad. Amin Khan informed Sayad Badshah that if this special allowance was not given to him at once, and before the Lieut.-Governor's visit to Ali Masjid, he would fire on Sir C. Aitcheson and suite if they ventured into the Pass. I strongly urged that he should be turned out of his maliki forthwith, and that the tribe be informed at the darbar which was to be held that morning that they must select another representative, as we could not possibly accept this man as their chief. The Lieut.-Governor thought otherwise, and preferred warning the Kuki Khel jirga at the darbar that he made them answerable for the behaviour of their selected chief. He put off his journey to Ali Masjid also, and limited his trip to Jamrud.

Reports were afloat immediately after this darbar that an Imperial darbar was shortly to be held at Rawal Pindi, and that H.H. Amir Abdur Rahman Khan was coming down from Caubul to attend in person to seek a personal interview with H.E. the Viceroy and Governor-General of India. These reports proved correct, and my business was to supply the Amir and all his retinue with food, wood, grass, and everything they required at Landi Kotal, Shagai (near Ali Masjid), and Jamrud. At Landi Kotal the only commodities procurable were wood and grass, even water had to be brought from Landi Khana; Shagai, thirteen miles nearer to Peshawar, could only furnish wood, grass, and water; Jamrud was nearly as bad, except that it was only ten miles from Peshawar. Moreover, I was to see that His Highness's camp and person were carefully guarded in my Khyber limits. When the time arrived to receive our illustrious guest, the whole regiment of 1st Bengal Cavalry (Skinner's Horse), under command of Colonel Chapman, was told off as escort. The Commissioner of the division, his assistant, and myself, with Legh from the King's Royal Rifles, who was in charge of a number of carrier pigeons, had our camp alongside of the 1st Bengal Cavalry, with whom we had been kindly asked to take our meals—a very great boon on the march. The Amirs of Afghanistan are not slaves to Time, as we found to our cost; but a week's sojourn at Landi Kotal helped me to complete my commissariat arrangements of supplies. It is often said that the presence of our troops in independent country irritates the inhabitants; but here was an entire cavalry regiment encamped on the Shinwari lands, and during the two or three parades that took place before H.H. the Amir arrived some little damage must have been caused to the crops and boundaries of the fields, yet no complaint was ever made by the residents. Large crowds collected to witness the parades, and no attempt was ever made by day or night to steal anything from camp.

About 4 P.M. on the evening of March 26 an Afghan high official—Farrash-Bashi—was announced, and desired to know where he was to pitch the Amir's camp, as His Highness would arrive on the morrow. I received this high official with due ceremony, and, after making the usual inquiries after his health, I sent men to point out to him the ground cleared and portioned off for the Afghan camp. I learnt later on that this individual was the head executioner of the ruler of the 'God-granted kingdom,' and so I gave him a wide berth afterwards. Next morning we were to meet His Highness at our boundary line, Tor-Kham, and proceeding there early, we waited in 'review order' for fully two hours before His Highness's cavalcade came up. The customary introductions having taken place, we had time to look at the Amir, who was surrounded by a crowd of attendants (*pesh-khidmats*) on foot. Just behind him rode the Dabir-ul-Mulk, Gholam Nabbi, his Commander-in-Chief, Sipar Salar Gholam Hyder Khan, Charkhi, our British Agent, Sardar Afzal Khan, C.S.I., and one or two lads mounted on good horses. Our cavalry was directed to go in front, as the Amir preferred having his own men near and round him. The carrier pigeons bearing a message to Peshawar of his arrival were now let go whilst the Amir was changing his mount, a very strong pony about 13.2 in height. Another animal of the same height and build was brought up close to the one he was riding, facing in the opposite direction. His Highness took his left foot out of his stirrup, and placed it inside the near stirrup of the saddle on the fresh mount; having done this, the right foot with the support of several attendants was brought over the neck of the animal he had already ridden, and swung over the saddle of the fresh mount, and he was then ready for a start. In this way the trouble of dismounting to the ground and then mounting again was avoided. One of the Afghan *cortège*, a young lad of some twenty years of age, attempted to show off his own wonderful equestrian ability in the narrow ravine, and his horse, letting out, injured three animals belonging to the Bengal Cavalry. One excitable commandant of infantry cracked his whip repeatedly, and made his foot soldiers stamp their feet violently as they marched up the sloping road leading to Landi Kotal. Behind the infantry came the royal drum, if one may call it so, which boomed out at intervals, then H.H. the Amir's cavalcade, followed by the Durrani horse, then the mountain guns, the rear being brought up by the Uz-Beg cavalry ('them House-Bugs,' as the British soldiers at Rawal Pindi called them). The Amir's officials, highly trained, kept perfectly silent throughout this and every other ride, and regarded us like images of stone. The plateau of Landi Kotal was reached at last, and near the caravan serai and lines of the Khyber Rifles a crowd of some 2,000 hillmen, mostly armed, some seated, some standing, were waiting expectantly the arrival of the Amir. Then followed a scene which I could not understand. The Amir looked round, and one of the mounted attendants rode up, whom he addressed in Persian. I only caught the words, 'Do your duty.' The attendant gave some instructions to half a dozen mounted men, and as the Amir's cavalcade approached a group of armed men, one of the attendants rode up and halted his horse in front of them until His Highness had passed. All the way down the Pass and on the return journey this scene was repeatedly enacted, no matter whether the armed Afridis were standing on the level ground or perched on a rock twenty feet above the Khyber road. Arriving at his camp, Abdur Rahman dismounted, and took his seat in his darbar tent at the head, whilst some four or five of us following the Commissioner were supplied with chairs, the Afghan staff standing outside. Tea in the Russian fashion was brought round in glasses, whilst we who had been up since 4 A.M., and were famished with hunger, longed for the entertainment to break up, so that we might go to our breakfasts at the mess tent of the 1st Bengal Cavalry. There being a difficulty in commencing a conversation, the Commissioner turned to His Highness, and asked him if he had seen the pigeons that had been let loose at Tor-Kham. The Amir said that he had not noticed them, and asked why and with what object they had been brought. The Commissioner attempted to explain the matter, and inquired if carrier pigeons were ever employed in Afghanistan. His Highness then told him that 400 were flown daily between Caubul and Herat. There was a silence for a minute after this, when Sardar Muhammad Omar Khan, brother of Sardar Muhammad Afzal Khan, C.S.I., the British Envoy at the court of the Amir, asked His Highness what the distance might be between Caubul and Herat. His Highness explained the geography of Afghanistan in a manner which exemplified the proverb 'that silence was golden,' especially in the presence of Amirs. In 1884 the Amir's officials had desired to build their post at Landi Khana, but were warned that their boundary did not come east of Tor-Kham, and on this account we had started very early to meet His Highness at the exact spot where our limits ended and those of Afghanistan commenced. It was a matter of necessity for us to be on this ground before His Highness arrived there. The Amir's retinue consisted of 1,622 men, 1,734 ponies and horses, besides numerous camels. The rain that had been keeping off for some time now commenced in earnest, and, with hardly any cessation, kept on to May 31, 1885.

The march on March 28, 1885, from Landi Kotal to Shagai did not commence at the hour expected, and we remained outside in the drizzling rain for nearly an hour and a half before the Amir came out of his tent and made a move. The day's journey passed off without any special incident until we got beneath the lofty battlements of Fort Ali Masjid and the stupendous heights of Rhotas opposite. The cavalcade went past the numerous forts of the Zakha Khel Afridis, where here and there were small groups of women and girls, their faces covered with the *chaddar*, trying under difficulties to have a peep at the show. Just after we had passed the narrowest part of the gorge, going by the road made by us along the cliff, His Highness halted his horse, and looking back at Sipah Salar Gholam Hyder Khan, said: 'What made you hold a place like that? You should have been driven out of it in a few minutes; the fort is untenable.' Gholam Hyder Khan wished to represent that in 1878 the Rhotas hill had been assigned to Bahram Khan of Lalpura and his Mohmands, who had retired when the British troops advanced, but his excuses were ignored, and the Amir's double hit pleased his courtiers. The camp at Shagai after sunset looked very picturesque, with the watch-fires of the picquets of the Khyber Rifles perched here and there on the hillside round about the encampment. March 29 saw us approaching Fort Jamrud, where the Amir was received by General (now Sir T.) Gordon, who had been specially deputed by the Foreign Office on this duty, whilst the half-battery sent out from

Peshawar thundered forth a salute, and the 12th Bengal Cavalry were drawn up to take their share of escort duty from Jamrud to Peshawar. The guns and horses of the field battery having reached Fort Jamrud on the evening of March 28, had been housed in the inclosure facing west. During the dark night some rascally Kuki Khel Afridi, or, what is more likely, some Peshawari outlaw living in their villages, crept up to the tanks that adjoin this enclosure, mounted one of the pillars of the gateway, and fired his rifle loaded with three or four slugs in the direction of the horses, and then slunk away. It was a stupid trick, as two horses were slightly wounded, and the Kuki Khel Afridis suffered to the extent of Rs. 600 fine. That evening, about 5.30 P.M., the Commissioner spoke severely to Malik Amin Khan and the Kuki Khel elders, who had been collected for this purpose, and said that they ought to look better after the bad characters of their tribe. In this particular case Amin Khan was innocent, as he was with us at Shagai when the shot was fired.

The 12th Bengal Cavalry, occupying the northern inclosure of the fort, kindly asked me to dinner and to have my morning meal with them, as the 1st Bengal Cavalry had pitched their camp a good distance from the fort, in the direction of Peshawar. It was about 10 P.M., our dinner was over, and we had drawn near the fire for a smoke, whilst the rain was coming gently down outside—when three shots in quick succession rang out. 'They are at the horses of the 1st Bengal Cavalry!' I cried, and rose up to go to my quarters; but I was deceived by the direction of the sound. When I got to my quarters, some 200 yards away, a messenger told me that the

Commissioner wished to see me, as his tent had been fired into. However, after due inquiry it turned out not so bad as that. A Mullagori sentry over his camp, having been relieved off duty, had walked towards a couple of thieves who were making their way to the Amir's camp. Thinking they were discovered, they fired over the sentry's head and fled up the ravine, whilst he discharged his rifle at them. Satisfied with this explanation, which was correct, we retired to rest.

The next day in pouring rain we continued our march to Peshawar. From there it was my lot to take the first batch of the Amir's infantry by rail to Rawal Pindi, and, again in heavy showers, we reached our destination about 11 P.M. I was most lucky in finding several native officers of the Bengal and Panjab cavalry on the platform ready to help me, with detachments of their men. All were Muhammadans and conversant with Persian and Pushtu, so their aid was of the greatest value. The officer in charge of the arrangements for H.H. the Amir's camp was my friend Turner of the Panjab Frontier Force, who in 1879 had come down from Caubul in charge of ex-Amir Muhammad Yakub Khan. Reaching his tent, I was warmly welcomed and provided with food, after having had a nine hours' fast between Peshawar and Rawul Pindi.

I had to go two or three times before His Highness on some duty, and Amir Abdur Rahman Khan always gave me a kindly welcome, but spoke to me as if I had just arrived from the Khyber, although I assured him that I had been all the time in his camp at Rawal Pindi. The darbar and parades being over, General T. Gordon one morning directed me to accompany him, as the Amir intended visiting the fort at Rawal Pindi, and examining all that was to be seen there. The General commanding the Rawal Pindi Division, with his full staff, was there to receive the Amir, who came with his Sipah Salar and a selected few. We were first taken down into the powder magazine, in which were stored 200,000 pounds of gunpowder. The Amir, walking with some difficulty, was next conducted through the various wards filled with rifles. A model of the latest 16-pounder field gun, which was being built at Woolwich, was standing in the centre of the arsenal. I believe that at that period it was the only model in India, and not a single field battery outside of England was then supplied with this arm. The weapon was brought to the Amir's notice, upon which His Highness told us that he had already three batteries of field artillery equipped with this gun at Caubul! Then, correcting himself, he replied, 'No, only two batteries, as the gun carriages of the third are not yet ready.' Ascending the stairs to the rampart, His Highness rested on the slopes of one of the gun redoubts just above the caponiere facing the park, and commenced making inquiries about the cost of the fort, the time it took to build, and what the caponiere was meant for. Then, looking at a hillock in the midst of the park, and not very far off, he asked what was its use. He made the same application regarding another mound. Then, rising up from the sward, he said in sharp, quick sentences, 'It is a good fort; it must have cost a lot of money to build, but it is commanded.'

Everything comes to an end, and as the Amir's visit to Rawal Pindi was drawing to a close, I had the pleasure of journeying with the first part of the Afghan soldiery by rail to Peshawar. After a few days' halt there I met His Highness at a garden party given by the Commissioner, at which Colonel Euan Smith was also a guest. Amir Abdur Rahman Khan had a grave, concerned look on his face, as if he was not quite satisfied with all that had occurred. On April 16 the camp was again at Shagai, and that afternoon General Gordon, the Commissioner, and I were present at a long interview with His Highness, at which he opened out his mind pretty freely. The next morning we started about 8 A.M. for Landi Kotal, and, riding almost immediately behind the Amir, I noticed his *pesh-khidmats* swerve to one side of the road, and the ruler of Afghanistan halt his pony in front of a dead body on the ground and a man of the Mullah type kneeling beside it with his hands up in supplication. I thought, 'Here is a nice event, for one of the Amir's people to be murdered just one day before leaving our limits!' However, it was not a case of murder. The Mullah's brother had been very ill, and to save paying the Khyber tolls they had joined the Amir's encampment and come up free to Shagai. There the ailing man had died, and the Mullah had adopted this plan to have his brother's body buried at Abdur Rahman Khan's expense. His stratagem succeeded.

On arrival at Landi Kotal the Khyber maliks asked to be allowed to see the Amir of Afghanistan. That night after dinner General Gordon, the Commissioner and I, had a final three hours' interview with His Highness, and came away from his tent about 1 A.M. in the morning. Then it took another hour to write down all that His Highness had said to us.

April 18 found us journeying westwards towards Landi Khana. A Zakha Khel thief had been secured at Dakka in the very act of house-breaking, and now his old mother, running alongside the cavalcade, solicited his pardon and release from Abdur Rahman Khan. But in such matters His Highness was very firm. 'You must have brought your son up very badly as a mother for him to be a thief now,' was the reply given to the old lady's solicitations by one who had cleared many thieves out of his own country with a strong hand.

Just then the Amir reigned in his horse, and called out, 'Does anyone know which is Madu Kwala and Tor-Kham?' On this the cavalcade halted, and I explained and pointed out each locality. The Amir was making inquiries about the spot where the boundaries of Afghanistan and the Khyber Charge met on this road. Urging his pony up a little hillock on the right-hand side, and followed by all the European officials and some of his own staff, the Amir directed his Commander-in-Chief to build his Afghan post on the crest of that hillock. This post has not been built yet, and although fourteen years have elapsed since that morning of April 18, 1885, the dispute between the Amir's officials and our own regarding the Afghan boundary line being at Tor-Kham or Landi Khana has not been disposed of up to date. As a matter of much importance, Tor-Kham was made our boundary limit immediately after the signature of the treaty of

Gandamak. But in those days the present Ruler of Afghanistan was at Samarcand.

The time had now come to bid adieu to our Royal guest. Wishing us farewell, Amir Abdur Rahman Khan, followed by all his dignitaries of state, his troops, *pesh-khidmats*, and the Zakha Khel lady asking pardon for her son, moved on into the limits of his own 'God-granted Government.' (The Amir and all his officials in their correspondence call Afghanistan the *Saltinat-i-Khodadad*, i.e. the 'God-granted Government.') We all dismounted to take a few minutes' rest before returning to Landi Kotal, and in this interval the Commissioner busied himself in writing his despatch announcing the departure of the Amir, and, placing it in the usual way, released the only pair of carrier pigeons that we had brought with us to start on their risky journey to Peshawar. There are some very high cliffs at Tor-Kham on the left-hand side of the road, and before the carrier pigeons had made a couple of circles one of them was snapped up by a peregrine. The second pigeon gave a longer flight, and we watched the chase anxiously; the pursued bird actually flew inside a huge hollow in the rock, but was chased out again. At last it was secured, both the peregrine and the pigeon coming down to the ground within 100 yards of the line of the 1st Bengal Cavalry, who, dismounted, were anxiously watching the flight. A rush was at once made towards the birds, and the peregrine, clearing off, permitted the men to secure the pigeon. It was the bird that carried the quill conveying the message. Its feet were much torn by the talons of the hawk, and it was of course in great terror. We returned to Landi Kotal, remained there that day, and on the 19th journeyed to Peshawar, our kind hosts, the 1st Bengal Cavalry, breaking their journey at Jamrud.

The Amir's visit through the Khyber Pass, taking up six days coming and going, had been no sinecure to the Khyber officials. As I have noted before, every item of food and all supplies had to be brought from Peshawar. The camps had to be carefully guarded, both by night and day. There was the fear of some Afghan striking an Afridi, and the latter using in return his rifle or his long knife. There was even the greater danger of some evil-minded person ascending a hill-top and firing into the Amir's camp. At Ali Masjid I saw a couple of Uz-beg cavalry dash their horses into the stream, and attempt to spear a couple of tame ducks belonging to a Kuki Khel Afridi householder. Then at Jamrud the two thieves, making their way towards the Amir's camp on a dark, rainy night, were interfered with by the Mullagori sentry. But happily nothing occurred during this week of anxiety to add to our troubles, and we rejoiced that our guests had journeyed safely through the Khyber. The first night, however, that His Highness encamped at Dakka, after parting with us, thieves broke into his camp and removed six Martini-Henry rifles from the care of his soldiery.

The rain and the cool weather still continued, and it was very fortunate for us that we were so luckily situated. For about the end of May we had to drag up the six heavy guns which the Government of India had presented to the Amir. A good deal of delay had been incurred in forwarding these heavy, obsolete weapons, since none of the men employed on the elephants and bullocks were willing to go beyond Landi Khana, and on this account servants of the Afghan state had to be sent down from Caubul to replace them. Captain Brunker, of the Royal Artillery, was placed in charge of the cavalcade, and the escort was composed of 300 men of the 9th Bengal Infantry under Captain Waller, whilst I evaded the first day's heat of the march by going out early to Jamrud. A start was made from Peshawar about 8 A.M., and Jamrud was reached at 4 P.M. The next day we commenced at 4 A.M., and the ascent took us twelve hours to Ali Masjid. A stout, robust colonel of the Afghan Artillery, mounted on a fine grey 'Kataghanni' horse, watched the proceedings with great interest, and the nearer we got to the Afghan Border the greater his anxieties became. Poor man, no one could tell what his berth had been before he was made Colonel of the Top-Khana, and given this troublesome duty; but it was evident that he was quite new to the work, and did not know what to do or what order to give for the simplest movement. And his face of despair when Brunker brought the guns up into line close order at Landi Khana, and handed them over to him to look after for the future, was a sight to see. Wishing him a courteous farewell, we turned back to Landi Kotal.

The following letter, dated Simla, May 14, 1885, from the Under-Secretary to the Government, Panjab, to the Commissioner and Superintendent, Peshawar Division, referring to H.H. the Amir's passage, was duly received: 'I am desired by the Lieutenant-Governor to acknowledge the receipt of your letter No. 1757 P of the 28th April, forwarding the Khaibar Political Diary from the 15th to the 21st April, and to say His Honor fully endorses your remarks regarding the services of Major Warburton, the Khaibar Rifles, and the Khaibar maliks and tribes on the occasion of the passage of His Highness the Amir and his retinue through the Pass. I am to request that you will convey to Major Warburton an expression of His Honor's appreciation of the excellent arrangements made by him on this occasion.'

Again, a letter dated Lahore, June 26, 1885, from the Secretary to Government, Panjab, to the Commissioner and Superintendent, Peshawar Division, noted: 'I am now to add that the Lieutenant-Governor is much obliged to Major Warburton for his exertions, which were highly creditable to him.'

But those who deserved most credit of all were the officers and men of the Khyber Rifles, who unflinchingly through cold and rain carried out all their difficult duties without a murmur.

CHAPTER IX

H.H. AMIR ABDUR RAHMAN KHAN

1885

No attempt will be made here to deal with any political bearings touching the life and reign of the remarkable man who has been Ruler of Afghanistan for now more than nineteen years. The history of that country, from the time of the death of the great Amir Dost Muhammad Khan to the period which made Sardar Abdur Rahman a fugitive and a pensioner at Samarcand, is well known to all readers of Central Asian history, and they must be equally familiar with the attempts made to conciliate Amir Sher Ali Khan from 1869 to the time that our troops advanced on November 21, 1878, to invade Afghanistan. Whatever may have been the causes which prevented our winning the affection of the Afghan ruler, his sardars, and his people must be left to the judgment of those experts at Calcutta, Simla, or the India Office in whose hands lie the destinies of India. I shall only deal here with the marvellous luck and good fortune that have always attended Abdur Rahman from the time he started from Samarcand in the early part of 1880 to win for himself the rulership of that troublesome country known to us as the land of the Afghans.

In the spring of 1880 we were holding Candahar, Kurram, Caubul, and the line *viâ* Jelallabad and the

Khyber Pass to Peshawar. The very powerful coalition formed by Muhammad Jan Khan, Mushki Alam, and the sardars and chiefs of the Sher Ali Khan faction had been defeated in their attack on Sherpur, but they were not crushed, and their power was still very great. Westwards from Candahar to Herat the whole country was virtually in the hands of Sardar Muhammad Ayub Khan, and what is known to us as Afghan-Turkestan, including Badakhshan, was held for the Sher Ali Khan dynasty by General Gholam Hyder Khan, Wardak, a trusted soldier of Amir Sher Ali's. This was the condition of the country when the present Amir with his small following left Samarcand, and made for the north-east quarter of Afghan-Turkestan, and, crossing the Oxus, entered Badakhshan. The first notice we had of his arrival on Afghan soil was sent to me by Sayad Mahmud Badshah of Kuner, and delivered at Jelallabad about the very day that Mr. Lepel Griffin had arrived there *en route* to Caubul. Although in a demi-official letter to the Foreign Department, some time before this, I had explained the advantages of placing Abdur Rahman Khan on the throne, yet the chances of his being permitted to get an entry into Afghanistan were so remote that it seemed a positive certainty of one of the late Amir Sher Ali Khan's family being accepted as Amir when our troops withdrew from the country. Sardar M. Ayub Khan was paramount at Herat, and nothing that the opposite faction could do would have shaken his authority in that province for one single second; and he further knew, or must have surmised, that sooner or later the British troops would be withdrawn from Caubul, and that the only individual he and his dynasty had to fear as a rival was Sardar Abdur Rahman Khan. It was also known that the only quarter of Afghanistan where this rival could then enter and make himself dangerous was Afghan-Turkestan. To Afghan-Turkestan Sardar M. Ayub Khan should therefore have gone at all costs, and prevented by every means in his power his sole and only rival from crossing the Oxus, or, if he succeeded in that venture, to destroy him when he had made good his landing. Instead of carrying out this far-seeing policy, Sardar Ayub Khan entered into that fatal march of 370 miles from Herat to Candahar, and wasted precious time and his army in trying to knock his head against the great British power which caused his destruction; whilst his rival, having reached Afghan-Turkestan, advanced towards Caubul, the capital of Afghanistan, by the shortest and quickest route available, and made his terms with the British Government. Fortune had been generous to him, for with little in hand he had dared much, and Sardar M. Ayub Khan, with every point in his favour, had lost the game. This was the first great win for Abdur Rahman Khan's side.

The next trump card was played by him immediately after securing the Amirship. The whole Caubul province was seething with malcontents who belonged to Amir Sher Ali Khan's lot, and who were anxious to see the Amirship handed over to the victorious soldier Sardar M. Ayub Khan. The head of this conspiracy was Muhammad Jan Khan, supported in the background by Mushki Alam. But Abdur Rahman Khan had between the years 1864 and 1880 tasted much of the 'hot and cold' of this world, and he had no intention of being caught napping again, so he struck whilst the great leader of the

Ghazis was arranging to strike. In this way Muhammad Jan Khan was secured, and sent away in the direction of Afghan-Turkestan, under charge of one of the Amir's much trusted *pesh-khidmats*, and he has not yet returned to his faithful friends at Caubul.

Whilst Muhammad Jan Khan's career was being thus cut short, Sardar Muhammad Ayub Khan, who had returned to Herat after his defeat at Baba-Walli, was raising up another army and getting together another field artillery, and when his plans were ready he again marched towards Candahar, and on this occasion was lucky enough to defeat Amir Abdur Rahman Khan's general, and secure Candahar. Friends urged him time after time to advance upon Caubul. His name was then high in favour; the powerful Ghilzai tribe, who revolted afterwards, were wavering, and might have joined him. His presence at Candahar was injurious to him, because the people there knew we were supporting Amir Abdur Rahman Khan, and Ayub's followers declared afterwards that it was this support which ruined their master's cause, and not anything which Amir Abdur Rahman Khan did. But Ayub lingered at Candahar, and permitted his rival to march down through the Ghilzai country, increasing his own influence thereby, crushing the faction of his enemy, and in the end winning at Candahar, whilst his general, Sardar Abdul Kudus Khan, marching from Afghan-Turkestan by way of Maimena, was fortunate enough to secure Herat city and district. Sardar M. Ayub Khan had no further resource left but to save himself by flight into Persia. And in this way Amir Abdur Rahman was able to tide over the most dangerous crisis of his career since he became the recognised Amir of Afghanistan.

The next incident was the rising of the Ali Sher Khel, Mandezai, Saugu Khel, and Sipah Shinwaris of Ningrahar in the Jelallabad District, the first of whom are related to and are a branch of the Shinwaris of Loargi (from *Lwara*, highland), and sometimes known as Landi Kotal (*Land*, or short, Kotal), who have come under us by the treaty of Gandamak. These four Shinwari clans claimed certain posts between Landi Khana and Dakka on the Peshawar Jelallabad road, and since His Highness had opened his portion of the road to caravans, and was taking tolls from travellers and merchants, these hill-men thought they had a right to make some demand for their share also. But instead of pleading their cause in a gentle, suitable manner, they attempted to secure it by force of arms, and this was a very dangerous game to play with His Highness. Troops were immediately launched into the Shinwari country, and during the sixteen years that have elapsed since the first commencement of this trouble the power of the four clans has been entirely crushed, and they have been compelled to become revenue-paying subjects of the Amir. About the same time the Mangals and the people of Kuner became fractious, but their resistance was not of so persistent or tenacious a nature as that of the Shins.

The great Ghilzai tribe were now about to try their luck against the fortunate ruler of Afghanistan, and although at the outset some spark of success attended their exertions, and one or two of the Amir's generals were hard pressed, still, in the end the greater unanimity in the councils and the greater resources of the Afghan Government made victory assured and certain. The Ghilzais were compelled to bow the knee, and forced to surrender all their arms. Just about this time Sardar M. Ayub Khan made his venture from Teheran in the direction of Herat, but on arriving at the confines of that province he learnt that all his friends were dead and buried, and that the new generation knew him not.

Sardar Muhammad Ishak Khan, cousin of the Amir's and son of Amir Azim Khan, who had for eight years ruled Afghan-Turkestan as Governor on behalf of Abdur Rahman Khan, selected the year 1888 for raising the standard of revolt against His Highness. The command of the Caubul army was entrusted to Gholam Hyder Khan, Orakzai (known as Landai, on account of his short stature), and the battle of Ghaznighak, which should have been a victory for Ishak Khan, was turned into a defeat by his conduct and the brave energy of Gholam Hyder. Sardar M. Ishak Khan with all his family crossed the Oxus, and he is now located at Samarcand, waiting patiently for the time when he may be once more called to make a bid for the throne of Caubul.

The campaign against the Hazaras was a long and trying one, but in the end His Highness was victorious and the Hazara power was broken. It may be resuscitated some day when Russia occupies Herat and Afghan-Turkestan, and feels it worth her while to secure the people of the Hazarajat as allies in any movement towards Kelat-i-Ghilzi, Ghuzni, or Candahar. But this is not a subject which should be allowed a place here. The overthrow of the Kafirs, that race which had held its own against all the great conquerors of Asia—Sultan Mahmud of Ghuzni,

Genghis Khan, Timur-i-Lang, Baber, Nadir Shah, Ahmad Khan, Durani, and a host of Moghul emperors—should bring a pang to the English heart, because English encroachments and English action led to their destruction. The very first move made by Robertson into the land of the Kafirs induced the far-seeing Ruler of Afghanistan, Abdur Rahman Khan, to make up his mind to the procedure he intended to adopt. And no sooner had the Durand treaty of 1893 placed Kafiristan within his sphere of influence than troops were launched from north, south, and west against the badly armed residents of the Kafir mountains, and the Mullah cry of 'Jahad' was preached with success to a fanatical Afghan population. What could men, however brave, armed only with ancient bows and arrows, do against a brave, hardy soldiery armed with good Martini-Henry rifles, and supplied with modern artillery? The Kafirs in a very short time were conquered and converted to Islam. And the old race may now be considered as wiped off the earth's surface.

Under the able rulership of Abdur Rahman Khan the city of Caubul has been vastly improved—almost rebuilt—and roads have been taken in hand which lead to strategical positions. Magnificent workshops have been constructed at the capital, and modern machinery of the newest type for manufacturing rifles, guns, ammunition, etc., has been brought from Europe and laid down. In other arts and manufactures also great progress has been made. But what appears most wonderful of all is the very great protection to life and property accorded to every individual who resides under the shelter of Zia-ul-Millat au Dina, H.H. Amir Abdur Rahman Khan, Wali of Afghanistan.

CHAPTER X

IN THE KHYBER

1886–1888

SAYAD BADSHAH, officiating Commandant Khyber Rifles, died suddenly of heart disease during September 1885, and his place was taken by Malik Afridi Khan, second in command, pending the return of Sardar Muhammad Aslam Khan, absent with the Afghan Boundary Commission. One day in the winter Afridi Khan and I had to go to the Sipah village of Ilam-gudar, which lies about two miles in a south-westerly direction in the bed of the stream from Fort Bara. The village is on the left bank of the Bara River, and consists of a succession of hamlets, each with a tower or two to defend the site and crops, extending for a distance of three to three and a-half miles towards the hills. Until you actually come on to the bank, and look down on the houses, nothing but the standing towers are visible. Once upon a time, during the Sikh rule, a Kuki Khel Afridi led the Sikhs on and helped them to surprise the village, and the residents had a very hot time of it. In spite of the strong hostility that prevailed between the Aka Khel, who mustered about 3,000, and the Sipah Afridis, whose numbers hardly came up to half this, the Ilam-gudar Sipahs were split up into two parties having a deep-rooted blood feud one against the other, and they nearly came to blows in my presence. Arriving at the tower which lay nearest to Fort Bara, and having taken seven or eight of their men, we went in a direction due west through the open plain, keeping away from the river and its habitations. Having completed the purpose for which we had gone out, we returned along the left bank towards Fort Bara, passing all the buildings and towers. It was a good old custom once general throughout India, but which has disappeared in these days, that whenever an English officer came to a hamlet the village headman would come out and offer him a rupee, which he merely touched and politely returned. This good custom, I am glad to say, still holds good in the Khyber Range, and if the people know the Sahib, they produce a sheep and a handful of rupees and offer them to the English guest. The custom is to put your hand on the rupees, thank the donor, and ask him to keep them for you until required. On this occasion we had carried out our duty with the inhabitants of two towers and their hamlets, who happened to be friendly to the Sipahs who formed our party from the start. Coming towards the third tower we saw nine or ten armed men standing to receive us, and I suddenly heard the click click of the rifles of the men with me, each individual placing his piece at full cock for instant action. This warned me that we were on dangerous ground. 'Sahib, there will be bloodshed if we do not look out,' cried Malik Afridi Khan; so we stopped for an instant to see what could be done, as the rival parties were now only thirty yards apart, and up to that moment I had not been warned of the two sides being enemies. Sending Afridi Khan to make a *détour* to our left with our party, I approached those who had just come out to receive me, and the usual formalities were gone through. I remained talking with them until Afridi Khan had got some two or three hundred yards away with his following. I asked all to return quietly to their homes, which they did whilst I rode after and rejoined Afridi Khan. It was to me always a pleasure to go to these Afridi villages, but there was an occasional drawback when some Peshawari outlaw was produced and you were asked to obtain his pardon. However, when they learnt that this procedure was distasteful to me, they gave it up. I made it clear to them that no pleading on my part could secure a pardon for the offender.

Sardar Muhammad Hassan Khan, ex-Governor of Jelallabad, had been in Afridi and Orakzai Tirah ever since the commencement of the Shinwari revolt in 1883, and had done his best to stir up the Amir's subjects against him. Owing to our former acquaintance, he opened up communications with me and asked me to obtain permission for him to journey in safety through India to Persia. I did so, and pleaded his cause to the best of my ability, and in time the sanction came, but with a reservation that on no account would the sardar receive any allowance or pension from the revenues of India. These orders I communicated to him, and intimated that if he came to me I would see that he was not interfered with. However, he preferred to carry out his own ways of procedure, and riding quietly into the city of Peshawar he got into the train and left without giving me any notice of his movements. The next morning his horse was recognised as it was being taken by Ilam-gudar, and I was apprised of what he had done. There were only two spots in India where he could go to and receive a welcome. One was Dera Dun, to see ex-Amir Yakub Khan; the second was Karachi, where resided Sher Ali Khan, Candahari, one of the favourite sardars of the late Amir Sher Ali. I telegraphed to the political officers in charge of both the sardars, and when Sardar M. Hassan Khan arrived at Karachi, Sher Ali Khan, knowing that the authorities were aware of his coming, informed them that he had arrived. He was permitted to leave for Persia without molestation, and on arrival there he wrote me a letter conveying his thanks for all that I had done for him. His was a strange, tortuous career. Brought up with the ex-Amir Yakub Khan, he shared with him all the sorrows and privations of the Afghan wars between 1864 and 1869, which gave the final victory to Amir Sher Ali Khan's faction. For five years he and Yakub Khan were prisoners at Caubul, and were released together when Amir Sher Ali Khan fled to Mazar-i-Sherif in 1878. Appointed in succession Governor of Ghuzni and Jelallabad, he fled from us in December 1879, fought against the British at Jagdallak, Patkao-i-Shahana, Char-Asia (in Logar), Ahmad Khel, Maiwind, and Baba-Walli. He was with Sardar M. Ayub Khan when the latter took Candahar, and was ultimately defeated by Amir Abdur Rahman Khan in 1881. Dressed in the garments of a Darwesh he recognised me at the railway station of Naushehra in September 1882, and after trying his fortunes in Kuner, Tirah, he endeavoured to move secretly into Karachi, with the object of getting back to Persia. When I went with the Afridi maliks to Karachi in February 1888, Sardar Hassan Khan had arrived there with the first batch of Sardar Muhammad Ayub Khan's friends, and was in receipt of Rs. 100 a month from us. I called and paid him a visit, and had a long interview with him. He left India again for some reason unknown to me, and in 1895 he went to England in Sardar Nasrulla Khan's suite, and is now one of H.H. Amir Abdur Rahman Khan's most devoted servants at Caubul.

Strange events occur in the history of these frontier tribes. Outsiders will hardly credit some of the stories told, but numbers of reliable witnesses can testify to the veracity of the following one. Amongst Afridis and Pathans the disposal of a widow lies in the hands of the nearest male relation to her deceased husband. If the son is of age, of course he is the first consulted; but an Afridi mother with a grown up son is not often of much cash value in the Khyber market. If, on the other hand, the woman is attractive and the son very young, the deceased husband's brother, should he be the guardian, either marries her himself or sells her to someone else. The widow of a Zakha Khel Afridi, living at Karamna in the Bazàr Valley, found herself in this unhappy predicament; she had a young son, and an exceedingly objectionable brother of her dead husband to claim her in marriage or to dispose of her for cash. She therefore took the matter into her own hands, and fled to the country of the Mullagoris, and married a man of her own choice. There is a very strong enmity between the Zakha Khel and the Mullagori, and all the years that I have had the management of the Khyber Pass arrangements I have never known them to be on friendly terms with each other. Some time before

1878 the females from the house of Malik Khwas Khan went to fetch water from the spring at Shipola in the Khyber, and whilst there were surprised by a band of Mullagori raiders, who carried them off. Amongst the captives was a wife of the then Khan of Lalpura, and her sister married to Khwas Khan. It took the utmost influence of the Khan of Lalpura, who had then control over the Mullagoris, to secure the release of these ladies. This incident may have intensified the feud between the two tribes. Coming back, however, to my tale; the Mullagori who married the widow from Karamna had no idea that she had left a young son on going to him, or, if he had, the recollection had passed out of his mind. The son, on the other hand, grew up, and, nourishing his wrath, looked forward to a meeting with his stepfather, having taken care to make himself acquainted with his appearance. He was in the Khyber Jezailchies at Landi Kotal when one day he saw the man who had married his mother, and he followed him, rifle in hand. The Mullagori, seeing that he was followed, asked the young man where he was going, and in reply the latter pointed to a Shinwari village not very far away. The older man was put off his guard, and as he was passing over some rough ground the younger individual knelt down and fired his piece at him, inflicting a slight flesh wound. Drawing out his long Afridi knife the wounded man chased the treacherous lad, who was unable to reload, into the Shinwari village, whose residents secured both persons and prevented further damage being done. The Mullagori complained that, without any just cause or reason, the young man had tried to murder him close to the Shinwari village. Having heard the charge the Zakha Khel shouted 'No cause or reason! Did you not wed my mother without my permission?' The Shinwaris took care to let one depart a good time before the other, so as to prevent any further attempts on the life of the stepfather by his angry stepson.

The gateway of Fort Ali Masjid faces due south towards the hills above Chora. The gateway is generally closed, the wicket only being kept open, and the sentry walks up and down the short passage that shelters him from the west wind which blows with such violence down the Pass. Exactly north lies the stupendous Rhotas Range, which on the map is marked over 6,000 feet. The side facing Ali Masjid rises up in sheer cliffs 2,000 to 2,500 feet overhead. To the naked eye there is no path visible which can take a human being to the highest crest of this ridge. When a Viceroy of India or other important personage paid a visit to Ali Masjid, a party of six or seven men of the Khyber Rifles were sent up to this crest to hold it, and had to remain there until the visitor moved away. It was about the spring of 1886 that a party of the Khyber Rifles were seated on the ground sunning themselves by the gateway of Ali Masjid, and looking in the direction of Rhotas. The men had their own rifles, all muzzle-loaders, with a few Enfields, and commenced arguing whether a bullet fired from a rifle on the top of Rhotas would reach the gateway. One said to another of the party: 'Go up with your rifle to the top and fire it in this direction, and we shall see where the bullet goes.' The man addressed took up his rifle, and after a laborious climb got to the crest. The bullet of the first shot was not traced. The

AFRIDI VILLAGES BELOW ALI MASJID.

second, by the merest accident, caught one of the lookers-on in the forehead and killed him on the spot. There was no possibility of communicating between the two parties by voice, so when the marksman came down he was astonished to see what he had done, and more astonished still to find himself made a prisoner. Some of the guard, however, connived at his escape, and he managed to get away. There was no occasion for this, as there was no law or rule by which he could have been punished.

In the spring of 1886 I had arranged to move our camp up to Tor-Sappar, which lies about seven or eight miles due north of our encamping ground at Landi Kotal, which was nominally the old caravan ground, roofless, exposed to the sun and rain and storms at all seasons of the year. We had stopped at Tor-Sappar for two to three weeks in 1884, but this visit was curtailed owing to Sardar Aslam Khan having been selected to go with the Afghan Boundary Commission towards Herat and Panjdeh, and various parts of that quarter of Afghanistan.

Peshawar is very pleasant up to the end of April, and it is not till about the end of the third week in May that the heat makes a change to cooler climes necessary. The Government of India had sent up a splendid elephant as a present for H.H. the Amir of Afghanistan, and shortly after its arrival at Peshawar the beast showed signs of being 'mást.' He managed to break away from his keeper and chains, and roamed at large for two or three days until he was captured somewhere in Yusufzai and brought back. Then his 'Mahaut' refused to put his foot inside the precincts of Afghanistan, and the Amir's officials at Peshawar had to send post-haste to

Caubul and get one or two men down who were accustomed to train elephants. In a short time these men arrived, and the huge animal, appearing to be docile, was taken up to Jamrud, then to Landi Kotal, and marched to Jelallabad, where His Highness had gone to in February to escape the rigours of a winter at Caubul. On the journey the keeper fed the elephant on such quantities of heating food that the day after its arrival at Jelallabad the animal became more 'mast' than ever, and, tearing through the camp, destroyed one or two lives and caused an immense deal of damage. Some time afterwards I met the Amir's official who had been in charge of the party with this animal, and in the most solemn manner he affirmed 'that it was a mercy of Providence that the brute had gone mad the day after he had given up charge of it, for if his insanity had come on twenty-four hours earlier his head might have answered for the incident.'

Lord Roberts, who had been appointed Commander-in-Chief of the Army in India during November 1885, visited Peshawar this spring and journeyed up to Landi Kotal, where after a day's halt a trip was made to Pizgah. As we were returning to camp a very violent storm of rain came on, and poured in torrents for hours and late into the night. It happened to be a caravan day, and large numbers of Ghilzai Kuchi families were going back from Peshawar to their homes in Afghanistan, and during the twenty-mile march from Jamrud to Landi Kotal, in this pelting rain, their women, girls, and little children suffered very severely. The next morning we returned to Peshawar. I was greatly pleased at this trip, for in Lord Roberts I found a

Commander-in-Chief who took the highest interest in everything connected with the Khyber Pass. When on his annual official tour to Peshawar he regularly made a trip through the Khyber to Ali Masjid and Landi Kotal, and once to Tor-Sappar, to see for himself how things were progressing amongst the tribesmen of the Khyber Range.

The camp was moved to Tor-Sappar, my companion up there being Malik Afridi Khan in place of Sardar Aslam Khan. I had become very fond of this place, and in my opinion it had a climate far superior to Murree, Dalhousie, or Simla, although its highest point was not more than 5,600 feet. The prevailing winds were east and west, the latter blowing over the Caubul River, and the first over the moist delta of the Doaba, and on this account there was never a hot wind as at other hill stations. The sky was always clear, and the rainy season limited to five or six showers, so that we were free from the three to three and a half months of incessant mist, fog, rain, thunder, and lightning which are the normal characteristics of the Himalaya hill stations from the middle of June to the end of September.

We had great gatherings of all the tribesmen, morning and evening, before and after our work was over. They gradually opened their hearts to me regarding their joys and sorrows, and I on my part tried to explain various things to them, which they could not comprehend, amongst others the mystery which greatly puzzled them of what became of the sun every night.

It being necessary to pay an early visit to the great Shilman Valley, I took advantage of a rainy morning, and, accompanied by Malik Afridi Khan,

Malik Walli Muhammad Khan, and two troopers, started at 4 A.M. to do this journey. During the occupation of the Khyber by military troops, one survey party composed of three companies of regulars (natives) had carried on their operations through the Shilman, and a second party, accompanied by a guard of similar strength, went through the Mullagori country. I was therefore anxious to see whether the feelings of the residents towards us had undergone any change. We were received with a very kindly welcome throughout our journey. In other respects we had a very distressing day, as the clouds disappeared by 10 A.M., and a fierce sun came out and beat down on our heads with great severity. Several times I dismounted, and dipped my head into water wherever it was to be found. Malik Afridi Khan had a slight touch of heat-apoplexy. By 3 P.M. we reached the house of Malik Kamran, in the Kam-Shilman Valley, and took shelter in his garden, but it was not till 8 P.M. that we found ourselves back at Tor-Sappar.

The month of September found me again at Peshawar, but I had to take Mr. Bensley, our Civil Engineer, to see Landi Kotal, and to arrange for the repairs to the various posts, which were now being carried on regularly every year. There had also been a similar provision made for the road, which was now kept in excellent order, although the sum sanctioned for twenty-five miles of a road in the hills came only to £200 in English money. Our greatest enemy was the flood, which swept down the Pass after every very heavy rain, carrying away hundreds of yards of the roadway. Against this enemy we had no remedy, and could only exercise patience and begin the work afresh. The opposition of the maliks by this time had ceased. Malik Khwas Khan was the only culprit who still carried out a tortuous policy, but only at rare intervals now. He made one final attempt in 1888, failed, and after that collapsed for good. The Foreign Secretary and Major Evans Gordon went up the Pass, and remained two nights at Landi Kotal. Mr. (now Sir Salter) Pyne also went through to Caubul, to lay the foundation of H.H. the Amir's arsenal and workshops. And so in many ways progress was being made in the Khyber.

In the lines of the 1st company Khyber Rifles, at Landi Kotal, there was a smart, good-looking boy of about twelve, whose name was Hathi. He was an orphan, who made his living by going on errands for the men, and except a sister about a year younger than himself, living in one of the Zakha Khel hamlets, he had no other relative in the whole of Afridi land. He had a very handsome, taking face, and all were kind to the orphan lad, for he seemed then to have no mischief in him. When Lord Roberts came up to Landi Kotal for the first time, this young man, on his own initiative, collected a number of young boys, trained them according to his fashion in presenting arms, and, dividing them into three groups at intervals on the Khyber Road, met the Commander-in-Chief with a general salute. This happy custom, thus started by young Hathi, was always carried out when any illustrious visitors journeyed up to Landi Kotal. When the Khyber Rifles were told off to attack the 'Gora Phar' Hill in the Black Mountain expedition of 1888, this young boy, who had gone through the campaign unarmed, behaved in the most gallant manner. He helped

Sardar M. Aslam Khan to ascend the hill, helping him at each step. 'Get away, boy; you will be killed,' was the Sardar's warning to him. 'Never mind if I am killed, you can throw my body into the nearest ravine,' replied the lad, and he stuck to his work and ascended that terrible hill with the best of them. The boy never knew what fear was. Later on he enlisted in the Khyber Rifles, but was killed in a brawl whilst absent on leave from his corps.

The period had now arrived when arrangements were about to be made for doing something in the Khyber, both as regards its defence and for the purpose of improving its water supply. The Inspector-General of Military Works, accompanied by the Superintending Engineer Military Command, Rawal Pindi, proceeded up to Landi Kotal and had a careful look over the whole plateau, making a most minute examination of its defensive capabilities. There are few positions so strong as the Landi Kotal plateau looking westward in the direction of Jelallabad. It was from here that Nadir Shah, advancing at the head of a victorious army 100,000 strong, was kept at bay for six weeks encamped below Landi Khana, whilst a joint force of Afridis and Orakzais barred his passage through the Khyber Pass. In these days we are apt to complain of the difficulties that an army will have to experience in the way of food transport if it steps into the land of the Afghans; but if history is to be credited, Nadir Shah, advancing from the direction of Persia at the head of an army presumbly 100,000 strong, chiefly cavalry, besieged and took Herat. He then advanced on Candahar, and it took him a full year to conquer that strong fortress. A move was then made to Caubul, which also succumbed to his arms. Then came the march towards the Khyber and the six weeks' halt at Landi Khana before he turned the Khyber, by marching through the Bazàr Valley, guided by an Orakzai chief in his service, who betrayed this route to him. How he arranged and managed to feed his large force at a desolate spot like Landi Khana passes all comprehension.

From Landi Kotal we came down to Jamrud, and the whole position from Fort Bara to Burj-Harri Singh and further northwards was examined by the military experts. Lieutenant (now Major) Macdonald was sent up to inspect the water supply, and his first visit from Jamrud to Kaddam and Gudar was successful; but wishing to inspect Kaddam once more on the following morning, he was stopped by a few Kuki Khels of this village just as he got up to tho place. I think the fault of this was due partially to the mistake of the second in command of the Khyber Rifles, Malik Afridi Khan. On the first day Sardar Aslam Khan had taken Lieutenant Macdonald to Kaddam and for two miles further up the stream, and the Kuki Khel elders had been exceedingly friendly. In the evening he went to the city of Peshawar on short leave, directing Afridi Khan to take charge and help Macdonald in any matter that that officer required. Macdonald desired Afridi Khan to take him out to Kaddam again early next morning, as he wished to measure the volume of water in the stream at that spot. Afridi Khan, for some reason unexplained, failed to send on notice of this intended trip to the elders and jirga of Kaddam (according to the usual standing orders given by me), as a timely warning of this nature gave the residents a chance of telling their women to keep away from the presence of strangers. To whatever cause this *contretemps* was due, Macdonald had to give up the trip, and came away much annoyed. Later on the jirga apologised for the rudeness of their young men, and brought sheep and money as a peace offering to Macdonald.

All this work in the Khyber, at Landi Kotal, and in the Afridi country had to be carried out without any aid from the Government of the Panjab, and if any rebuff or stoppage occurred one had to take it cheerfully, and, after exercising patience, make another attempt later on. An individual called Khayasta Khan of Sarkai, one of the Kuki Khel Afridis, had received several acts of kindness, which he repaid by interfering with some workmen employed on the water duct near his house. Either on the day of his contumacious behaviour, or some twenty-four hours later, he was walking about his fields which lay in the ravine below his fort. Two of his enemies issued out of Subadar Amir Khan's fort, which was some 600 to 700 yards up the ravine, and, creeping into the water course, dragged themselves to within some 400 yards from Khayasta Khan, who had no idea of what was in store for him. Taking aim, both rifles cracked together, Khyasta Khan fell with a broken leg, and the women of his family, rushing out, carried him into his house. Subadar Amir's men were now in a perilous position. They lay flat in the not very deep water course, whilst marksmen from Khayasta Khan's fort and from Jam sent bullet after bullet at them. There they remained until sunset, when darkness enabled them to escape. Later on I shall relate how Khayasta Khan was revenged. I on my part told him that his broken leg was a punishment for his bad conduct, after having received so many acts of kindness from us. After this his behaviour was always excellent, and in 1889 H.E. Lord Lansdowne, seeing him at Ali Masjid on the occasion of the Viceregal visit to the Khyber, very kindly directed him to be presented with a wooden leg, to replace that which had been amputated.

In the summer of 1887 the Inspector-General of Military Works, General Sandford, and the Superintending Engineer Military Works, Rawal Pindi Command, Colonel (now Major-General) Lovett, and Colonel R. M. Stewart went up to Landi Kotal with me, and there was another long consultation over what was required to be done. Mr. Macdonald and another R.E. officer were also there, making plans for a fortified serai at the plateau. The former officer was also directed to make a careful inquiry into the water supply question at Loargi, and in the whole of the Khyber Range northwards towards the Caubul River, including the Shilman and Mullagori countries. My portion of the duty was to see that Mr. Macdonald was protected whilst busy at this work, and that no friction or unpleasantness should occur between the tribesmen and ourselves. So far as I could judge, all suspicion as to our intentions had disappeared, and if we required anything done a good clear and true explanation of our purpose at the commencement was always implicitly accepted. Leaving Mr. Macdonald and his assistant to do their work at Landi Kotal, the other officers journeyed down to Peshawar, and the three who had come from Simla and Rawal Pindi returned to their stations.

But a matter of far greater interest was now to be carried out, and I fondly believed that it would be really an accomplished fact. On July 12, 1887, Mr. Baker, Engineer of the N.W. State Railway, came to my house and explained to me that he had been busy on the survey of the railway extension from Peshawar to Jamrud. Commencing at the Cantonment station, the line was to be carried behind the Saddar Bazàr, round by the cavalry lines, through the southern portion of the Brigade Parade Ground, and then, going westward, would cross the Jamrud road near Burj-i-Harri Singh, and so pass on to the north of Fort Jamrud. I may say that five to six surveys from the Cantonment and City stations were made in as many years, but on the last occasion Mr. Mackinnon assured me that he had come to lay down the line, and asked my assistance in the way of escorts. He lived for a month or more at my quarters at Burj-i-Harri Singh, and then suddenly departed. Needless to remark, the Peshawar-Jamrud Railway was not in existence when the Afridi war of 1897–1898 broke out.

A strange episode occurred close to my house and on the road leading from the cricket ground, passing in front of the military prison in the direction of Michni. I had occasion to visit Jamrud, and having been out the entire day, had returned late in the evening to Peshawar. I had not got up very early the next morning, but my attendant called me, saying that a rough-rider of the battery under command of Major Dunnage, R.A., had been fired at by a Pathan on the road whilst exercising his horse. Fortunately the Ghazi fanatic, although he fired two shots, missed his aim and ran away. He was, however, followed up and secured. He turned out to be a resident of a village close to the Mathra police station in the Peshawar District; he had committed house-breaking at night in the neighbouring village of Shahi, and had very badly wounded a Mullah (priest) who was much venerated in the neighbourhood and in the villages across the border. He had fled for shelter to Kaddam, then to Gudr, villages of the Kuki Khel Afridis, but they had requested him to move on. Then he proceeded to the Mullagoris, and they had asked him to quit also. He had therefore come in to Cantonments, and made up his mind to kill the first Englishman he could lay his hands upon. He was tried under the Frontier Outrage Act by the Commissioner of the Peshawar Division and sentenced. Between 1882 and the close of 1895 there were four Ghazi outrages at Peshawar; of these two, Fulford and Stevens, were fatal, a soldier of the Devon Regiment, wounded at very close quarters, had a wonderful recovery, and the case that I have attempted to describe above was the only attack in which the unsuspecting victim escaped all injury.

I am now coming to the most interesting part of my command or charge in the Khyber Range. It was the month of November 1887, and Peshawar was exceedingly full and very gay, for Lord Dufferin, Viceroy and Governor-General of India, and Lady Dufferin, with all their staff, Lord Roberts, Commander in Chief in India, with the Head Quarters Staff, the Lieutenant-Governor of the Panjab, with his secretaries, were there, and numerous visitors from all parts of India had thronged in to witness the darbar and share in whatever amusements and pleasures might be going on. The darbar took place on November 25, and, like all such functions, was an exceedingly brilliant affair, representatives from all the different tribes on the borders of Hazara, Peshawar, Kohat, being in attendance, and they were each in turn brought up and introduced to Lord Dufferin. I have often wondered what the trans-border hillman thought of these darbars, and in what light he considered them, when the pageant was over. A darbar as we have made it and as it is, and as it was understood in old Oriental Governments, are two different things. The monotonous presentations at last came to an end. There were two or three laughing incidents in the march past, when the young son of Muhammad Sherif Khan, the present Khan of Dir, insisted on forcing his gold pieces on the Governor-General. Then the Madda Khel jirga, trooping by the Viceroy, all suddenly squatted down on the carpet, much to the chagrin of the Deputy Commissioner who was in charge of the party. Last of all the Assistant in the Kohat settlement, who looked upon his large printed presentation card as a Viceregal heirloom, to be preserved by his family for all time to come, and to be produced hereafter as a record of his good and faithful services, would shout out for his card (*mira ticket*) as we wheeled him into his proper place in presence of Her Majesty the Queen Empress of India's representative, his last cry being 'Mira ticket,' as he was pushed out by the door of the tent. The darbar over, the crowd soon dispersed, when the Viceroy and the grand officials cleared out of the great tent, and the only lot who lingered were some hundreds of trans-border men, whose *chaplis* or shoes, made from the leaf of the dwarf palm, had been taken off when they were ushered inside the tent, and were now jumbled up in a huge heap, where it was impossible for any individual to recognise what really belonged to him.

What of course interested me most was the Viceregal visit to the Khyber, which came off immediately after the darbar. The Viceroy and Lady Dufferin, the Lieutenant-Governor of the Panjab and Lady Lyall, drove in carriages from Peshawar as far as Ali Masjid. Lord Roberts and others rode from Jamrud to the middle of the Pass. Whilst Lady Dufferin and Lady Lyall stopped at Ali Masjid to examine the fort, the Viceroy and the rest of us, mounting our horses, made for Landi Kotal. As I rode on the left of His Excellency, the Commander in Chief, who was on the right of the Viceroy, said to Lord Dufferin, 'Warburton is most anxious to have a road made from the Landi Kotal plateau, which will go through the hills to the north of the Khyber Pass and debouch into the Peshawar Valley.' The Viceroy, turning to me, asked what would be the advantages of this road. I replied 'that if by any misfortune or disaster the Afridis attempted to close the Khyber Pass, the route from Landi Kotal through the Shilman and Mullagori country to Peshawar would always remain open and could never be closed, as those two tribes were far too weak to make any attempt of the sort. And even if the Khyber Pass did remain open, it would always in case of war westwards give us two routes from Peshawar to the Landi Kotal plateau, and *vice-versâ*.' I shall touch upon this road question again when I come to the year 1889. We had about thirty-five riding in this cavalcade, His Excellency being taken to the General's camp at Landi Kotal to have a look down towards Landi Khana; we then retraced our steps to Ali Masjid. The dust, however, was so great on the ride up and down that it was hard to distinguish the features of the horsemen as they dismounted at Ali Masjid to partake of lunch. The Viceregal carriage and escort turned into the Peshawar Mall by the club, as it was getting dark. It had been a pleasant visit without a single hitch, and I rejoiced that under my guidance a Viceroy of India had been able to traverse up and down the whole length of the Khyber, welcomed by its people.

When the Khyber maliks had the honour of being introduced to Lord Dufferin at Ali Masjid they asked to be permitted to see Calcutta and some of the wonders of India, and His Excellency promised to accede to their request. I shall describe this visit in the next chapter.

CHAPTER XI

THE TOUR OF THE KHYBER MALIKS

1888

ON January 5, 1888, my party of sixteen Khyber maliks assembled at the Cantonment station of the N.W. State Railway at Peshawar, and started by the morning train for Calcutta. A few of them had been taken as far as Attock in the year 1883, but to the majority of them the country east of the 'Father of Rivers,' the Indus, was an unknown and unvisited land. Nothing that they had seen—whether in the way of the rivers they had passed, or the magnificent railway bridges they had crossed over, or the palatial buildings they had had glimpses of—seemed to have any effect on the stolid minds of the residents of the Khyber Range. They passed by everything without a change of feature, as if large stations, broad rivers, magnificent bridges, and huge cities were to be seen and met with at every step in the Khyber Pass. But when we had passed Allahabad, and the train, going at the rate of thirty miles an hour, disclosed nothing but green fields, interspread by villages here and there, on either side of the line as far as the eye could see, there began to dawn on some of them the breadth and length and size of that empire which acknowledges the rule of the Queen-Empress of India. At 4 A.M. on the morning of Sunday, January 8, our train halted at Howrah, and we were met by my friend, Kazi Sayad Ahmad, C.I.E., Attaché at the Foreign Office, who made all the arrangements for housing my people under his roof during their stay at Calcutta. This was an excellent plan, as the Kazi was a native of Peshawar City, and understood the language, customs, and religious views of his visitors. Being a Mussulman himself, he knew what their wants were in the way of food, and lastly he could watch and be careful that they saw no sights during their stay at Calcutta which would bring into odium the 'white man and his people.' I was sheltered by Mr. Panioty, C.I.E., Assistant Private Secretary to H.E. the Viceroy, a gentleman of great abilities who had held this post under several successive Viceroys, and whose hospitable house was always open to me. The situation, too, suited me exactly, as Government House was close at hand, the Foreign Office was across the street, and the Private Secretary's office was in the building occupied by my host.

A day or two after our arrival at Calcutta there was a garden party at Government House, and the Khyber maliks were honoured with an invitation. H.E. Lord Dufferin received them with extreme kindness, and, making careful inquiries after their comfort and health, introduced them to the Governor of Bombay, and then, conducting them personally to the refreshment tent, directed the table attendants to supply them with ices and cakes. I felt some anxiety as to the result of this, and as we were walking down I whispered in Pashtu to the Sipah chief, 'Take care you do not object to partaking of anything that is offered to you, because nothing that is objectionable will be presented to you; for this I will be answerable.' 'Sahib,' replied the Sipah malik, 'if you give us poison at this juncture, we will eat it.' An immense crowd had by this time collected round us, and watched the Khyberis with interest. The refreshments over, the men asked peımission to say their prayers, and, laying their *lungis* down on the ground there and then, looked in the direction of Mecca, knelt, and prayed.

During their stay in Calcutta they were taken to see every place and object worth visiting. In this way a day was spent at the Howrah workshops, another at the Mint, a third at the Bank of Bengal. Then a visit to tho small arm and cartridge manufactory at Dum-Dum, followed by a trip down the river in a launch to the Botanical Gardens, finishing off with a lunch at the King of Oude's Palace given by his son-in-law. The Admiral also kindly permitted them to see an English man-of-war. They were invited by the leading Mussulmans of Calcutta to a great feast. The head of the Telegraph Department received them in his palatial offices, and permitted them to send and receive a few messages from their friends and relations at Peshawar. The first messages were of a hum-drum nature, and it seemed to me as if the Afridis thought we were trying to humbug them. There was one man, called Feroz Khan, Malikdin Khel, who always looked as if in great pain. Whenever asked what was the matter with him, he only answered, 'I do not feel well.' He requested that a message might be sent direct from himself, asking 'who at that moment were in the telegraph office at Peshawar.' The reply came almost instantly that, with others, his maternal uncle, Malik Sarfaraz Khan, was at the office. The next message was, 'How is my uncle now?' The answer came, 'Quite well now; the fever has gone. How is your boil?' This message caused amusement as well as extreme surprise. The uncle had been ill at his home in Chora when the nephew left him on this trip. The nephew was also suffering from a very painful boil, about which he did not wish to speak either to his Afridi companions or to anyone. And when the telegraphic message from Peshawar revealed both the uncle's recovery and the nephew's disorder, the reputation of the *tar-barki* (telegraph) was established at once, and never doubted afterwards.

The day of our departure came at last, and H.E. the Viceroy having seen all the Khyber maliks at a final interview at Government House, we left Howrah by the evening train for Bombay. Near Jubbulpore the maliks had a narrow escape, the wheel of their carriage having in some way been injured just before we reached that station. It was then 10 P.M., and the carriage had to be taken off and replaced by another. The guard said it was most lucky that the original carriage had not collapsed, or half the Khyberis would have been killed or injured. However, we reached Bombay in the morning without meeting with any more dangerous adventures, and placed ourselves under the guidance and management of the late Sir Frank Soutar, Commissioner of Police. A magnificent residence had been provided, and from the roof of this building my wild men of the Khyber for the first time caught a glimpse of the sea. 'What is that, Sahib?' asked Malik Walli Muhammad Khan, Zakha Khel, pointing to the ocean. 'That is the Kala Pani [*Tor-Obo*, i.e.

Black-Water in Pashtu] or ocean,' I answered, 'which stretches past Aden in that direction.' 'I wish we had some of that in the Khyber,' replied the Malik. They all went to the water's edge and tasted a small quantity, when their eyes opened with astonishment at the salt flavour. After four days of Bombay we embarked on board the 'Kilwa' for Karachi, having been treated with much kindness and great hospitality.

The sea was perfectly calm, hardly a ripple on its surface; the deck was crowded with passengers, and in this happy condition we made our way undisturbed till 11 at night, when we retired to rest. As their cabin was rather stuffy and hot, the captain of the 'Kilwa' permitted some of the Khyber maliks to sleep on the quarter deck. About 5 A.M. I was roused by finding that a great quantity of salt water had come into my cabin, and made me fairly wet. The motion of the vessel, instead of being smooth, was now very jerky and pitching. One or two of the Khyber maliks were suffering from *mal-de-mer*, and their more fortunate brethren were shrieking with laughter over their sorrows. But a rough sea is no respecter of persons, and as the turbulence of the waves began to touch up the others, they all dropped their hilarity and crept to their cabin to hide their sufferings from public gaze. We had unexpectedly come in for a 'blizzard,' which, blowing due east from the Persian Gulf, swept with considerable violence through the whole of India within so many degrees of latitude, and expended its strength in the furthest limits of Eastern Burmah. The sea had become exceedingly rough, and the waves washed repeatedly over the deck, causing much misery to the poor deck

N 2

passengers. I went to comfort the unhappy Afridis for a few minutes, but we were all delighted when Karachi was reached, and we had glided into its harbour safe from all further tribulations from the sea.

We remained four days at Karachi, and the authorities kindly allowed the maliks to see Manora Point, where they had explained to them the system of harbour defences by the agency of sub-marine mines. The terrors of the sea voyage from Bombay to Karachi, however, were too much for old Malik Sultan Muhammad, Malikden Khel, and nothing would induce him to go near the sea again. 'You may kill me, Sahib, but I will never go near that Kala-Pani again,' so he was the only one of our party who did not see the wonders of Manora Point.

Leaving Karachi by the night train, we journeyed up through Sind, and by the Harnai route arrived at Quetta, where Sir Robert Sandeman made us at home for four days. The weather was dreadful, heavy snow lay on the mountains, and the greater part of the Peshin Valley was white, whilst an icy cold wind blew from the direction of the snow-covered Khojak. Sandeman had served in the Peshawar Valley prior to and during the Ambeyla campaign of 1863, and many of the Khyber maliks were personally known to him, and he asked many questions as to what had occurred in their midst and towards their country during the quarter of a century he had turned his back on Afridi land. We left Quetta on a splendid morning, and journeying this time by the Bolan railway, we reached Jacobabad, Sukkur, Montgomery, Lahore, and finally landed on the platform of the Peshawar Cantonment Station N.W.R. on Ash Wednesday, February 15, 1888. Sardar Aslam Khan and a host of relations and friends of the Afridi maliks were there to welcome us back. The maliks were dismissed to their homes at an early date in order to visit their relations and tell them of all the wonders and strange sights they had seen in their tour of six weeks through India.

Some three weeks after this Malik Tar Muhammad Khan returned from Chora and appeared in my office, looking very grave. 'Well, have you told your people all that you have seen?' I asked him. 'Yes, Sahib, but they will not believe a word I tell them, so I have stopped answering their questions.'

I have described the circumstance of the youthful son of Muhammad Sherif Khan, Khan of Dir, being present at the Viceregal darbar held at Peshawar on November 25, 1887, when the lad wished in his childish way to force his gold pieces upon the Viceroy. His father had not come into Peshawar upon that occasion. But during the spring of 1888 H.H. Amir Abdur Rahman Khan came once more down to Jelallabad to escape the rigours of the Caubul winter, which generally begins to be exceedingly severe about the month of February. Muhammad Sherif Khan, anxious to secure the support of the Government of Afghanistan, or thinking the journey would in some way be beneficial to himself, moved into Jelallabad and appeared before His Highness. Umra Khan of Barwa promptly stopped his return, and in this way Muhammad Sherif Khan had to come to Landi Kotal, and march down to Jamrud and Peshawar, to enable him to get back to Swat and make a strike for his country, which had been secured by the rapacious Umra Khan. This incident is mentioned merely to show the reasons of the Khan of Dir coming down the Khyber Pass.

The month of August 1888 I always regard with special respect, as this was the month in which the fortified serai at Landi Kotal was commenced. Captain Macdonald, whose work at Landi Kotal during the year 1887 has already been notified, made all his plans, surveys, collected all his data, and then went up to Simla to lay them before the Defence Committee and the Inspector-General of Military Works. His programme was now reȧdy, and he was coming down to introduce it. Hardly was it circulated amongst the contractors at Peshawar that works were to be commenced at the Loargi plateau, when Malik Khwas Khan, Zakha Khel, who was chief over half the Zakha Khel Afridis and had a strong fort on the Khyber Road, made up his mind to give trouble and prevent the works being started. He had no special objection to such works being built anywhere in the Khyber provided they brought some money into his purse, and money he loved beyond everything in this world. He had collected something like 40,000 to 50,000 rupees, chiefly by depriving his tribesmen of their share of the Khyber allowances for a series of years, which allowances had been paid to him for distribution to them, but the most of which he had placed to his own credit. His brethren, according to their savage fashion, had worried and harried us in every direction, because they were cheated by their chiefs, until at last Malik Khwas Khan and his rival, finding they could not control the action of their powerful clansmen in the Bazȧr Valley, had asked for their allowances to be handed over direct to their own selected tribal representatives, and then these Zakha

Khel annoyances and raids ceased. Malik Khwas had seen with his own eyes that the border military police post we had commenced to build at Jola Talao in the Peshawar District in August 1881 had been levelled with the ground by the Aka Khel Afridis, who objected to this building being erected in their direction, and that up to the spring of 1886 no attempt had been made to recommence the works destroyed five years previously. He also knew the tactics played by the Kohat Pass Afridis, about 1,100 strong, who for fifty years had prevented the powerful British Government from doing anything to repair or make workable the eleven miles of road that, passing through their country, connected the district of Kohat with that of Peshawar. If he was backward in any matter which might be injurious to the British cause, there were abundance of evil advisers in the city of Peshawar to guide him in that way. He himself used to tell this tale regarding his father with great satisfaction. One day his father, a very tall Afridi, riding a pony, was passing through the Kissa-Khani Bazàr that leads from the Edwardes Gate of the city of Peshawar towards the Kotwali, when he noticed a large crowd assembled, and in the centre was a clergyman, possibly missionary Lowenthal himself, addressing the crowd, with a copy of the New Testament in his hand. Listening attentively for a short time, Khwas Khan's father yelled out at the pitch of his voice, 'Oh, Padre Sahib, what is the use of your offering us the New Testament? If you desire to convert us, bring us gold, gold.' Malik Khwas loved gold even more than his father did, and he knew that, if he could get his elders and Malik Walli Muhammad Khan, the rival chief, with his party, to combine with him in opposing the building of the fortified serai at Landi Kotal, the game would be in their hands. However, at this juncture Malik Walli Muhammad Khan and the elders of both sides remained true to me, and the works were commenced and completed without a hitch.

On August 7, 1888, Captain Macdonald, Sardar Aslam Khan, and I journeyed up to Landi Kotal and pitched our tents near the site where the serai was to be erected. It was not a site which I should have selected had the choice remained entirely in my hands. There was a cemetery to the south, and a ziarat with a second graveyard to the north of it, which necessitated reducing the breadth of the western portion of the serai by about fifty yards; and there were other objections which should have been considered when choosing this spot for such a building. However, the selection had been made, and we had to carry out orders. The extent of ground required was measured off, and its value fixed by the maliks of the Loargi Shinwaris and the price paid to the owners. Captain Pringle, of the Royal Engineers, came up to do the building, whilst Captain Macdonald, under directions from Simla, was to carry out other special duties, and, what was of the highest importance both for us and the Loargi plateau, to make a survey of a road from the Landi Kotal serai through the Shilman and Mullagori countries to the Peshawar District, and lay it down six feet broad. At first our work remained at a standstill from natural causes, as there was not water in the large tank for us to make bricks from; and, secondly, our work had just been started at the 'Ullus Well' for bringing down water to our camp, and as this entailed laying

LANDI KOTAL.

down some two miles of pipes and sinking heavy tanks at the well itself, it would require certainly a month or more before this business could be placed on a satisfactory basis. Rain was what we wanted, and on August 4 rain fell and gave us 283,000 gallons of water in the tank, sufficient to make 700,000 bricks, whilst our requirements were 2,700,000. But very heavy rain on August 23 and September 3 and 6 filled our huge tank entirely, and there was then no further cause of anxiety on that score. The 'Ullus Well' scheme advanced satisfactorily. This well, excavated at the eastern end of the Loargi plateau, belonged to no particular village, but was the joint property of the Shekhmal Khel Shinwaris and was known as the 'Ullus' or people's well. It had never been known to dry up in the driest season, and when all the tanks and wells at Landi Kotal failed, the women used to carry their pitchers to this place for their morning and evening wants. When fairly cleaned out, the daily supply was about 5,000 gallons, and of this the Shinwaris gave us about 3,000 every day free of any payment. If this well had been at Peshawar, under conditions similar to those at Landi Kotal, the owners, aided by pleaders and barristers, would have made the Indian Government pay very heavily before parting with the precious water, and if there had been any objection to meeting their claim they would have gone to law at once over their right. Captain Macdonald had inspected the Tangi water supply, when he received a telegram from Simla directing him to leave at once and join the staff of the Black Mountain expedition of 1888. He departed from Landi Kotal on September 16.

Now further changes were in store for us. When the Black Mountain expedition had been discussed in the Indian papers as likely to come off during the autumn of 1888, subsequent to the deaths of Major Richmond Battye and Captain Urmston, the corps of Khyber Rifles had volunteered for service, and submitted their application on June 30 to be employed in the coming campaign. Nothing more was heard of this application until September 16, when a telegram was received from Simla directing 350 men of the Khyber Rifles to be sent to the front. Major Aslam Khan had left on the 13th on a visit to his family in the city of Peshawar, and a warning in accordance with the Simla telegram was forwarded to him. Ten tents, 135 men and officers of the Khyber Rifles, with 100 mules were required from Landi Kotal, and having made the necessary selection, the men were paraded and I addressed a few words to them to this effect: 'Do nothing that will bring disgrace or discredit on the Khyber Rifles and myself.' They were then marched down the Khyber Pass to Jamrud, where they were to join the rest of the corps selected to co-operate with the British and native troops. On September 21 they left Peshawar by train for Hassan Abdal, and marched thence to rendezvous at Abbotabad. Telegrams were also received regarding the movements of a British mission from Simla towards Caubul, and I was asked to arrange about Shinwari mules to accompany the British officers from Peshawar westwards. Just then war broke out between H.H. Amir Abdur Rahman Khan and his cousin, Sardar Muhammad Ishak Khan, Governor of Afghan-Turkestan, when the latter's troops were defeated at the battle of Ghaznigak, and

Ishak Khan, compelled to cross the Oxus, took shelter in Russian limits. This unfortunate war and the Amir's approaching journey to Afghan-Turkestan, which he had not seen since the spring of 1880, are said to have prevented our mission going to Caubul in the year 1888. According to information brought down by the Caubul caravans, H.H. Amir Abdur Rahman Khan left his capital on October 25 to march towards Mazar-i-Sherif in Afghan-Turkestan.

I was compelled to journey down from Landi Kotal to Peshawar on October 1, and my place was taken up by my native assistant, Akbar Khan, as there was still a chance of some friction with the tribesmen. However, we had been exceedingly fortunate and lucky so far, and there was no reason why friction should come about now, when everything was making such excellent progress. During October the campaign in the Black Mountains progressed, and both from the papers and letters news came to hand that the men of the Khyber Rifles had behaved well in the various fights and skirmishes at Abu, Khund, Kunhar, Thakot, and Goraphar. Colonel Ommanney, C.S.I., Commissioner of the Peshawar Division, who was with General Sir J. McQueen, K.C.B., in the Black Mountain expedition, wrote to me: 'Your Khyber Rifles have behaved admirably, and have won the respect and confidence of the General and all the troops; you may well feel proud of the good work done by you in the Khyber in managing the Afridis so as to have led to their volunteering and acquitting themselves so well.' But another incident gave me even greater pleasure. Not a man of the Khyber Rifles had been killed in the various fights, and only five wounded. These men were sent down to the hospital of the 30th P.I. at Peshawar, and when I went to see them, and asked how they were getting on and whether they were in need of anything, one of them turned round and said, 'We Khyber Rifles have not disgraced you, Sahib, have we?' This was with reference to the little speech I had made to them at Landi Kotal on September 17, when they were being sent down to join their comrades at Jamrud, and it was a treat to hear this and to know that the words had been remembered.

The Khyber Rifles returned to Peshawar on November 26 and halted there one day, and under Colonel Ommanney's instructions the Municipality of the city of Peshawar supplied them with a dinner. A kind, thoughtful act like this was greatly appreciated, and drew the soldiers to the man who had considered their comfort and welfare on the eve of their returning from service to their homes. On November 28 they went on to Jamrud.

The following native officers and men of the Khyber corps were rewarded with the Order of Merit for their services in the Black Mountain expedition: Subadar Major Mir Akbar Khan, for conspicuous gallantry on the following occasions:

1. On October 8, 1888, at the attack on Abu village, Black Mountain, in having single-handed charged five or six of the enemy, and saved the life of a wounded Sepoy.

2. On October 24, 1888, at the attack on the village of Ghori, when he was the first man to enter the village under a heavy fire.

3. On November 1, 1888, at the capture of the

Ghoraphor Pass, when he led the right attack and displayed great personal bravery.

4. On November 3, 1888, at the attack on Pokal, when he led his men over difficult ground under a heavy fire, and cleared the enemy from the left flank, inflicting on them heavy loss.

5. On the same occasion, in having carried a wounded Sepoy to a place of safety under a heavy fire during an attack on the rearguard, when returning from Pokal.

6. On November 4, 1888, in having with thirty of his men dislodged a large body of the enemy who were occupying the summit of the Chel Mountain.

Jemadar Muhammad Ghalli (Madgalli), for conspicuous gallantry on the following occasions :

1. On October 10, 1888, at the attack on Khund, Black Mountain, Hazara, when he led the attack and was the first man to enter the village.

2. On October 12, 1888, in having with four Sepoys driven thirty or forty of the enemy out of a village near Betban.

3. On October 15, 1888, in having, near the village of Mer Khanai, when in command of a flanking party, during the return march from Kunhar, rushed forward with a few of his men and repulsed a party of the enemy who had opened fire from the heights.

4. On October 28, 1888, in the vicinity of Thakot, in having with a picquet dislodged the enemy from a sangar, killing several of their number.

5. On November 1, 1888, in having at the capture of the Ghoraphor Pass been conspicuously to the front in storming the heights under a heavy fire.

6. On November 3, 1888, in having, when returning from Pokal, during a series of most determined

attacks on the rearguard, been the last to leave his position, on each occasion allowing the enemy to come to close quarters, and thus securing the retirement of his men.

Naick Habib, for conspicuous gallantry on October 28, 1888, in the vicinity of Thakot, Black Mountain, Hazara, in having, with three Sepoys, captured a sangar occupied by the enemy.

Sepoy Akhtar Shah, for conspicuous gallantry on October 8, 1888, in having, in the attack on the Abu village, been the first man to reach the village under a heavy fire. On this occasion he was severely wounded.

No. 29 Sepoy Mir Abbas, and No. 583 Sepoy Ajar Din, for conspicuous gallantry on November 1, 1888, in having, at the storming of the Ghoraphor Pass, Black Mountain, Hazara, been the first of the Khyber Rifles to reach the crest.

On the morning of November 29, 1888, H.E. the Commander-in-Chief in India with all his staff arrived at Peshawar, but unfortunately, an attack of fever coming on, Lord Roberts was unable to journey to Landi Kotal on December 1. On that date Generals Elles and Chapman and staff, accompanied by Sir Charles Dilke, rode there and examined the progress that had been made in carrying out the works commenced in the month of August. It was a great source of satisfaction that so much had been done under the management of Captain Pringle, who had besides made himself greatly liked by the Shinwaris of the plateau.

A few days later, on December 6, Captain Macdonald, who had returned from the Black Mountain expedition, was desirous of examining the Tangi water supply, which is situated about two miles above Kaddam. In fact, he wished to go to the same spot to which he was journeying in 1887 with Afridi Khan when the youngsters of Kaddam prevented him. On this occasion a long warning was given to the Kuki Khels as to what our intentions were. We were going to Tangi, and when the water supply had been carefully inspected by the Engineer officer, we were to have our lunch on the banks of the stream, and then go back towards Peshawar, through the desert, stony plain between Burj-Harri Singh and the independent Khyber Hills, and see whether we could not secure an 'obara' with the hawks belonging to Sardar Aslam Khan and his second in command. A large cavalcade started on this trip, consisting of Sardar (now Major) M. Aslam Khan, Captain Macdonald, R.E., Captain Trevor, 15th Sikhs, and myself, with Afridi Khan, an escort of about fifty of the Khyber Rifles, and a few troopers with the hawksmen, besides some 200 of the Kuki Khel elders.

Talking and laughing, the whole party reached the narrow gorge Tangi, through which the united waters of the Chora and Ali Masjid streams dash, before the water is taken into irrigation channels, and distributed into the fields of the Kuki Khels; but a very large proportion sinks into the ground, and, passing under sand and stone, forms a fair sized swamp some twelve miles down on the Peshawar-Michni road. The examination of the ground and the discussion with the jirga as to what should be done with the bed of the stream to augment its water supply being over, lunch was discussed and we prepared to journey back. Our road to the stony plain passed up the right bank of the ravine just below the village of Uccha (Dry) Gagri, so, parting with the Kuki Khel jirga, we rode up the bank and joined our troopers and the men in charge of the hawks. A line some 500 yards broad was formed, we dividing it at certain intervals, and, with our faces towards Peshawar, we started to look out for the bustard. Just then Major Aslam Khan called out that a shot had been fired at us, as he had heard the whiz of the bullet. Looking at the crest of the high conical hill above Tangi, from which the shot was thought to have been fired, the distance seemed to me fully 1,800 to 2,000 yards. We gave chase and fired some shots towards the top of the mountain, hearing which disturbance all the Kuki Khel jirga came rushing to our assistance. But it was impossible and hopeless to capture an Afridi on a hill top 2,000 yards away; besides, night was coming on rapidly, and we had to ride twelve miles to reach our homes.

Within two days the names of two offenders were disclosed to me, both belonging to the village of Kaddam. One was a son of a very venerable looking elder, Mulla Dostai by name, and the other was a *hamsayah* of his; both culprits were lads of eighteen to nineteen years of age. The Kuki Khel jirga were told that in their attendance and presence this outrage had been committed, and that they must punish the offenders. The jirga fined Mulla Dostai Rs. 1,000 and brought the money in, and burnt the house of the *hamsayah*.

Some months afterwards, when I happened to be stopping at Landi Kotal, both Mulla Dostai's son and the young man who had fired on us from the top of the hill came to see me on a friendly visit.

CHAPTER XII

THE SHILMAN ROUTE

1889

Captain Macdonald, being now at liberty to resume his survey work on the Landi Kotal-Shilman-Mullagori road, went up there after the incident on the Tangi Hill, and pushed on vigorously with this duty. The people themselves readily gave every assistance, because the Shinwaris hated the Zakha Khel Afridis, while the Mullagoris detested the whole Afridi race, and both wanted a good road made through their countries to Peshawar which would render them entirely independent of the Khyber Pass, so therefore they rejoiced greatly when they heard that we had commenced the work in earnest. They gave aid in land, in men, and in advice: 'Do not go too near the Mohmands, for you may find them as troublesome as the Afridis,' was the exclamation of one of our best friends amongst the Shinwari elders. The Afridis, on the other hand, were greatly chagrined at the very idea of such a highway being proposed or even considered, and their annoyance was much more increased when they actually saw the work begun. By the middle of February 1889 the survey was expected to be completed; and, although I was never shown the estimate, I was told that the actual cost had come to Rs. 50,000, or about £3,000 in excess of the estimate, and to reduce this the road was to be made twelve feet wide instead of fourteen, until further funds were available, when the additional two feet width could be arranged for. Colonels Hildebrand and Garwood came up to Peshawar, and we journeyed to Landi Kotal accompanied by Major Aslam Khan. After a short rest there we travelled along the new road which had been made by Captain Macdonald with a gradient of 1 in 50. With the greatest ease we walked along this alignment, across the Loargi plateau, and dipped into the Kam Shilman Valley, halting the first night at a ruined hamlet between the villages of Malik Kamran and Malik Jamal. The second day I crossed the Dabrai Kotal, but Colonel Hildebrand, objecting to the numerous zig-zags that had to be made up and down that hateful hill, went round the bend over the Caubul River with his assistants, the precipices there being too much for me. Major Aslam Khan and I were in camp at Shahid Miana when the four officers came in, and I could see from their faces that they had failed. Captain Macdonald said to me, 'If we cannot find a way round by the river, they will never sanction a road with these numerous zig-zags over the Dobrai Kotal.' Old Malik Papino, of Shahid Miana, was watching us with interest, and his fine stalwart son was standing by his side. I said to the boy, 'I will give you a *lungi* worth 30*s*. if you will show Macdonald Sahib a road round that hill.' The lad said he would try, and old Papino, who had seen Macdonald repeatedly place lighted matches inside his mouth and close his lips, firmly believed that he was gifted with supernatural powers, and grinned in response to his son's reply. I did not like to stay an hour longer than was actually necessary in this place, because the village cultivation did not look more than three or four acres in extent, and the old man was cutting down his barley with an ungrudging hand for our horses; but we were compelled to wait another twenty-four hours and make one more attempt to circumvent the hill. The next day the four officers made an early start, and were back in time for lunch, and from the look on the face of Papino's son I felt sure he had succeeded, and so it proved. The third halt was at Lwara Miana, which had been twice visited before; and on the fourth day, which was March 19, 1899, we descended into the plains of the Peshawar District. The tour had commenced on the 11th, and ended on the 19th.

With regard to the road, so far as I was able to judge, after seeing every portion of it except the quota about a mile in length round the bend of the river, it was even now six to eight feet in width, passing through shaley hills, which rendered the working on them light and easy; the gradient was excellent, and all that was required was to increase the present width to twelve or fourteen feet to permit tongas, ekkas, and country carts moving up and down. Everything was ready, the coolies available for carrying on the work; there was no friction or trouble with the tribesmen about making the road through their country, or appropriating land for this purpose, and all that was necessary was for a command to come directing us to renew operations and complete the work which had been already commenced and continued so far with success. A command did come—to stay all further proceedings, and under this mandate a most useful and necessary work was stopped, and the arrangements for completing the road scattered to the winds. We had cause to regret this act afterwards, especially in 1897.

Leaving Jamrud at 10 P.M. on May 31, 1889, Major Aslam Khan and I reached Landi Kotal at 6 A.M. the following morning. We rode at a walk the whole way, the darkness preventing our moving faster. Our escort consisted of but two troopers, and the ride was weird in the extreme. Arriving at Malik Khwas Khan's fort, we sent a man to obtain a drink of water, and soon the individual himself, roused from his sleep, appeared without anything on his head. He and his sons had committed some outrage against a section of the Zakha Khel Afridis living in the Khyber, and they had turned on him and made close prisoners of himself and his family. And for several months afterwards, when I desired to see the intriguing gentleman I had to send a party to the opposite side to let him out, except on Tuesdays and Fridays, which were caravan days, and then he could journey out of his own accord. At first I had a great dread of these fights, fearing that they might interfere with the caravans; but I altered my mind on the advice of a friendly Shinwari chief, who said, 'Let them fight, Sahib; they will soon get tired of it, and ask you to lay the stones (make peace) between them.' And so it proved. The men kept up their use of arms, and got expert with their rifles, but they husbanded their ammunition, and after every petty fight their demeanour was more conciliatory, because money had to be made and saved for a fresh supply of ammunition purchased from wherever it was obtainable. The malik, having to supply all his own following, was sometimes a loser to the extent of 300 to 400 rupees for a couple of days' amusement, as his tag-rag were not going to spend their cartridges in his cause.

During our stay at Landi Kotal our existence was very comfortable, much more so than in former years. The serai was completed, and five officers' quarters, consisting each of one room and bath-room, were now available, and water was laid on to each quarter. There was a mess-room in the same block, where we had our meals, which chiefly consisted of country bread, poultry, vegetables brought up from the Peshawar Valley, but we never saw butcher's meat unless we killed a sheep ourselves. The machine-gun towers to the south of the serai were being finished, and would serve to defend the road from Landi Khana to the Loargi plateau. A well was being bored for in the serai just thirty yards south of our quarters, and everything betokened progress and encouragement.

Subadar Major Mauladad Khan, C.I.E., of the 20th P.I., came up to see me at Landi Kotal, and it was a treat to meet this fine old soldier, and, as his regiment was then located at Rawal Pindi, we were able to secure his aid in quieting his trouble-some malik, who was determined to do everything in his power to exhaust our patience. My visit to the Shinwari plateau lasted this time from June 1 to August 21. We led the same life as I have once before mentioned. A large gathering assembled every morning and came out for the early walk and returned to quarters by 8.30 A.M. There was then held a sort of small darbar, at which every topic pertaining to the locality or referring to matters in the Khyber, in Tirah, in Peshawar, or in Afghanistan was discussed, each man who came offering his opinion, or asking for an explanation from those who were able to give it. When the morning meal was announced the people dispersed for their food, and then the regular work of the day was carried out till 5 P.M. Then came a walk, very often to and through villages, where all the people turned out to welcome us and produced cots for our party to rest on.

Our warmest welcome came from the children, who always shouted out the Afghan greeting, 'May you not be tired,' when we approached them. To which the proper reply was, 'May you become great' or 'May you never be poor.' If they saw our procession coming anywhere near to their village, or resting on any ridge close to their hamlets, the little folk always ran down to meet us. As our acquaintance improved we arranged little feasts for them, one at the time of going to and the other on returning from Landi Kotal. Two to three hundred children, chiefly boys (they would not bring girls over six to seven years away from their habitations), and a few lassies would be collected, and twenty shillings' worth of native sweets would make them perfectly happy and please the mothers at home.

The lives of the grown-up girls and married women amongst the Shinwaris might be taken as a sample of the customs and habits amongst the fair sex in the trans-border independent land. During the eighteen years I was connected with these people in the Khyber Range, I hardly spoke to a woman on more than three or four occasions. A woman or girl above ten years old is never permitted to address any male not connected with her by relationship. A stranger has always to be avoided, and if by any chance a woman comes across one in a narrow lane or road, she generally covers up her face and stands with her back towards him until he has passed. At Landi Kotal all the women living in the villages towards our serai used to collect in the early morning and proceed in a body to the hills in the direction of the Bazàr Valley, and remain out cutting grass and wood until 3 P.M., when they returned homewards. If the Shinwaris were at war with the Zakha Khel of the Bazàr Valley, which was usually the case, guards armed with rifles would go ahead of the girls and women, and take up positions most suitable for protecting them. These outings were looked forward to with great interest, and at these female pic-nics they played their national games; but woe betide the man who ventured into their haunts, for then the males of the whole tribe had to sit in judgment on the culprit, who was most lucky if he escaped with only a heavy fine in money. When the girls and women had finished their work, and wended their way homewards with their loads of grass and wood, the guards would follow in rear of the party until they got out of the hills and separated for their homes.

The Shinwaris would sometimes tire of this guard duty, and become neglectful after being on it for several weeks. It was then that the savage Zakha, who had been on the look-out for his chance after months of patient waiting, would pounce down on the defenceless women and carry off some half dozen or more. If the women got a fair start they were more than a match for the men in running, but the Zakhas usually alarmed them by a display of rifles, and through fear of being fired at several would allow themselves to be captured. Then the Shinwari world was stirred up and raised a hue and cry; but it was generally too late, and many hundreds of good rupees had to be paid ere the Zakha Khel released the captured women.

On the night of August 31 I started by the midnight train from Peshawar and reached Simla at 9.30 P.M. on September 2, after an absence of nearly twenty-five years from that favoured hill station. The last time I went down the road to Kalka was about the close of July 1865. My present trip was undertaken with the special object of finding out whether there was any prospect of completing the Loargi-Shilman-Mullagori road, which was already more than one-third finished. Also to ascertain the reason of the inexplicable behaviour of the railway authorities with regard to the extension of the line from Peshawar to Jamrud; why so many surveys had been carried out in the past five or six years, and on what grounds a railway engineer had lately been to Peshawar and assured me that he had received definite and final orders to lay down the rails to Jamrud, but, after remaining about fourteen days, had cleared away suddenly, without sending me a word in explanation of his hurried departure. On September 4 I was invited to the Viceregal Lodge and honoured with an interview by H.E. the Viceroy. Lord Roberts was also kind enough to grant me two interviews, and I was permitted to discuss the frontier question. All I could learn was that Lord Lansdowne intended visiting Peshawar and the Khyber, and that any matters which had to be decided would be settled on the spot, and that I was to be in attendance at Peshawar when His Excellency would make the Khyber trip about the end of October 1889.

October 30 came round, and at 7.35 A.M. H.E. the Viceroy, with Sir James Lyall, Sir John Ardagh, and myself made a start from Peshawar to Ali Masjid, Lord W. Beresford, Surgeon Lieut.-Col. Fenn, C.I.E., Captain the Hon. Charles Harbord, Mr. Barnes, and Captain Streatfield, A.D.C., were also of the party. Arriving at Jamrud, His Excellency was received by 360 men of the Khyber Rifles under command of Major Aslam Khan, C.I.E., with a royal salute. Lord Roberts and the Quartermaster-General, Sir James Browne, had already ridden on ahead to Ali Masjid. The Viceroy, after inspecting the Khyber Riflemen, followed.

Reaching Ali Masjid, we had just sat down to breakfast when a shot was heard outside, and the Military Secretary, coming into the tent, said that a man had been accidentally shot in the leg. The Viceroy jumped up from his chair, and, followed by the Commander-in-Chief, went out of the tent, and passing through the mass of Afridis, armed with rifles and daggers, stood by the cot on which the wounded man lay. His name was Ismatulla, a Paindeh Zakha Khel of the Bazàr Valley and brother to a jemadar in the Khyber Rifles. The Afridis had been warned that if they came to salàm to the Viceroy at Ali Masjid they were not to bring their rifles with them; but it was most difficult to get this order thoroughly carried out, and on this morning some rifles had been brought and placed against a wall in front of which the Afridis sat. A Snider rifle, touched by some individual accidentally, rolled to the ground, and being loaded, and possibly at full cock, went off, sending the bullet through the right ankle of the unfortunate Ismatulla. As Lord

Lansdowne stood by the wounded man's cot making inquiries after his injury, Ismatulla said it was nothing, and, baring his left arm, showed His Excellency where two bullets had already left their marks on him. The Viceroy shook the wounded man by the hand, and directed that every care should be taken of him. The injured man, however, died on the third day.

Mounting our horses, a start was made for Landi Kotal, and on reaching the Zakha Khel Khyber the rival factions lined their side of the road and respectfully saluted the representative of Her Majesty the Queen Empress of India. Landi Kotal was reached, and the maliks of the Shinwaris and of Shilman were in attendance to do their share of similar duty. I then took His Excellency two miles higher to the point of Pisgah, where a glorious panorama lay revealed before us. On our left, commencing with the lofty peak forming the western limits of Rajgal, the snowy Safed Koh extended westwards for over one hundred miles. To our right was the white mass of Kafiristan mountains, extending northwards into a sea of snowclad tops, representing ranges in Bajawar and towards Chitral. To our right front and far away below flowed the Caubul River, past the Koh-i-Bedaulat, going west to east, making its northern bend at Kam-Dakka. The dark arena below us was the Valley of Jelallabad, bounded on the extreme east by the Karkatcha Range and the mountains of Laghman. 'I would not willingly have missed this,' His Excellency exclaimed in admiration of the view. Turning back to Landi Kotal, it was a good ride of thirteen miles down the Pass before we reached Ali Masjid, where we found the Marchioness of Lansdowne, attended by Colonel Ommanney, the Commissioner, and Captain Brazier Creagh. After lunch His Excellency went down the line of the Khyber maliks, and asked the name and history of each. Bidding adieu to all, the Viceregal party journeyed towards Peshawar, which was reached at 7.30 P.M.

I may note that all the excellent arrangements for their Excellencies' visit to the Khyber were made and carried out by Captain Inglis and Major Aslam Khan. My leave had not expired, and although, in obedience to orders, I had to attend, it was merely as a spectator. The whole credit of doing everything that helped to make this trip so comfortable and pleasant for the illustrious visitors was due solely to the exertions of these two officers and the native officers and men of the Khyber Rifles.

A grand parade was to be held on the great Brigade ground facing the Khyber Hills at 11 A.M. the next day (October 31), and His Excellency the Viceroy had kindly expressed a wish to personally distribute the orders of merit to the six men of the Khyber Rifles whose names have already been given for their gallant conduct during the Black Mountain expedition of 1888. The Khyber Rifles, about 350 strong, under command of Major Aslam Khan, C.I.E., were to take part in the ceremony with the regular troops. They were drawn up on the left of the line in open order when the Viceroy and Commander-in-Chief in India rode on to the ground, and after the usual inspection was over, and the Governor-General with all the staff had taken up their positions at the saluting point, there came the march past, the infantry going by in grand companies, returning in close column, and then going past at the double.

This was the ordeal I dreaded for the Khyber Rifles in the face of a critical audience, for the men had had no experience of drill of this nature, for, being scattered over a length of twenty-fives miles and employed six times in the week on caravan duty, it was difficult, if not impossible, ever to get a sufficient number together for ornamental parade movements. But the Khyberis, under their gallant commander, did right well, and I rejoiced to see them go past, as the Regulars did, in correct dressing and distance, with heads erect and eyes looking straight before them. An Afridi, accustomed to wearing shoes made of the dwarf palm, invariably keeps his eye fixed on the ground as he walks, and it requires a good bit of training and correction to break him of this habit. After the march past the Khyber Rifles were brought back and halted in front of the Viceroy. Lord Lansdowne pinned the Order of Merit to the breast of each man entitled to receive that reward for his bravery, and then addressed a kindly speech to His Excellency the Commander-in-Chief regarding the conduct of the Khyber corps and their services in the Black Mountain, which Lord Roberts directed me to translate to the Commandant, which I did in Persian, and Major Aslam Khan repeated it in Pashtu.

By a piece of good luck we had been relieved from a serious dilemma. When the case containing the six Orders of Merit arrived at Peshawar it was not opened and examined, but placed for safe keeping in the Peshawar Treasury. On October 30, when opened, we found that by some mistake no ribbons had been sent. Here was a dilemma! The parade was at 11 A.M. the next day, and no possible chance

SIR ROBERT WARBURTON, LIEUT.-COL. ASLAM KHAN, OFFICERS AND MEN OF THE KHYBER RIFLES.

of purchasing the ribbon required either at Peshawar, Rawal Pindi, or Lahore. Fortunately the native orderly officer to Sir J. Lyall, hearing of the trouble I was in, very kindly gave me enough for my wants and relieved my anxiety. And nothing would induce the fine old Sikh to accept anything in return for his goodness. It was enough reward for him to know that I was grateful for his considerate act.

His Excellency Lord Lansdowne was the second Viceroy I had the honour and privilege of taking through the entire length of the Khyber Pass within a period of two years.

The Marquis and Marchioness of Lansdowne and the Commander-in-Chief, with their respective staffs, left Peshawar by special train on November 1, and the Lieutenant-Governor, Panjab, with his secretaries, departed the same day for Lahore. The Viceregal party were to halt at Attock, and then go down the Indus in boats, and do the whole frontier as far as Quetta before returning to Calcutta. Meanwhile, a few days' fighting amongst the Shinwaris at Landi Kotal interfered with the working of the 'Ullus' well; but this was satisfactorily arranged for by our taking up the question, and telling the people that they might fight if they liked, but the working of the well was not to be interfered with. This order had the desired effect, for in nearly every case the savage of the independent hills was clever enough to interrupt our work by his inter-tribal quarrel, so as to force us to interfere between them, and by our influence and power decide the question which had caused the uproar.

A piece of very bad news came to hand this month, and that was that the completion of the

Landi Kotal-Shilman-Mullagori road was to be shelved for the time being, because the Government desired to have, first of all, a survey carried out for a railway from Peshawar to the right bank of the Caubul River facing Fort Michni, and then up the stream, within our limits only, towards Dakka. I felt certain that this road—which was of vital importance for the defence of the Landi Kotal plateau, and which was absolutely necessary whether the Caubul River railway was made or not—was now doomed to be set aside altogether, and so it was.

The months of November and December passed away without producing anything of extraordinary notice or importance. The new year came round, and it was my good fortune to find my name in the Honours Gazette as a Companion of the Star of India. I knew to whom my thanks were chiefly due for this recognition of my humble services—namely, to his Excellency Lord Roberts, Commander-in-Chief of the Army in India.

AT ALI MASJID. PRINCE ALBERT VICTOR, SIR E. BRADFORD, COL. OMMANNEY, AND OFFICERS OF H.R.H.'S SUITE.

CHAPTER XIII

THE VISIT OF PRINCE ALBERT VICTOR

1890

In the early part of January 1890 rumours reached Peshawar that there was a chance of H.R.H. Prince Albert Victor, Duke of Clarence and Avondale, visiting the Peshawar Valley, which rumours became certainty on the morning of the 30th of that month, when His Royal Highness, accompanied by Colonel Sir E. Bradford, Captains Holford, Edwardes, and others of his suite, arrived at the Peshawar Cantonment station of the N.W. State railway. He was received by Colonel Ommanney, Commissioner of the division, the General Officer commanding the district, and the leading local officials. After the usual formal introductions His Royal Highness drove with Colonel Ommanney to the Commissioner's bungalow, where he was to stay during his brief visit of two days. There was a luncheon and garden party afterwards at the Commissioner's, to which the whole world of Peshawar was invited and went. I had then the honour of nearly an hour's interview with the Prince, who asked me many minute questions regarding the affairs of the Khyber Pass and the frontier tribes, telling me that it was his wish to go through the Pass on the following day, 'when,' he added, 'I shall have more time to enter further into these matters.' That evening the Royal Irish Regiment entertained

His Royal Highness and his Staff at dinner; and although the party did not break up until past midnight, the start for the Khyber was made shortly after daylight. At 6 A.M. the Prince took his seat on the Royal Artillery drag, and we proceeded to Jamrud. Here the Prince had agreed to receive and decorate certain Native officers who had distinguished themselves in the Black Mountain expedition. The ceremony was briefly but effectively gone through, His Royal Highness pinning the medals on the breasts of the recipients and afterwards making a short complimentary speech to them which I interpreted. This address from the Prince was repeated by my deputy, Colonel Aslam Khan, to the whole body of the Khyber Rifles, copied into the regimental order book, and again read at two separate parades. The kind and graceful manner of His Royal Highness was greatly appreciated and much talked of afterwards by the Native officers and men.

As it was considered advisable that the Prince should get through the Pass and back before sunset, we moved on quickly to Ali Masjid. This was not from any apprehension of danger from the tribes, but, the most trying time of the day in the Peshawar Valley being just at sunset, when, owing to the rapid fall of the temperature there is liability to sudden chills, it was only a wise precaution taken for health's sake. During our progress His Royal Highness questioned me frequently, desiring me to point out to him any famous spots in the once dreaded Pass. He asked to be shown where the fight had commenced on November 21, 1878, when the troops under Sir Sam. Browne proceeded to attack Ali Masjid. This with the position taken up by the heavy guns when they

AT JAMRUD. H.R.H. PRINCE ALBERT VICTOR ADDRESSING THE OFFICERS OF THE KHYBER RIFLES

opened fire against the fort was shewn to him. As we came down the road from the Shagai ridge where it first touches the bed of the Ali Masjid stream, the small water-mill on the right bank facing the road was also pointed out. Hundreds of visitors pass and re-pass this tumbledown old water-mill, with its two or three stunted mulberry-trees, without knowing or heeding that it is a spot of historic interest so far as British India and Afghanistan are concerned. For it was there, under those stunted mulberry-trees, that the meeting took place between Cavagnari, as the Envoy of the Viceroy, and Faiz Muhammad Khan, Sher Ali's Governor of Ali Masjid, when the request that the British mission to Caubul should be allowed to advance was refused; a refusal which brought on the war with Afghanistan—a war which entailed the sacrifice of so many lives on both sides, and which caused an expenditure of two hundred millions of rupees from the revenues of India. It was a momentous meeting, and Cavagnari, knowing how great were the issues which hung on every syllable of his, did all that tact, forbearance, and courtesy could do to win over the stubborn representative of the Amir. But this was not to be. 'You are setting Afridis against Afridis to cause strife and bloodshed in this country, yet you call yourselves friends!' shouted Faiz Muhammad as he closed the interview and declared that his master was prepared to take the consequences. They were not long in coming. Two months to the very day on which that interview took place Ali Masjid was abandoned before the advance of the British troops, Faiz Muhammad a fugitive, and his master quaking on his throne. But saddest of all the reminiscences connected with that meeting is the recollection that it was the prelude to the tragedy which closed the life and promising career of the brave and brilliant diplomatist Louis Cavagnari.

At Ali Masjid the Prince and party halted for breakfast, and we then started for Landi Kotal along the new road by the cliff, intending to return by the old route through the bed of the stream, the narrowest and most beautiful part of the Khyber Pass. Katta Kushtia, where the turning movement was made by the Guides and 1st Sikhs of General Macpherson's Brigade, when, after a march of twenty-four hours, their appearance caused the evacuation of Ali Masjid, and the small bend round the rock where some three hundred of the Amir's troops were then made prisoners, were shown to His Royal Highness. Then passing on to the Ziarat of Gurgurra (sloe-tree) where the Zakha Khel boundary begins—a guard from the tribesmen holding the blockhouse on the right-hand side—the Prince was shown the lonely shrine, about which were heaped loads of wood and other things all unguarded, for no true Mussulman would think of stealing even a straw from the precincts of a sacred shrine. But the story of this shrine is a curious one. The Zakha Khel Afridis bear a most unenviable name as being the greatest thieves, housebreakers, robbers, and raiders amongst all the Khyber clans, their word or promise never being believed or trusted by their Afridi brethren without a substantial security being taken for its fulfilment. Naturally a race so little trusted were not fortunate enough to possess a holy man whose tomb would have served as a sanctuary to swear by and thus save the necessity of the substantial security. One day, however, a Kaka Khel Mia came into their

PRINCE ALBERT VICTOR DECORATING NATIVE OFFICERS KHYBER RIFLES AT JAMRUD.

limits with the object of seeking safe conduct through their territory to the next tribe. They received him with all politeness, but finding in the course of conversation that he was of saintly character—a holy Kaka Khel Mia—they came to the conclusion that he was just the individual wanted to put their character for truthfulness on a better footing. They therefore killed him and buried him, making his tomb a shrine for all true believers to reverence, and a security for themselves to swear by! The Zakha Khel chiefs of the present day do not admit that the holy man was murdered in the manner described, but say that he was attacked by some Shinwari raiders and died of his wounds. However, there stands the shrine.

Leaving it, the journey through the Pass was continued. At Malik Khan's fort and on the road to the south of Malik Walli Muhammad Khan's the rival factions stood to salute and welcome His Royal Highness. The Prince was particularly struck with the three young sons of the latter—lads aged five, seven, and eleven years, who walked, spoke, and behaved with that quiet, refined dignity which seems inherent in high-born Oriental youths.

At Landi Kotal the Khyber Rifles were formed up as a guard of honour and the Shinwari chiefs were presented. Here we rested for a short time, and the Prince made me point out to him all the places of local importance or interest. He had evidently well read up the history of the Khyber, and showed by his intelligent questioning that he simply wished to be corrected concerning any points or details which he was not quite certain about. We then rode back to Ali Masjid, taking the route through the watercourse and the narrow channel immediately below the fort, which I always regard as the finest and grandest part of the Pass. After lunch and the presentation of several Afridi maliks and jirgahs, a start was again made, and at sunset we were at Peshawar.

Thus this anxiously looked for and interesting trip of His Royal Highness through the Khyber Pass of such evil fame of old, was successfully made and concluded.

That evening the Prince dined with the General and started at midnight by special train for Rawal Pindi to witness next day a grand review and march past of all the troops at that station. I was given a seat in the same train, and my friend Malik Walli Muhammad Khan, who had hurried down from the Khyber in our wake, went to Pindi by the ordinary night train to see the tamáshá also. I had a good position at the review close to the flagstaff—Lord Roberts, the Commander-in-Chief, having kindly called me up to the carriage in which he and Lady Roberts were seated; His Excellency was incapacitated that day from mounting a horse owing to a strain in the leg which he had met with tent-pegging at Muridki camp of exercise. The Prince, after being received with the usual salute, placed himself on the other side of the Chief's carriage and the march past took place. At its conclusion it was noticed that in the space allotted to Native spectators were Muhammad Ayub Khan and some of the Afghan Sardars and chiefs who had followed his fortunes, and who were now closely watching the soldiers against whom they had lately fought and been defeated by. A few words which I did not hear passed between His Royal Highness and the Commander-in-Chief, and then the Prince rode off alone and unattended to within a few paces of the carriage of the Afghan soldier who had fought us at Maiwand and Candahar, but who now by the fortune of war was a refugee and almost a prisoner in British hands. Reining in his horse, the Prince deliberately and with dignity raised his hand to his hat and saluted the fallen soldier. This act, simple and spontaneous as it was, seemed to electrify the Native crowd. No act that His Royal Highness could have performed could have done more to ingratiate him with the Asiatic beholders than his touching, gentle tribute of respect to a fallen but once powerful foe. The Khyber maliks who saw it were loud in expressions of admiration. 'The grandson of the Queen Empress and the future heir to the throne of England to ride up and salute a man who has ever been an enemy of England is marvellous! No wonder the Sarkar is always victorious!' a Zakha savage was heard to say aloud in his native tongue to his fellows. I expect that many a blessing and prayer were uttered that day on behalf of Prince Albert Victor.

The Prince left Rawal Pindi on his homeward route that night, no doubt thinking little of the incident I have recorded. But next day several Afridi chiefs and their followers came to see me, and amongst them was my old friend Walli Muhammad Khan, whose carriage had been close to that of Ayub Khan's at the review. He was quite excited over the act of the Prince, and after explaining what he and others felt about it he concluded with these words: 'Sardar Ayub Khan has always been an enemy of the English Government. He was defeated at Candahar and took refuge in Persia, but finding everything fail he has been brought to Pindi and kept there as a pensioner of this Government. And now I have seen the future King of England and ruler of India go forward and in my presence and sight salute his own captive! It was a noble act! It shows that you English are fit to be rulers of this country.'

Within less than two years after this the telegraph wire flashed the fatal news to Peshawar that Prince Albert Victor was no more. Carried into the defiles of the Khyber the savage residents of that range sympathised too with the Englishmen who mourned. Having seen with their own eyes his kindly, courteous demeanour, his fearlessness in mixing amongst their armed throngs, and having heard of the incident at Rawal Pindi, there was genuine regret amongst my stern, unemotional wild men, and the prayer 'Would that the Almighty had spared the Shahzada!' was echoed by many in and about the Khyber Pass.

PRINCE ALBERT VICTOR'S CORTÈGE, ALI MASJID, JANUARY 31 1890

CHAPTER XIV

THE CAUBUL RIVER SURVEY

1890–1891

CAPTAIN MACDONALD arrived at Peshawar during the first week of February 1890, with orders to make a survey from the Peshawar City station for a railway line to be carried to a point on the right bank of the Caubul River facing Fort Michni. This part of the line was in the jurisdiction of the Deputy Commissioner of Peshawar; further westward, the survey was to be taken up the right bank of the said river to Samsai, the whole of this part being under the management of the Political Officer, Khyber. Beyond this lay the country of the Amir of Afghanistan, with which we were to have no concern. Captain Macdonald, with reference to the survey through the district under his charge, which was British territory, had little trouble. Then came my quota, which gave considerable trouble and entailed several days' hard fighting, but the blame of this was in no way caused by any of the tribes under my charge. All the headmen and maliks of the Mullagoris and Shilman were sent for and introduced to Captain Macdonald, and it was explained to them on what duty he had come to Peshawar. When he reached Warsak all the Mullagori maliks were to join him, to guard his camp, and to supply him with everything he required. They were to pass him through their lands, and hand him over safely to the care of the Shilman elders when he entered their territory. Two hundred men of the Khyber Rifles, under command of one of our best native officers, Subadar Muhammad Ghalli—the same who had received the Order of Merit for distinguished bravery on six different occasions—were to join Captain Macdonald's party at Warsak. My advice to him was under no consideration or temptation to cross over to the left bank of the Caubul River, or to enter any territory belonging to the Government of the Amir Abdur Rahman Khan, because then complications would most certainly arise. To enter into the country of the 'God-granted Government,' or to cross the river to the left bank, would be foolish. It is necessary to diverge a little to explain the mistakes that followed.

By the treaty of Gandamak, signed on May 26, 1879, by Muhammad Yakub Khan, Amir of Afghanistan, on his own part, and by Major P. L. N. Cavagnari, C.S.I., on the part of the British Government, the control of the Khyber and Michni Passes, which lie between the Peshawar and Jelallabad Districts, and of all relations with the independent tribes of the territory connected with these passes, was to be retained in the hands of the British Government. In accordance with the above treaty, the right bank of the Caubul River, from Samsai to the spot where it touched the Khalil lands in the Peshawar District, had been taken over by our Government and formed a portion of the Khyber political charge. For eleven years the terms of this treaty had been fully carried out, and had been accepted by Yakub Khan when Amir, and after him by Abdur Rahman Khan; but now two petty sections of the Mohmands living on the left bank of the Caubul River, and who have large possessions in the Peshawar District, came forward to contest our right of action, both in the Mullagori and the Shilman limits, on the grounds that they had a right to share in any benefits which might accrue from our surveying for and making a railway up the right bank of the Caubul River, within British rights. It may further be noted that the deep Caubul stream entirely separated these claimants from the Valley of Shilman and the uplands of the Mullagori country. These tribes were the Tarakzai and Halimzai sections of the Mohmands, who live in the country outside of and to the west of the Peshawar District from the Caubul River to Fort Abazai. The Tarakzais live in the quarter due west of Fort Michni and north of the Caubul River, and are presumed to have an armed strength of some 3,900 men, but they have fourteen villages within the Peshawar District, covering about 10,000 acres. The Halimzais come next with an armed strength of 2,400 men, but they have only one village of 4,000 acres outside their own country in British territory. Contrary to all representations, the jirgas of the Tarakzais were first permitted to cross the river and attach themselves to Captain Macdonald's camp on the right bank, with which these people had no concern. To those who saw this procedure in another light, the best way to have prevented the Tarakzais from interfering with Captain Macdonald's movements was to have warned them that if a single shot was fired from the left shore of the Caubul River all their free grants in the fourteen villages would be attached. Or, if they desired to show their zeal, they could locate their jirga on their left bank, until such time as the British survey party on the right bank had finished work and passed away from the country facing their bank. For it could not be doubted for a moment that the Tarakzai jirga, by remaining on their own shore, were in a better position for controlling the unruly members of their section than by crossing a deep river and going to the opposite bank. Captain Macdonald left Peshawar on February 7, and four days later news came to hand that Mullah Khalil, a regular firebrand of the Afghan war of 1878–80, who was in receipt of a pension of Rs. 5,000 from the Afghan Government, and was living in the Mohmand country at this period, was stirring up the Mohmands to resist the survey party. Representations were again made by the Khyber officials that the proper way to prevent the Mohmands, who were supposed to be under the Amir's rule, from attacking our party was to write to the Sipah Salar and explain to him the whole position, and ask him to do what was needful in preventing Mullah Khalil and his Mohmands from interfering with us in our own country. This was done later on after much delay, but in the meanwhile there was a good deal of fighting between Captain Macdonald's guard after passing the Kam Shilman ravine and the Mohmands on the other bank, and for ten or eleven days the firing from both sides was brisk. Then the order came from the Afghan Commander-in-Chief, and the Mohmand opposition vanished at once. When the fighting was all over, and four days after the last shot was fired, the Halimzai jirga walked into Captain Macdonald's camp. At Peshawar six weeks later these men threw down at the Deputy Commissioner's feet the bag of 100 rupees that had been given to them as a reward for their services, and one malik of the Tarakzais burnt his lungi before all his jirga on the banks of the Caubul River, as they were journeying from the City of Peshawar to their own villages. Whatever happened in this matter concerned the Peshawar District authorities only. What the Khyber officials had to rejoice over was that Captain Macdonald's work was happily and successfully finished, that the Khyber Rifles had behaved well, and that the conduct of the Mullagori and Shilman tribes had been excellent. One shot was fired during a dark night towards Macdonald's camp when it was in the Shilman Valley, and for this I fined the tribe Rs. 500. The survey party came on to Tor-Sappar, and from there journeyed down the Khyber Pass to Peshawar on May 9, while Captain Macdonald and Sir James Browne, Q.M.G. in India, proceeded on a raft by the Caubul River to Michni, and thence by road to Peshawar, arriving there the same day that we did.

Whilst Captain Macdonald was fully occupied in the direction of the Caubul River, and had a guard of the Khyber Rifles, this was the time selected by Amin Khan, Kuki Khel, for another of his foolish acts in the direction of Jamrud. Supported by a gathering of 200 men, bearing a flag rigged up by one of his confederates, this mob went parading and dancing about the stony ground to the south of the Khyber Road, outside the boundary pillars of the Jamrud Cantonments. This act was tantamount to gross impertinence on the part of Amin Khan, but as he had committed no breach of any rules touching the Khyber Pass management one had to exercise patience, and some three or four Khyber maliks were sent out to argue with and try to bring the young man to reason. But when he attempted to stop the Peshawar khafila on the caravan day, and his tag-rag had to be brushed aside by the Khyber Rifle escort, the matter assumed a different aspect. The whole united Khyber jirga fined the Kuki Khels 2,000 rupees, and owing to the constant trouble and fighting about the distribution of their allowances, had it handed over in their presence to selected elders representing each section. And in this fashion this troublesome job came to an end; how troublesome it was will be described when I come to the chapter on Amin Khan and his final escapade in 1892.

Some 120 Mohmands came stealthily one night from the village of Lalpura, during April 1890, and tried to secure the person of Armia Khan, Malik of the Mandezai Shinwaris, who had taken shelter in a Shinwari fort at Landi Kotal just below Pisgah, the furthest enclosure in the direction of Afghanistan. The guard in the fortress, not knowing what this gang had come for, fired at and killed one of the Mohmands, on which the rest scampered down the hill side. A day or so later travellers coming up from Dakka and Lalpura explained why and for what purpose these Mohmands had come into our limits. It was useless to make any representations for redress.

On May 23, 1890, Major Aslam Khan, Mr. Barrat, assistant engineer, and I reached Tor-Sappar, which was to be our home for the next three or four months. Tor-Sappar, to my mind, was a place of very great advantage to us. It was a natural hill-fortress, capable of holding 1,500 soldiers (Europeans), with

SIR ROBERT WARBURTON AND LIEUT. COL. ASLAM KHAN, C.I.E.

a splendid climate, and ranging from 5,300 to 5,600 feet high. The rainfall was slight during the summer months, and its temperature was as cool as that of Murree. Lying far away from Mohmands and Afridis, there was no reason why we should not have made a hill station of this spot, which was inestimably superior to Cherat in every way—in climate, in extent, in its superior water supply, and its safety from lurking thieves. And, what was more to the point, the whole hill could have been secured without asking leave of Afridis, Shinwaris, or Shilmans. The place had no owner. If the Caubul River railway be ever made, Tor-Sappar would lie within ten miles of the nearest station, thirty-two miles west of Peshawar, and would help to strengthen the northern corner of the Loargi plateau and command the Shilman route. Its water supply was sufficient to give 1,200 gallons on the spot, and 15,000 gallons a day just $1\frac{3}{4}$ miles from the furthest point of the Tor-Sappar Range. Compare this with Cherat, where water has to be carried over a distance exceeding three miles!

On July 17, 1890, a telegram was received from His Excellency the Commander-in-Chief in India congratulating Major Aslam Khan on the high honour conferred on him by Her Majesty the Queen Empress in bestowing on him the honorary rank of Lieutenant-Colonel in the Army. This reward he had worthily deserved for his good and meritorious services extending over a period of thirty years.

The officers of the Caubul River Railway Survey—Captain Macdonald, Lieutenants Gloster, Austin, &c.—had remained with us until their work was over, and, having made our sojourn more pleasant by their presence, they had gone away down the Khyber Pass to Peshawar, and left us to our own resources. Subadar Major Mauladad Khan, C.I.E., who had now retired on a pension from his regiment, the 20th Duke of Connaught's Own Panjab Infantry, had been with us from the very first day of our reaching Tor-Sappar, and had remained till the day of our departure. We had our daily visitors in maliks and jirgas from the Afridis, Shinwaris, Shilmanis, and Mullagoris, the last three predominating, as we were nearer to their countries. We had reached our summer home for 1890 on May 23, and on the morning of September 15 we made our start for the Loargi plateau, and then descended into the Kam Shilman Valley, a descent of about 4,000 feet, and halted for the night at the village of Malik Kamran. This was the last time we had the pleasure of accepting this kind, good man's hospitality, for when our party went to Kam Shilman again my friend had been carried off by fever. He was a great loss to me, for in all the years I knew him he had never once tried to deceive me, and what little he had to give he bestowed with a generous, ungrudging heart and for the sake of the Sarkar. From the cold of Tor-Sappar we had suddenly jumped into the heat of a confined valley; however, it was very pleasant in the shade, and the nights were cool. The next morning we ascended the Dabrai Hill, and descended into the Shahid Miana Valley, which was to be our encamping ground for September 16. The Dabrai Hill is another spot where 2,000 Europeans could be well and safely located for the summer months, in a climate far more suitable for them than either the Gullies, Murree, Dalhousie, Simla,

Mussoorie, or Landour, hill stations with which I am well acquainted.

Hitherto on all previous sojourns at this dreadful spot, Shahid Miana (which means the hamlet of those who had sacrificed their lives), our camp had been pitched alongside the road, but on this occasion, hearing of the excellent spring about a mile or more up the ravine, our party went to investigate pending the arrival of our baggage. What a change as we penetrated the gorge for some distance! The hill sides were perfectly green with grass, and very large trees, imported from Hindustan, for they did not belong to the Khyber Range, abounded, showing that once upon a time some resident of these hills had made a good garden in this sheltered locality. And, what was of even greater interest, a splendid spring, giving 100,000 gallons of water daily, gushed out of the mountain side. The springs issuing from the mountains in the Khyber and Tartarra Ranges are generally warmer in the autumn, winter, and spring seasons than the waters that lie on the surface, and on this account the residents name them hot springs, but during the summer season they are cold. Every drop of this abundant spring sank into the sands and stones, and, flowing underground, fell into the waters of the Caubul River, about a mile to the north-east of Shahid Miana. A very pleasant halt was made on the side of the ravine facing the spring, and when our baggage arrived we made this spot our resting-place for two entire days. On September 18 we journeyed to and encamped at Lwara Miana. In the tract between these two stations there are places suitable for locating 2,000 Europeans or even more during the hot months, with abundance of water. The band of the Khyber Rifles, consisting of Afghan pipes and drums, played during the days of our sojourn for two hours every afternoon, and attracted some 300 lads round them, whilst the housetops were dotted with figures in black, showing that the Mullagori ladies were partial to music. On the last night there was a huge bonfire, which lit up a burlesque performance, aided by the pipes and drums, and which lasted some three hours, witnessed by a large admiring audience. I expect that night of September 19, 1890, will long be remembered by these simple people of the Tartarra Range. The next day I went into Peshawar, whilst the escort and band of the Khyber Rifles marched into Jamrud.

The month of October passed without anything extraordinary taking place. A large camp of exercise was about to be formed at Khyrabad, which we were all looking forward to, as this would give me a chance of letting the Khyber maliks and elders see a really grand march past of all our three arms in great force. His Excellency the Viceroy and Governor-General had kindly given permission to three native officers of the Khyber Rifles to go down to Calcutta at the Government expense, and I had hoped to take privilege leave of absence about the same time and journey with them. This leave, however, was refused by the Panjab Government on the ground that my services could not be spared. Besides, Mr. O'Callaghan, C.S.I., C.I.E., Secretary to the Government of India for State Railways, was expected very early in November, and I had to take him up to Landi Kotal, and then down by the route which Lieutenant-Colonel Aslam Khan and I had travelled between September 15 and 29, as Mr. O'Callaghan was most anxious to see as much of the country through which the Caubul River railway was to be taken as he could. He arrived at Peshawar on November 13, and we at once went to Jamrud to pass the night. On the 14th we were at Landi Kotal; 15th, Kam Shilman; 16th, Shahid Miana. That evening Mr. O'Callaghan walked with me to the Caubul River, which comes down with great violence here and forms a whirlpool with a backwater, where rafts of wood floating down the stream are at times likely to break up, when the Mullagoris take the opportunity of securing some valuable pieces of timber. We returned to Shahid Miana before sunset, and after examining the river from Lwara Miana the following day we were back at Peshawar on November 18. This was the last I heard of the Caubul River railway. Like the improvement of the road through the Kohat Pass, and many other good intentions which should have been carried out, this Caubul River railway project was crushed at its very birth by that dead weight of passive resistance which has brought pain and sorrow to many advocates of a firmer policy than has yet been carried out in the Land of the Five Rivers.

The manœuvres at the Attock camp of exercise were in full swing when His Excellency Lord Roberts arrived there on November 21. It was notified that the grand march past of some 18,000 British and native troops was to be carried out on December 4, and, with the consent of His Excellency, I sent down a large party of Afridi, Shinwari, Shilmani, and Mullagori maliks and elders to Khyrabad on the morning of the 3rd, so that they could pass the night there, be close to the parade ground, and see the show next morning. I was also summoned down by His Excellency, who desired to see me with reference to his visit to Landi Kotal and Tor-Sappar. The march past came off in glorious weather. Some 18,000 of the finest troops in India went by in front of thousands of admiring spectators, chiefly collected from the city and most of the villages and hamlets of the Peshawar Valley, whilst mingled with them was a large contingent from the hills of the independent tribes. When I met my Khyberis after my return from Tor-Sappar, they said: 'Sahib, we have seen your British and Native cavalry, your horse, field, and elephant batteries, your European and native infantry, and can comprehend all such matters of parade and march past; but we cannot understand why a large white goat was conducted in front of a British regiment.' This was the white goat of the Royal Welsh Fusiliers. I had dined with the regiment on St. David's night, and eaten my leek in proper style as I stood upon my chair, and had heard from the colonel of the gallant corps the origin of the goat being connected with the corps, but just at that moment, do what I could, the story would not come back to my mind. So in despair I replied, 'Because those men come from a hilly country, whose residents are fond of drinking goats' milk.' This stupid story was fully credited, and the men bent their heads and said, 'Now we understand.' After the parade was over I was permitted to journey in the Chief's special train to Peshawar, which was reached on the evening of December 4. The next morning Lord Roberts, General Sir James Browne, Quartermaster-General in India, left Peshawar with me for Ali Masjid, and by evening we were in the serai at Landi Kotal, and on the following day, escorted by two troopers of the Khyber Rifles, we rode to Tor-Sappar. On the way Sir James Browne, turning to His Excellency, said, 'Here are the Commander-in-Chief and the Quartermaster-General in India, with the Political Officer, Khyber, riding in these hills with an escort of only two troopers. If this fact was repeated in England, or to any officers of the old Panjab school, they would not credit the story.' The people came out in numbers to welcome His Excellency. By 6 P.M. we were back at Peshawar, and at 10 His Excellency was journeying to Rawal Pindi *en route* for Lahore and Calcutta.

The war clouds had been collecting for a long time over the Miranzai Valley and Samana, and now at the close of 1890 the Kohat Border was to taste the fruits of the policy which has proved disastrous in whichever part of the Panjab Frontier it has been tried—i.e. that of employing middle-men to deal between the 'Sarkar' and the tribes of the independent hills. In vain did the late Sir John Coke, at one time Deputy Commissioner of Kohat, object to a Bangash Khan being made Sub-Collector of Hangu and the Miranzai Valley and given power to deal with the hill men across the border; his views were overruled, and in 1854 he resigned his berth as Deputy Commissioner, and preferred returning to take command of that fine regiment which I believe he raised, and which is still known on the whole of the Panjab Frontier as Coke's Rifles. And now, thirty-seven years afterwards, Muzaffar Khan of Hangu and his firebrand son, Bazgul Khan, had to be secured by the Panjab Government and deported to Lahore. In the Black Mountain fresh complications were expected, and the Khyber Rifles again volunteered for service. The Khyber maliks and elders, knowing that I was anxious to go with the corps—not to supersede Lieut.-Colonel Aslam Khan, but to assist him in his work—sent in a written assurance that the peace of the Pass would not be disturbed if I were permitted by Government to go with the Khyber Rifles. This document was forwarded by me to the Government of the Panjab, with an application from myself, but the result was a refusal.

The three officers of the Khyber Rifles, Subadars Mursil and Muhammad Ghalli, and Jemadar Gholam Muhammad, who had been permitted by the Government of India to journey down to Calcutta, and with whom I was not allowed to go, returned to Peshawar on January 4, 1891. The Foreign Secretary and the officials and people of Calcutta had been very kind to them. They had been taken over the mint, railway works at Howrah, the Bank of Bengal, the telegraph office, Fort William, many shops, &c. The Admiral sanctioned their being shown over a man-of-war; then they journeyed down the river in a launch, saw the shipping and Zoological and Horticultural Gardens; and, last of all, the Viceroy, Lord Lansdowne, with that kindness of heart which always marks the true gentleman, very graciously accorded them an interview at Government House, accepted their humble presents of Afghan knives, and gave to each a large silver medallion with his own and Lady Lansdowne's profile engraved thereon. With tears in their eyes, these men related to me the kindnesses they had received from our people at Calcutta. One of them, Subadar Mursil, who had formerly served in the Queen's Own Corps of Guides and had fought on our side at Ambeyla, had received in his day more than thirty wounds from bullets, swords, knives, in different fights, public and private, in which he had been engaged during his stormy career. He was in command of the fortified serai at Landi Kotal after August 18, 1897, when Captain Barton, Commandant of the Khyber Rifles, was peremptorily ordered to forsake his men and retire to Jamrud. He had one son with him in the serai, and two sons were with the Afridis when they appeared on the Loargi plateau about August 25, after having been allowed to burn and sack Shadi Bagiar, Fort Maud, Fort Ali Masjid, and every post between Jamrud and Landi Kotal. Eye-witnesses who were inside the serai, and who were fortunate to escape, informed me of the good stand made by Subadar Mursil against overwhelming odds. His two sons were sent forward to ask him to surrender, but he refused, and threatened to shoot them down if they did not retire. The Afridis suffered a loss of 118 killed and wounded before they were able to secure the serai, which was only done when this brave and loyal Subadar had been killed by a bullet through his head.

Just at this period we suffered a very great loss in the sudden death of Subadar Major Mauladad Khan, C.I.E., of the 20th Panjab Infantry. He was a gallant soldier, thoroughly loyal to us, and yet devotedly loving his clansmen, the Kuki Khel Afridis. 'I do not want my race to be destroyed by any conflict with the powerful British Government' was the great maxim of his life, and he always did his best to prevent any cause of rupture taking place.

The malady which caused this fine man's death could have been cured easily if he had been taken before any medical officer at Peshawar on January 3. Instead of adopting this procedure, his relations put him on a cart and rattled him all the way to Jamrud; then, placing him on a cot, he was carried to his house at Gudar, and as no one there knew what was the matter with him, or what was the possible remedy, he was allowed to die.

The month of January 1891 was extremely cold; heavy rain had fallen during the previous week, and of course this meant snow in the Khyber and Tirah Ranges. A heavy fall came on January 15, and at Landi Kotal there was three feet depth of snow on the ground. It was during this inclement weather that the Miranzai field force had to advance and ascend the Samana Range, something like 6,000 feet high, to punish the Orakzai clans for their bad behaviour, carried on through a long series of years, in pursuance of the policy of our own Bangash Khans. I warned all the Afridi maliks and the elders and jirgas of every section as to what the origin of this quarrel was, and with which they had nothing to do. I told them that if, in opposition to my advice, they went to the assistance of the Orakzai clans they would first of all have to face General Sir William Lockhart's troops, and would be shot down; secondly, that their Khyber allowances would be stopped; and, lastly, that they would be debarred from British territory. Mir Bashar, Golundaz, Mullah Idris, all three men in the pay of the Amir of Afghanistan, and all the Mullahs in Tirah, including Sayad Akbar Akhundzada of the Aka Khels, who was answerable for all the troubles amongst the Afridis and Orakzais during the year 1897, did their utmost to induce the Afridis to combine and aid the Orakzai clans, but, with the exception of about 200 men, they all refused; and when Sir W. Lockhart had moved into the Mamuzai country, which is quite close to Afridi Tirah, the Afridis even then refrained from mixing themselves up in the quarrel, and kept their men in hand and under proper control within their own boundary. Those who believe or put any faith in the idea that the 'Forward' policy had anything to do with the Afridi rising of 1897 should inquire into the particulars of this Miranzai campaign of 1891.

The Black Mountain expedition of 1891 was also about to commence, and the troops who were to participate in that venture were concentrating in the required localities. On February 12 some 300 men of the Khyber Rifles, under command of Lieut.-Colonel Aslam Khan, C.I.E., marched from Jamrud into Peshawar, and, as the weather was exceedingly cold and inclement in the Black Mountain, they were ordered to remain a few days encamped at Peshawar. Thirteen days later, on February 25, the Royal Welsh Fusiliers and the Khyber Rifles marched out together to share in the vicissitudes of the coming campaign. It was an unlucky business for the Khyber Rifles, in this wise. On March 21 some eighty of the enemy had made a breastwork on a hill near Abu, and held it. Lieut.-Colonel Aslam Khan, with 140 of his men, was ordered to turn them out. Having in support 200 of the 5th Ghurkhas, this was easily done, and the enemy were driven off a second hill, where our men had to remain for the night. On this hilltop were two very large sheds, in which the Black Mountaineers put up their cattle when it rained or came on to snow. One of these huge sheds was taken up by the Ghurkhas, and the other handed over for the use of the Khyber Rifles. Night was falling and it commenced to snow, when Lieut.-Colonel Aslam Khan turned out all his men to collect wood and light fires to warm themselves. There then remained inside the shed Aslam Khan, his three orderlies, his horse tied to the centre upright of the building, a guide of the country, and some doolie bearers. Suddenly the shed came down, killing the horse, four doolie bearers, the guide, and wounding two of the orderlies. Aslam Khan happened to be standing at the right corner of the shed, beneath a beam, which came down slowly, dragging him to the ground, but, its end resting on a little two-foot mud wall, protected his body from the certain death which must otherwise have befallen him. It was a miraculous escape, and he was dug out with some difficulty. What the weight of the roof was may be judged from the fact that it took twelve hours' hard work to get the dead and wounded out. Aslam Khan was carried in a doolie to Derbend, and removed to Peshawar, and the Khyber Corps were left without an officer to command them who knew and understood their ways and how they should be managed to produce the best results in a mountain campaign. I had been prevented from going even as an Aide to Lieut.-Colonel Aslam Khan, and my constant appeals to obtain two or three European officers for the Khyber Rifles had been entirely ignored; so here were my people in an unexpected and unfortunate dilemma, through no fault of their own.

The headman of the Kuki Khels still continued to

give trouble, and one of his side managed to fire two or three shots from a hill-top at a cart conveying two officers as they were returning from the Khyber to Jamrud. A few words are necessary to explain this matter. The eastern entrance of the present Khyber road is commanded by two very lofty hills. That on the south, called Ghund Ghar, lies entirely in the lands of the Kuki Khel Afridis. The other, known as Rhotas, extends for many miles westwards up to and past Ali Masjid, and as it is possible for other tribesmen to get to the crest of this hill, high above the point where the Peshawar-Jamrud road enters the range, five or six men are always sent up from the garrison of Shadi Bagiar blockhouse to hold this crest on Tuesdays and Fridays, should European visitors be journeying through the Pass. The measure was merely taken to prevent some thief, robber, or rascal from ascending the hill, firing a shot, and then decamping, with the object of getting the Kuki Khels into trouble. One caravan day the guard at Shadi Bagiar had been changed, but the corporal in charge of the post had omitted to send up picquets, and this omission came to be known in the village of Sarkai, close to Jam. That very morning two officers of the garrison had obtained permission to drive out to Landi Kotal, and to return the same day. As this was a long business, it was necessary to leave Peshawar about 6 A.M., and you were lucky if you got back by 6 P.M. Passing early by Jam and Sarkai revealed to the residents that the Europeans were going to Landi Kotal, and could not possibly issue out of the hills before 4 P.M. So one young lad from Sarkai, belonging to Amin Khan's side, took his rifle, put a handful of cartridges into his pocket, and, inclining towards Gudar, ascended the Rhotas Hill without being seen by the garrison of Shadi Bagiar, a huge hill intervening. Hiding himself behind a rock, he waited there for several hours, until he saw the dog-cart pass below him some 800 yards, then, firing three or four shots, he decamped, as the Shadi Bagiar garrison—alarmed by the first shot—were turning out in pursuit. The sole object of the youth was to get the Kuki Khel Afridis fined, because they had objected to handing over their allowances to Amin Khan. The Khyber Afridi jirga fined the Kuki Khels 1,000 rupees for this business, and as Malik Amin Khan declined to come in to receive his share, the whole of the Kuki Khel Khyber allowances for a twelvemonth were handed over to the jirga, who were to divide their own portion according to the distribution list fixed in 1890, and to deal with the malik's portion as it pleased them best. For the malik had been selected by them and accepted by us. Amin Khan lingered at Jam for some time after this, and then went to Nathia Galli to appeal to the Commissioner (now Sir Richard) Udny, finally returning to his home at the western limit of the Bara Valley. The year 1892 revealed his character in its true light.

Having secured three months' privilege leave from August 31, I started for Simla, arriving there on September 2. Nothing happened during the next two months, but at the end of October I was summoned to Lahore, as the Lieutenant-Governor of the Panjab desired to see me, and I arrived there on the morning of November 5. There were two subjects which I had been constantly urging and pleading about. The first was the necessity of giving me a

British military officer as assistant, who would learn the duties in the Khyber on the lines carried out by me, and be qualified to take my place when the time came for my departure. The second referred to the command of the Khyber Rifles. As Aslam Khan was advancing in years, and his health was very bad, and, at all events, as he would have to retire in two years, I strongly recommended a European captain being made commandant on his retirement, with two European officers as assistants. I pointed out with all the ability I could that it was a dangerous experiment placing the command of a corps like the Khyber Rifles in the hands of a native gentleman of that country, and that, although we had been fortunate in having secured an excellent man in Aslam, there was not another native officer of the infantry or cavalry who was fit to take his place. I further urged that it was utterly impossible for one man to command 836 men, and that if it was desirable to make the corps—which was of the best material in India—thoroughly useful and efficient, there should be, at the very lowest estimate, three European officers with it. Further, in view of the Caubul River railway being made, I urged that two to three more companies should be added to the Khyber corps, and a couple of mountain guns be given to it. I had now the chance of personally making the same appeal to Sir James Lyall, and did so again to the utmost of my ability. What the result was will be revealed later on. Let the British public and the Panjab Government note what has been recommended for the Khyber Rifles in 1898 since my departure from India. In every respect it is what I had been urging for a long series of years.

CHAPTER XV

AMIN KHAN'S RISING

1892

EVERY visitor who has sanction from the Commandant to enter the inclosure which constitutes the Fort of Jamrud should ascend to the Keep, where the telegraph signallers used to have their residence, and, going up the last eight or nine steps, get to the highest platform of the fortress. The view from it will amply reward him. It is a splendid look-out, especially on a beautiful winter's day. Let him turn his back on the Peshawar Valley and look due west towards the mouth of the Khyber defile in the direction where the sun sets. The arena immediately below his gaze, bounded on the south by the ravine which, as it ascends, forms the real Khyber, on the west and north by a stony, profitless, hilly waste, belongs to the Kuki Khel Afridis. They own more land towards Lashora, Sapri, Ali Masjid, Lala Chena, and in the Bara Valley and Rajgal; but I will limit my observations to the quarter I have noticed, and to just three small hamlets in it. On the north lies Gudar, the birth-place of Subadar Major Mauladad Khan, with its two small forts, and its residents not more than eight persons capable of bearing arms. A mile south of Gudar, and about three hundred yards south of the Khyber Road, is Sarkai. There is no mistaking the place, one four-walled high inclosure with a number of caves on either side. Then further east, between Sarkai and Fort Jamrud, comes Jam. Due south of the last, on the left bank of the Khyber ravine and some four hundred yards from Jam, lies Khayasta Khan's tower, and about the same distance still further south the long building with two towers owned by the late Subadar Abbas Khan, at one time of the Panjab Frontier Force. I do not think these hamlets and inclosures all told could turn out 150 permanent male residents capable of bearing arms. At the same time they have supplied the Panjab Frontier Force and the regiments of the Bengal Army with some twenty first-rate native officers in the past thirty years. In no other quarter of the frontier or in India could you produce such a splendid show on the same data of villages and armed inhabitants. Let me mention a few of those officers whose names I can cull from memory, and whom I have personally known.

Subadar Major Mauladad Khan, of the D.C.O. 20th Panjab Infantry. This fine soldier, whose death I have recorded in the previous chapter, fought for the English cause in nearly every battlefield on the Panjab Frontier as well as in Egypt. He was decorated with the first-class order of British India, was a Companion of the Indian Empire, and in possession of four medals and six clasps.

Subadar Major Laman Khan, also of the 20th D.C.O. Panjab Infantry. This man was in the China campaign, and is the proud owner of six medals and seven clasps. Since his retirement from the 20th Panjab Infantry he shared in the Malakand fight 1897, and the Tirah campaign 1897–98, which will give him three more clasps. He was hale and well in April 1898.

Subadar Abbas Khan, *Subadar Amir Khan*, *Subadar Asad Khan*, 2nd Panjab Infantry, and *Subadar Major Mir Alam Khan*, of the 28th Panjab Infantry. The last named, a veteran of the China and Ambeyla campaigns and of every fight up to 1895, with his breast covered with medals, well and fit for much further service. *Rissaldar Kaddam Khan*, 4th Bengal Cavalry, who was sent to England to attend at Her Majesty the Queen Empress's Jubilee in 1897. *Jemadar Jalal Khan*, and three native officers of the Khyber Rifles.

In spite of their fine soldier-like qualities, and the fact of their having given us such first-rate native officers, the Kuki Khels of the villages in close proximity to Fort Jamrud, were the worst behaved of all the Afridis. The great majority of them were men who had served several years in the army or in the police, and had been compelled to take their discharge and return to their homes in pursuance of some blood-feud, vendetta, or heritage of revenge which necessitated their presence in their own homes or forts. These old soldiers, fairly well acquainted with law, tainted the rest, and as they knew how far they could proceed without kicking over the traces, dealings with them generally caused more trouble than working with several times their number of Afridis belonging to tribes living further away from the Peshawar District. These were the men who had selected Amin Khan as their representative chief on the death of Abdulla Nur in the early part of 1884.

The first year's Khyber allowances seem to have been fairly distributed about May 1, 1884, by Amin

Khan, before the Kuki Khels dispersed and migrated to their homes in the Bara Valley and Rajgal. But even then it must have dawned on Amin Khan and the men who led him astray that if this distribution was to be carried out every year on the same scale, the tribal allowances would go only to the tribe, and none of the plunder would fall to their share, as was the case in the time of Abdulla Nur during the years 1881, 1882, and 1883. With this fear in view, Amin Khan tried in 1885 to appropriate a large portion of what really belonged to the tribe, as well as his maliki share, and at the same time he attempted to bully us into bestowing on him the special allowance of Rs. 150 a month which had been bestowed on Abdulla Nur for his lifetime only.

As Amin Khan was now fully bent on stealing as much belonging to the Kuki Khels as he possibly could, they were equally determined to checkmate his manœuvres, and looked round to see whom they could place in opposition to him. By selecting a capable man they could rally round and support him, whilst without such a head the party would fall to pieces at once. First of all they looked to Akbar Khan, but just at that time there was no real feud between Akbar and Amin, and on this account Akbar did not care to endanger his life and spend his money in a profitless cause. The people then turned to Hyder, an elder brother of Amin Khan's, and for a time Hyder remained firm and gave considerable trouble to his younger brother. So much so that one evening in the month of December 1886, when Lord Rosebery was going from Fort Jamrud up the Khyber Road, with Lieut.-Colonel Aslam Khan, Mr. Munro Ferguson, and myself, accompanied by

Amin Khan and a small escort of cavalry, we came upon Hyder Khan marching down the road with about twenty to thirty of his friends armed with loaded rifles. Aslam Khan advanced to Hyder Khan, and, addressing him, explained who our party consisted of, where we were going to, and when we intended returning. In this way we parted, Hyder Khan going on to Jam with his large escort, whilst we rode on in the direction of Ali Masjid. I did not myself believe that Hyder Khan in our presence would take the law into his own hands and murder his brother on the Khyber Road for having usurped his post, which by right he felt belonged to himself as the eldest son of Abdulla Nur. But Amin Khan, who was thoroughly alarmed and frightened at this *rencontre*, was not going to risk his life a second time, or to tempt Providence afresh; so when our cavalcade were about to retrace their steps towards Fort Jamrud, he asked permission to depart for Lala Chena, the village quite close to Ali Masjid, where he had many friends amongst the Farid Khel Kuki Khels, and in whose company he felt himself safe. Hyder Khan, who was greatly wanting in capacity and was looked upon as half-witted, soon tired of opposing his younger and more ambitious brother, and was further bought off with a pension sufficient to feed himself and family, so he retired from the contest. Amin Khan's fortunes would now have brightened a little had he not in a moment of folly cruelly and treacherously murdered Candahari, brother of Rissaldar Kaddam Khan, of the 4th Bengal Cavalry, and cousin to Akbar Khan, of Jam. Amin Khan and Akbar Khan were both relations belonging to the same section of the Sher Khan Khels, and whilst

Akbar's fort was at the western extremity of Jam, Amin Khan's lay 200 yards away to the east of the village. Akbar Khan now, to revenge the murder of his cousin, threw himself heart and soul into a very unequal contest—unequal because, first of all, Amin Khan had 30,000 to 40,000 rupees which Abdulla Nur had robbed his tribesmen of, and his rival was poor in comparison; secondly, because the majority of the Rajgal Kuki Khels, who formed seven-tenths of the Kuki Khel Afridis, were on his side. However, the settled residents of the villages near Jam, the old soldiers and lawyers, stood by Akbar, and help in the way of money came from Kaddam Khan; but even with this the day would have gone against Akbar in the end had the village of Sarkai, immediately in his west rear and commanding his base, not come to his aid in consequence of a blood feud of their own. This feud is worth recording.

Sarkai, Khayasta Khan's fort, and the inclosure known as Amir's Garhi, belonged to one family. The residents, descended from the same stock, were all related to one another by blood. Sarkai, in which Subadar Asad Khan lived, may have had thirty armed men; Khayasta Khan's fort, about four hundred yards south of Akbar Khan's habitation, some fifteen men; whilst Amir's Garhi—which belonged to Subadar Abbas Khan, and on his death in 1881 came to his son, Subadar Amir, and is now held by Subadar Major Zaman Khan—had a small garrison of only eight men. There had been some bad blood between Subadars Amir and Asad Khan, but nothing likely to do much harm, until in an evil moment Amir, in the spring of 1884, killed two sons of Asad Khan who had come to his fort. Amir declared that these men had ventured into his abode to murder him, and that he had saved his own life by putting them out of the way. Whatever may have been the cause of this cruel act, the result in the end was fatal to Amir, who was a firm and devoted ally of Amin Khan's. In the village of Kaddam, which is situated about a mile or less further up the ravine and on the same left bank, the faction opposed to Amin Khan had gained the upper hand and were by far the stronger party in that locality. When the real fight between Amin and Akbar commenced, the latter was supported by Sarkai and Khayasta Khan's fort, whilst Amin Khan could only rely on Amir, whose inclosure was nearly nine hundred yards away and garrisoned by a weak party of eight persons. What made Amir's lot so much harder was that from May to December every year Amin Khan used to retire to the Bara Valley, and leave him and his small gang to fight the whole coalition opposed to them. Knowing Subadar Amir's life was never safe, I had him transferred to the Kohat Border Police, and accepted a pensioned Subadar, Muhammad Zaman, in his place. In the meanwhile the enemy commanded by their fire the north and west of his fort, and by erecting a breastwork on the right bank of the ravine facing the fort they secured control of the eastern quarter also. And so when Amir Khan and Subadar Major Zaman Khan went on leave to their homes, they could only do the journey under cover of the darkness of the night, and during the rest of their stay they were close prisoners inside their own inclosure. I often went to see this fine old man, Subadar Major Zaman Khan, at his home, and he complained bitterly of the 'cursed misfortune' that had launched him into the miserable feud, and made him a captive in his own home for months whenever he returned to it on leave. He was suffering for Subadar Amir's folly, but the time was fast approaching when punishment was to fall on Amir himself.

I have already explained the wounding of Khayasta Khan in a former chapter, and now I will relate how Amir came to his end. Just before the loss of his leg, Khayasta Khan rose up early one morning, and, field-glass in hand, carefully scanned his enemy's double-towered inclosure. It was barely light, and yet he could see a figure under the mulberry tree, facing the only entrance the inclosure had, washing his hands, a little outside the cover of the tower wall. He looked very carefully, and in the increasing light he discovered the figure to be that of his arch-enemy Amir Khan. Putting down the field-glass, and taking up his Martini-Henry, he took aim and fired. The bullet just touched Amir's beard, who, throwing himself back under cover, had a narrow escape that time. Instead of taking warning, Subadar Amir gave up his appointment in the Kohat police and went to live in his own fort. As three sides of it were under control of the fire of the enemy's rifles, he had a deep covered way dug out to the south of his building, with a square piece of level ground at the end, where he used to go and say his prayers without being seen or fired at from the three quarters held by the enemy. But in his caution he committed one error. I went along this covered way after his death, and saw that a man standing straight up was perfectly safe; but once you got to the square bit of ground where Amir sat and said his prayers, no wall or cover had been raised, and a person was fully exposed to the fire of anyone who could get a shot at him from 50 to 300 yards on the southern side of the inclosure. The difficulty was to get to within 50 to 300 yards of Amir without being seen and discovered by the watchmen on the two towers of the building. However, spies—possibly ladies of Amir's household, who were related to Khayasta Khan and Asad Khan's families—must have revealed the condition of affairs, and the want of protection of Amir's prayer house. One night in the hot weather, two smart men of Khayasta Khan's side started at 10 P.M., and took up their position 150 to 200 yards to the south of the square spot, and concealed themselves. There was hardly any cover, save a stone here or there, and the summer sun rising would reveal to the watchmen any movement or object of suspicion in that quarter. The two must have kept very close on that fearful hot summer's day, exposed to the fierce rays of a tropical sun, unable to move or stir, lest their situation should be exposed to the enemy's riflemen, and their own watch rewarded by a volley which at such close quarters would be certain death to them. Mid-day, two o'clock, five P.M., no sign of Amir Khan, but just as the sun was dipping down behind the Khyber Hills their patient watch of twenty hours was rewarded, for he came through the covered way and stood on his prayer ground, looking at the brown, burnt, parched-up hills. The two rifles rang out at the same moment, and Subadar Amir fell dead.

Amin Khan's action from 1884 to 1891 has already been recorded in these pages. He threatened, as I have already mentioned, to fire on the Lieut.-Governor of the Panjab in 1885 if he ventured to journey up the Khyber, unless Abdulla Nur's special pension was continued to him. In 1890 he was fined Rs. 2,000 by the full jirga of the Khyber elders and maliks for attempting to stop the Peshawar caravan, and the tribal allowances were distributed direct to the elders of all the sections of the Kuki Khel Afridis, instead of being handed over to their malik alone. In the spring of 1891 his man fired on two officers journeying down the Khyber in a dog-cart, and about the same time he declined to come in to receive his own chief's share. These are the chief items which I have recorded in connection with Amin Khan's name; but I have omitted to relate how for six years I was worried in trying to settle the quarrels between him and his tribesmen touching the distribution of their Khyber allowances. How I longed for the days of Mackeson, when our Indian Empire was yet no further north than Ludiana and Ferozepore, and a strong Sikh power intervened between the Khyber and British India, and when Frederick Mackeson had the authority and power to turn away any useless, troublesome malik who would not behave himself properly towards the officials of the British Sarkar! I shall pass over all the years of constant worry which fell to my lot, and shall now deal with Amin Khan's final plunge; and if I make the story a little longer than it may seem necessary, it is done with the object of explaining the mode and procedure of carrying out a tribal rising by the aid of Mullahs in Tirah, as was done in 1879, in 1892, and lastly in 1897.

After the death of the Sapri Mullah, there were in Tirah between 1890 and 1898 three Mullahs of note —Sayad Akbar Akhundzada, Aka Khel, the Malikdin Khel Mullah, and the Mullah of the Kambar Khels.

There were numbers of others in the various sections of the Afridi and Orakzai clans; but the above three were called by the Afridis 'mauzoons,' men who were permitted to preach and give advice at the great gatherings held at the mosque of Bagh every Friday. Sayad Akbar was young in years, avaricious, and energetic, but his whole energy was spent in trying to force the Sipahs to hand over to his tribe, the Aka Khels, a share of their Khyber allowance. He was also bribed by Malik Sher Muhammad Sipah to force the Sipahs to let him distribute their allowances —two measures that I opposed might and main. His ways did not please the Afridis. The Malikdin Khel Mullah was an old, God-fearing man, full of good advice to others, and highly loved and respected. The Kambar Khel Mullah was of lesser note, but he also was not vicious. Irrespective of the real Mullahs, there were in every mosque throughout Afridi- and Orakzai-land during the summer season three or four *talibs* (religious students), vagrant rascals who lived on charity, who never did an honest day's work, and who were at the bottom of every mischief that required hatching or circulating. These men used to collect at Bagh in hundreds every week to say their Friday's prayers. Presuming that the Mullahs wished to secure an Afridi rising against the British Government, this was how the plan was arranged and carried out. A notice was circulated, inviting all the Afridi clans to attend at Bagh on a certain Friday to say their prayers. On the day fixed, jirgas from all the sections of the Afridis, possibly to the number of three to four thousand men, would attend, and, after the usual prayers had been said, the business which had brought them together would be entered into. Now, amongst

Afridis and Pathan tribes a man's deadliest enemies are those cousins outside his own family who are heirs to his landed property. The Mullahs having discussed the subject, would ask if all were agreed to adopt an aggressive policy against the British Government. If a strong party was opposed to fighting, as was the case during the Miranzai expeditions, the subject was dropped at once; but if only one individual objected, the Mullahs would call him a 'wahabi,' and invite his cousins and the *talibs* to burn down his house. He was thus forced to acquiesce, and the same procedure was adopted towards all until complete unanimity prevailed. From 1884 to 1892 Amin Khan had done his best to get the Mullahs to secure an Afridi rising, but so far all his exertions had ended in failure. But in 1889 his brother, Zaman Khan, took service with Sipah Salar Gholam Hydor Khan, the Amir's Commander-in-Chief in the Jelallabad District, and a fresh item of disturbance was added to the firebrands already at work amongst the Kuki Khels.

May 1, 1892, arrived, and in accordance with orders received half the maliki allowance was given to Amin Khan and half to Akbar Khan, and the tribal distribution arranged for in 1890 was carried out. Everything was going on extremely well when, on May 6, Zaman Khan, brother of Amin, who had received an advance of Rs. 3,000 from the Sipah Salar and obtained leave of absence from Asmar in Bajawar, reached Peshawar with 100 men. His presence produced a lot of intrigue and trouble, but the jirgas insisted on seeing their orders carried out, and the Kuki Khels were dismissed to their homes. There was after this one secret meeting at the house of Khwas Khan in the City of Peshawar, at which were present the following maliks: Khwas Khan, Zakha Khel, Feroz Khan, Malikdin Khel, Sher Muhammad, Sipah, and Amin Khan, Kuki Khel. What passed at the interview no one would reveal, but when these four men came out, and Amin Khan went away, Khwas Khan was heard to say: 'We have given him a long pole to cross a deep stream, and he will either pass over in safety or drown in the venture.' On May 24 Lieut.-Colonel Aslam Khan and I went up to Landi Kotal, where we found Mr. Taylor, C.E., hard at work over the Tangi water supply. By this time Amin Khan and the Rajgal Kuki Khels had reached their homes. Amin Khan at once set to work again to win the Mullahs over to his cause, and this time he spent his cash freely. His first venture was to waylay my dak carried by two men of the Khyber Rifles. The attempt was made at 10 P.M. near Fort Maud by some fifteen of his followers. They secured the snider of one of the escort, but the other man, firing his piece into the thick of the gang, helped his comrade to escape with him towards Fort Maud, saving his own rifle and the mail bag, which was sent up in the morning to Landi Kotal with a report of what had occurred. Another small raiding party was sent by Amin Khan down the Bara Valley towards the Aka Khel *maira*, but by this time news came to me as to what was going on in Tirah, and every day I was kept fully informed as to Amin Khan's action. The dak was then brought up by day in place of at night; the garrisons of Shadi Bagiar, Fort Maud, and Ali Masjid were increased, and water vessels provided for them. The Mullah of the Malikdin Khels was written to by me and asked the reason of this agitation; he answered that he had nothing to do with it, and that the whole mischief was being caused by Amin Khan and the Aka Khel Mullah, Sayad Akbar. Day by day the reports became more threatening; all these were submitted to Mr. (now Sir R.) Udny, Commissioner of the Peshawar Division, and he was asked to represent the matter urgently to Government, and solicit troops being sent out to Jamrud to render assistance to the Khyber Rifles in the Khyber Pass. Ten days before Amin Khan made his final move to march down, this movement was explained in the clearest language to the Commissioner. The Shan Khels of Nekai and the Paindeh of Chena (Zakha Khel clans) sent jirgas to me at Landi Kotal, explaining that some 6,000 to 8,000 men were coming down with Amin Khan. On June 30 his *lashkar* reached Chena and remained there two days; an informer at once came and warned me of this march, and the jirga of Chena also came in. The Zakha Khel Maliks, Khwas and Walli Muhammad Khan, were then sent with these men to hold the ridge near Ali Masjid. On the 3rd Amin passed behind Ali Masjid, Lala Chena, and encamped at Shudanai, five miles from Jamrud. Hearing of this move, Lieut.-Colonel Aslam Khan and I, leaving Mr. Taylor at Landi Kotal, rode down the Pass and reached Jamrud about 2 P.M. In spite of my ten days' warning urgently pleading for help in troops, not a man had been moved from Peshawar to Jamrud to assist the Khyber Rifles or the garrison of Fort Jamrud. The telegraph wires were there and then set to work, and the condition of affairs explained to the Commissioner, to Simla, and to General Sir H. Collett, commanding the Peshawar District, who was then at Cherat. That day two companies of the 14th Sikhs were sent to Jamrud, and the next day two field guns under an escort of two companies of the Royal Scots Fusiliers arrived late at night. On July 4, which was a Monday, some 200 men of the Mullagoris, summoned by me, came to my aid. At mid-day the Kuki Khel jirga belonging to the villages round about Fort Jamrud was collected, and posts assigned to them, and they were sent off to secure and hold them. Those told off for Shadi Bagiar, Jehangira, and Fort Maud reached their posts before the attack was developed. Close upon sunset men were seen in large numbers carrying flags on the high hilltop to the left of the Khyber Road waving their swords, whilst the rattle of musketry told that the three posts held by the Khyber Rifles and Kuki Khel allies were being attacked. Soon a reddish glare arose in the direction of the Khyber, which increased in intensity as the night grew darker, there being no moon. The fire, which was a large one, kept on till the early hours of the morning. Lying down on a cot in the open ground, we tried to secure some rest, as our march was to commence at 4 A.M. and I was wearied out with eighteen hours' anxiety and work. July 5 was a Tuesday and the Muhammadan festival of the 'Bakra-Idh,' the holiest in their calendar, and besides it was our caravan day, and Amin Khan had vowed that on this day he would close the Khyber Road.

As I was about to get up at 4 A.M. Rissaldar Kaddam Khan came and whispered in my ear that he had heard casually that Amin Khan had fled; but the news was too good to be relied upon, so we advanced with the Khyber Rifles in skirmishing order, with our small force ready for any contingency. Fortunately the news brought down to Kaddam Khan was correct. We found Amin Khan and his gathering had really gone. When we got to the spot where the pathway turns on the left to Fort Maud we saw the mischief which had been caused by the attack. Two large outhouses to the south of the fort had been burnt and entirely destroyed. Within three to four yards of the walls we found bundles of grass scattered here and there, which showed beyond any doubt what the fate of the fort would have been had the Mullah *lashkar* got in. If the Kuki Khel and other Afridis had attacked on the afternoon of the 3rd, or on the morning of the 4th of July, nothing could have saved the three posts of Shadi Bagiar, Jehangira, and Fort Maud. Their capture and conflagration would have created so great a moral impression that there would have been a certainty of Ali Masjid and Landi Kotal then suffering the fate that befell them afterwards in 1897. For it must be remembered that the bitterness regarding the occupation of the Samana, the increase of the salt tax, the influence of Amin Khan's money, the action of the three maliks in assisting him, and our utter unpreparedness were factors of far greater importance in 1892 than they were five years later. Fortunately Amin Khan attacked at sunset, and in the darkness he was repulsed. He and his brother, Zaman Khan, were watching the fight from a mound just near Jehangira. Just after the repulse news reached him that Malik Yar Muhammad Khan, of Chora, had secured all Amin Khan's Hindus, with the mules bringing down supplies for his *lashkar*. He also learnt that we were advancing in the morning. These three events combined induced him and his gathering to make a retrograde movement to Tirah, and they never stopped once the retreat commenced until they reached their homes.

Passing the caravan on to Ali Masjid, we turned back to Fort Jamrud, as all danger was past, and our Zakha Khel allies were holding the ridge by Ali Masjid, whilst the Khyber Rifles occupied the fort. It may be called a Providential escape. At the same time, I firmly believe that the Afridi *lashkar*, as in 1879, only wanted a good excuse to get back to their country, and had no desire or wish to fight the British Government.

By this time the Commissioner had arrived at Peshawar from his summer home at Nathia Galli, and the General and his A.A.G. had hurried down from Cherat; at the conference held at the former's house Sir Henry Collett, Major Davies, and I strongly advocated assisting the Khyber Rifles with regular troops if the posts in the Khyber were ever attacked again.

Amin Khan was deprived of the half maliki which had remained to him, and, having spent all his accumulated wealth in this one plunge, he lost his prestige with his defeat and was unable to do any further mischief. But this result might have been secured eight years before if the Panjab authorities had only understood that an Afridi malik was not a Baluch Tumandar.

On July 8 Lieut.-Colonel Aslam Khan and I returned to Landi Kotal. The European troops and guns were then withdrawn to Peshawar and the Sikhs a week later. By that time all danger was over, and the Afridis had been warned that if the posts in the Khyber were again menaced regular troops would at once be sent to the aid of their allies the Khyber Rifles.

Malik Yar Muhammad Khan distributed the rations amongst his own people, and handed over the fifteen Hindus whom he had captured conveying supplies for Amin Khan to me. They were permitted to return to their homes with a severe warning. My native Orakzai assistant, who was in league with Amin Khan, was sent away on a pension; but all my endeavours to get him replaced by a European officer who would work loyally for the British Government, and never mix himself up in any tribal intrigues, failed. I wrote sheets of foolscap with no success. I preferred to do without an assistant rather than to have a native who might play me false again. I had had two such men between 1882 and 1892.

Amin Khan after his failure made no second attempt to move down with a gathering towards Jamrud or any of the Khyber posts. He now confined himself to urging Afridis serving in the various regular regiments, Khyber Rifles, and police to desert with their arms and bring the rifles to him, promising to reward them with Rs. 500 for each rifle produced. He could only bring pressure on the Kuki Khels of Rajgal, and some time in August 1892 two of them deserted from the 28th Panjab Infantry, carrying away their Martini-Henrys and accoutrements. I sent warning of their flight to all the Afridis, and as they were passing through the Sipah Bara Valley one of my Sipah elders secured the rifles, accoutrements, &c., and let the men go. Amin Khan tried hard to get the arms from the Sipahs, but they declined to hand them over to anyone except myself. On August 31 twenty-two Sipahs, armed excellently, appeared at Landi Kotal and delivered over the two rifles. About 1 A.M. on the morning of September 1 some four or five shots were fired at the gate of the serai where I slept. At dawn I learnt that twenty-five Kuki Khels, headed by Amin Khan, had given chase to the Sipahs, and, finding them too strong to tackle, had revenged themselves by firing at the iron-bound doors of the serai. On their flight to Landi Khana they had exchanged shots in the darkness with the garrison of Fort Tytler.

There was no further anxiety about Amin Khan, because at the close of July all the Khyber maliks and jirgas had sworn to support us against Amin Khan and every Mullah in Tirah. The word of the jirga was far more reliable than the oaths of the three deceiving maliks who had led the Kuki Khel Amin Khan to his destruction. We remained at Landi Kotal till October 28, and during the months subsequent to July 4, when the Afridis attacked the three Khyber posts, the attitude of the people towards us became more friendly every day. Anything we wanted, either on behalf of Government or of ourselves, was cheerfully granted. Even English married officers came up and took their wives to see Tor-Sappar, and enjoyed the rides over the plateau.

His Excellency the Commander-in-Chief had expressed a wish for Mr. Spenser Wilkinson to be allowed to see as much of the Khyber as he cared to inspect, and in carrying out Lord Roberts's wish Mr. Wilkinson journeyed with me to Landi Kotal on December 5, and we had the pleasure of the society also of Mr. Joseph Walton, now M.P. for Barnsley Division, W.R. Yorks, who had arrived at Peshawar with the intention of seeing the frontier. After inspecting everything, especially the Jelallabad Valley, from Pisgah, which reveals fully the wonderful excellence of the Loargi position, we returned to Peshawar.

The Peshawar District had been more than usually unhealthy that season, and was now threatened with a description of poisonous fever which had been deadly some twenty years before. It commenced to rain on July 29, 1892, and poured incessantly for sixteen to seventeen days; this turned the valley into a swamp, and the heat of the sun falling on this created a miasma which proved fatal to many Europeans as well as to natives of the district. This extraordinary unhealthiness extended to the skirts of the surrounding mountains, and was fatal even to several residents of Landi Kotal, which I regard as one of the healthiest places I have ever lived at, and this after many years' experience of the locality. Lord and Lady Roberts and family came up to Peshawar, and Lord Roberts, accompanied by his son the Hon. Frederick Roberts and by his eldest daughter, paid his farewell visit to Ali Masjid. He had for eight years taken the greatest interest in the Khyber Pass, and had always given his strongest support to any measure that benefited our hold on the Khyber Range, and had aided any measure likely to produce a good understanding with its residents. The name of Lord Roberts will always be cherished and loved by the Native army and by the peoples of India.

The Kuki Khels gave no further trouble. Settling their affairs and realising all the fines due on account of Amin Khan's misdeeds, I went on two years' leave from May 11, 1893. The representations that I had made for years to be allowed a military officer as assistant, who would learn the work in the Khyber and carry on the duties on the same grounds that I had been working on, and who would take my place on my departure, had not been successful. Sir James Lyall in November, and again in December 1891, had faithfully promised me that he would support my application for a military assistant, but that the question of appointing a captain and two lieutenants to the Khyber Rifles would be deferred until such time as Lieutenant-Colonel Aslam Khan meant to retire on pension. The documents went to England, and the appointment of my assistant was approved of by the Secretary of State for India and the file was sent back to India some time in 1892. But it was not till April 15, 1893, that Captain C. Minchin joined the Khyber staff at Peshawar. Many valuable years had been wasted in securing this appointment, but as Captain Minchin was new to the work, he was not put in political charge of the Khyber when I took my departure.

AT ALI MASJID. LORD ROBERTS, HON. MISS ROBERTS HON. FREDERICK ROBERTS, AND PARTY

CHAPTER XVI

ON LEAVE IN INDIA

1893–1894

Before giving over my Khyber charge, I wrote a courteous letter to the Private Secretary of the Lieutenant-Governor of the Panjab, explaining the procedure that had been adopted towards me, which had entailed great loss in pay to one not over blessed with the world's riches, and I asked him to bring my letter to the notice of Sir Dennis Fitzpatrick. I retained a copy of this document, and have it now, but no reply was ever sent or vouchsafed to me. A furlough income of Rs. 700 a month, or £540 a year, after thirty-two years' service did not permit of my going with my family to Europe, as I wanted to do, so we made up our minds to spend the summer months at Murree and return for the winter to Peshawar, where, amongst old scenes and old friends, the quiet and rest which I was in search of might be secured. On the evening of our departure the railway station swarmed with Afridis who had come to bid me farewell. It was hard parting with people with whom I had been in daily touch for eleven years; still, there was the consolation that in five months we should be back in Peshawar, and that the twenty-two weeks would quickly pass away, when these old acquaintances and friends would be seen again. With this earnest hope and a kind good-bye to our own people, and a 'Khoda Hafiz' and 'Salâm' to the dwellers in the valley and on the independent hills, our train steamed out of the Peshawar station.

Murree I am devotedly attached to and fond of. It lies thirty-eight miles from Rawal Pindi, and can be reached in five to six hours by Mr. Danjeboy's excellent tonga service. Starting from Peshawar by the evening train, I have dismounted from the tonga early next morning on the road to Kashmir, which passed beneath my garden. To Mr. Danjeboy I am indebted for many acts of courtesy during our acquaintanceship of twenty-three years. Having seen Murree, Dalhousie, Simla, Mussoorie, Landour, the palm for beauty of scenery must, in my humble opinion, be given to the first. With your head-quarters at the rooms near the tonga offices, immediately below the club, you could arrange for tours into Kashmir, or to the Gullies *en route* to Abbotabad, or to Thandiani; and nothing could be more enjoyable or glorious than those trips through the beautiful Gullies before and after the rainy season. House-owners who had to make their incomes by letting their houses, and merchants who had to secure their gains by sale of goods, bemoaned the day when the Panjab Government removed its summer seat to Simla and Mr. Danjeboy opened out his tonga service towards Kashmir. Former visitors to Murree were then drawn away to Simla and Srinagar; but in my opinion this was a gain to Murree by preventing it from being overcrowded. One drawback to Murree, however, was its red clay soil, into which you sank when the heavy rains were on, but which when dry became as hard as iron. The place is too cold for fruit, which seldom ripens; and as for gardening purposes, just as everything looks fair and prosperous, a destructive storm of hail will come and level everything with the ground. The most terrific storm I have ever witnessed occurred on May 28, 1893, smashing and tearing off all the fruit on the trees, destroying the garden produce, and breaking hundreds of panes of glass in the club and various houses all over the station. I saw another storm, not quite so bad, come down at the close of July 1896; and I had witnessed Murree white with hail on October 12, 1885.

During the first period of my leave at Murree my Afridi friends were very assiduous in their journeys and visits, which were made contrary to my wishes on two grounds. First of all, there was no serai or building near where travellers could put up near my house with the least degree of comfort, and as they had to make a long and, to them, an expensive journey merely to see me, I did not like to find them made uncomfortable for my sake. Secondly, there was a large Afghan colony already at Murree, and if the police authorities learnt that Afridis were in the constant habit of journeying up to the place to visit me they might suspect them of being the offenders in case any rifles were carried off from Kuldanna, Garial, or the depôt. A few words to one man had the desired effect, and my Khyber allies, knowing that I was not running away and would speedily return to Peshawar, refrained from making their journeys so frequently. On September 3, 1893, I left for Simla, and arrived there just before the departure of the Durand mission for Caubul, and during a short stay I arranged, with the permission of the Panjab Government, that I was to give up a year of my furlough and return to my Khyber charge on May 11, 1894. It was the last season of Lord Lansdowne's Viceroyalty, and there was universal sorrow and regret at the prospect of his and Lady Lansdowne's approaching departure from India in the coming spring. Calcutta would still have them for the winter season, but it was a far cry to Calcutta from Peshawar.

I was back at Murree by 6 A.M. on Wednesday, November 1. The journey by tonga from Rawal Pindi was very cold, especially as one was clothed in garments suitable for Kalka, Lahore, Rawal Pindi, and not for a hill station 7,500 feet high; besides, the wind blowing down the Murree-Rawal Pindi road about 3 A.M. on a November morning told severely as the tonga made its way rapidly up hill. A few days to pack up and despatch boxes to Rawal Pindi made us ready for our return to the Peshawar Valley. We experienced an exceedingly severe shock of earthquake, which came on about 9.30 on the morning of Sunday, November 5, and the marvel was that no damage was caused to the stone-built walls of the house or to any of the houses in the station. The weather in the sunshine was delightful, but exceedingly cold in Kuldanna Cottage, which, facing the Kashmir Hills, has a northern aspect, and is in no way protected from the wind which blows in the winter season from the snow-covered mountains. We found that no amount of wood fires would warm the rooms, so it was with considerable satisfaction that we stepped into our tonga on November 10th, and reached Peshawar at 4.30 A.M. on the 12th, having made one day's halt at Rawal Pindi to permit our servants and heavy luggage to come up with us and journey in our train westwards. The valley had in no wise changed since our departure, but the health of the troops was much better than it had been twelve months before, there having been little fever in 1893.

Owing to some cause or other, the valuable stores collected at the mobilisation go-downs of the 1st Army Corps, located to the east of the city station, were burnt down a few days before my return, involving a loss to Government of something like £50,000. It was never discovered how the fire originated, whether it was due to accident or was the handiwork of some person or persons who had something to gain by the destruction of these commodities.

The Durand mission arrived at Peshawar from Caubul on November 22. Sir Mortimer and Surgeon-Lieut.-Colonel Fenn left the same day, and the rest of the party moved away on the 23rd, except Captain Manners-Smith, who remained behind to square up accounts. The mission officers were full of the kind way in which they had been treated by the Amir, Abdur Rahman, and one of them who had seen him in 1880, and again in 1884, and for the third time in 1893, assured me that the Amir was now a changed man to what he was some thirteen years before. That this mission had made Abdur Rahman Khan happy and cleared away from his mind all suspicions was good news, and we all hoped that it might turn out to be true in the end, although there were one or two disbelievers in India who were not quite so sanguine.

Immediately after my return to Peshawar all my

Khyber friends came daily to see me, but some of them were under the impression that I was bound to interfere in certain matters which had been carried out during my absence. To these complaints I never attended, assuring them that whatever had been done by the officer acting for me I could not possibly interfere with, whether it coincided with my own views or not.

During my brief absence several changes had taken place. Malik Amin Khan, whose hostility to the British Government, commencing with the spring of 1884, culminated in the expedition from Tirah to close the Khyber in 1892, which ended in his ruin and the deprivation of his maliki, had been pardoned, and was to get back the half chieftainship which he had been in possession of at the end of May 1892. I was warned not to interfere with this resolution in any way. Amin Khan was to be introduced to me before I retook charge on May 11, 1894. The procedure was strange, and in no way likely to benefit Government; still, as it had been decided to carry out this step without asking or consulting me, there was nothing to do but to obey orders. The trouble would in the immediate present come on my shoulders, but in the future it would have to be carried by the Panjab Government and those who had given this advice. On February 22, 1894, Malik Akbar Khan, Kuki Khel, was shot as he was saying his prayers at his mosque inside the inclosure of his house. The miscreant who committed this act was a near relation, one of the four sons of a man whose house adjoined Akbar Khan's, and whose family had been aided and assisted by him with arms and money against a powerful rival. Akbar Khan, I regret to say, died from the wound received by him. What made the evil deed infinitely worse was the circumstance of this murderer having been turned out of his house by his own brothers, and, contrary to their advice, Malik Akbar had taken him in and sheltered him, supplying him with clothing and food. The miscreant fled, and took shelter with his brothers. Akbar Khan's party declared that Malik Amin Khan had promised Rs. 1,200 to see Malik Akbar put out of the way, and a sum of money did actually pass hands when Amin Khan came down from the Bara Valley. On the other hand, Amin Khan's friends gave out that the murderer had been selected to assassinate Amin himself. Considering that the latter was away some forty miles at the western extremity of the Bara Valley, and not likely to place himself in the power of any friend of Malik Akbar's, the story could not be credited. But whichever motive was the correct one, Akbar Khan's murder was a great loss to Government. He had risked life, fortune, everything for the 'Sarkar,' and stood up for just rule and order at a time when the Abdulla Nur faction was wealthy—and riches mean power among Afridis. He never hesitated to obey, and, if it was in his power, to carry out an order of our Government; and such devotion on his part, even if it brought him personal profit, deserved consideration from the Power he had done his best to serve.

The avenging came quickly and sharp. Malik Akbar's party, either by bribery or in some other way, secured an entrance into the fortress and tower where the murderer had taken shelter, killed him with two of his brothers and a couple of retainers, levelled the walls of the building with the ground, and then had the spot ploughed up. Only two of the family—Jemadar Jelal Khan and his brother Chenar—escaped, and they had to go to the other side of the village and claim shelter from the faction who had been inimical to their father Ahmad Shah during his life, and to the whole family after his death.

On April 9, 1894, Mr. and Mrs. Clements and son, Mr. and Mrs. Martin, two lady doctors, and party went to Jamrud, intending to journey westwards towards the capital of Afghanistan. This was the first time since the days of Lady Macnaghten, Lady Sale, and the dark period of 1841–42 that any English ladies had ventured to attempt this journey.

I went to Simla to spend the last month of my year's leave, and took up my family with me, leaving Peshawar on April 13, and arriving at Simla two days later. I had a meeting with Sir M. Durand on the 16th. During my stay at Simla I was presented to the new Viceroy, the Earl of Elgin. My first appearance at a *levée* in India was at Government House, Calcutta, in November 1862, when his father was Viceroy and Governor-General. There was no official mention made of any Viceregal visit to the frontier during the approaching winter season, although Lord Elgin said that there was every prospect—nay, almost certainty—of his paying a visit to Dharmsala, where his father lies buried. From what I was told by his staff, it seemed that a frontier tour had been discussed at the Viceregal Lodge, although nothing had been definitely resolved upon. I had a couple of meetings with, and made the acquaintance of, Mr. Babington Smith, Private Secretary to the Governor-General.

There was some uncertainty about the date on which the Panjab Government desired me to resume my appointment in the Khyber. However, nothing came in the way of altering my former plans, and so, leaving Simla on the morning of May 7, I was able to reach Peshawar on the 9th, and begin work on the forenoon of the 11th, having been absent exactly one year on leave in India. During my short stay at Simla in September and October 1893, I had seen Mr. Fanshawe, Secretary to the Panjab Government, and, when broaching the subject of my being permitted to give up a year of my leave and return to duty, I asked him to represent to Sir D. Fitzpatrick that I was losing a very great deal in pay by remaining on in the Khyber, and if my management of the Pass had been a successful one, could he not be induced to recommend an increment? The Secretary replied that he would bring the matter to the notice of the Lieut.-Governor, who would consult the Commissioner, Mr. Udny, on the subject. This decision soon came. I was told that my request had been negatived.

Amin Khan, Kuki Khel, who had come into Peshawar, was introduced to me by Mr. C. G. Hastings, C.I.E. (who had been officiating for me during the previous twelve months), at his house, and such portion of the Government orders that were necessary that he should know were explained to him by Mr. Hastings. He was particularly warned not to go near Jam in coming to or going away from Peshawar.

Sardar Habibulla Khan—who was the eldest son of the Amir, and had been spending February, March, and April in the Jelallabad District—now resolved to return to Caubul, as his presence was required there in carrying out some urgent social State religious ceremonies; and the Sipah Salar, who had been to see His Highness on certain official matters, possibly the coming Mohmand Bajawar demarcation, retraced his steps towards his command. The month of May passed, and, beyond hearing rumours of what was going on in Eastern Afghanistan—which rumours were carried down by men belonging to the bi-weekly caravans, or by informers sent by us to glean information—nothing was known for certain as to the feeling amongst the Bajawaris and Mohmands regarding the new demarcation. On our side the Commissioner of Peshawar, Mr. (now Sir Richard) Udny, who had been appointed as head of this Mohmand-Bajawar Boundary Commission, had signed and circulated a proclamation dated the 7th of the Muhammadan month of Zu'l-hijjah, 1311 H.=A.D. June 12, 1894, a translation of which is herewith given:

'*Proclamation.*

'From Mr. R. Udny, Commissioner and Superintendent, Peshawar Division.

'To all Bajawari, Mohmand, and other tribes inhabiting the country towards the Indian Empire, from the Caubul River to the southern limit of Chitral, from the boundary line now agreed upon between the British Government and the Amir of Afghanistan.

'(1) Whereas certain questions were raised regarding the boundary between Afghanistan and India, and as H.H. the Amir, as well as the Indian Government, desired to have these questions disposed of in an amicable and friendly manner, so that for the future there may not be a difference of opinion and thought regarding the above matter between these two kingdoms, who have treaties and engagements between themselves. The Government of Great Britain, with the consent of H.H. the Amir of Afghanistan, during the month of September 1893=Rabbi-al-awal 1311 H., sent a mission consisting of a few officers under the leadership of Sir Mortimer Durand to Caubul. And by the mercy of God Almighty, the two Governments in a friendly manner concluded an agreement, on November 12, 1893=2 Jamadi-ul-awal 1311 H., regarding the limits of the country of H.H. the Amir towards India, for hundreds of (krohs) miles from Wakhan on the north to Persia on the south.

'(2) In this agreement it was decided between the two Governments, already bound by agreements and engagements, that the Indian Government will never interfere at any time in the countries lying on that side of the line in the direction of Afghanistan, and that His Highness also will cause no interference at any time in the countries that may be lying outside the boundary line in the direction of India.

'(3) With the object of demarcating this long boundary with facility and celerity, it was agreed upon by both the kingdoms, already bound by treaties and engagements, to divide this boundary line into certain parts, and each part of this line should be marked where it is found necessary by the British and Afghan Commissioners.

'(4) Therefore I send this proclamation to you, that I have been appointed Commissioner by the Government of India to demarcate that portion of the boundary which pertains to the tribes noted at the beginning of this proclamation. In this condition of affairs I shall probably start shortly towards Afghan limits for Asmar, and being joined at this place by a Commissioner appointed by H.H. the Amir, demarcate the boundaries of Afghanistan from Chanak towards the Caubul River. I shall then, I hope, be able to point out the boundary on the spot. Until this is done it is not an easy matter for me to explain the exact features of the boundary. But at present a brief sketch of the boundary will be understood by you from the following details.

'(5) Whereas the kingdom of Great Britain has agreed that H.H. the Amir should retain in his possession the country of Asmar on the north to Chanak situated on the Kuner River, or the river of Kashkar, the boundary demarcation will commence from Chanak in a south-westerly direction up to Kuner, and at a distance of a few English miles from the bank of the Kuner River towards Bajawar. From Kuner the boundary line goes southwards, and, taking a bend, ascends the hills close to Satala Sar, which hills divide the watershed between the Kuner and Panj-kora Rivers. From Satala Sar the boundary line passes over the crest of the hill, on one side of which the waters flowing from the Dag Hills fall into the Panj-kora River, whilst the waters on the other side, passing through the Satala Valley, fall into the Caubul River. And in the centre of this hill lies the Kotal of Satala. The extreme end of the boundary touches the Caubul River in the vicinity of Polosi.

'(6) From a review of the above details you will understand that in addition to the countries watered by the Kuner River which lie towards the limits of the Indian Dominions, H.H. the Amir has agreed not to interfere in all that country the eastern waters of which fall into the Panj-kora River; nor to interfere or stretch his hand in that quarter of the Mohmand country the waters of which fall into the Caubul River below Polosi.

'(7) On this account your future concerns and relationship will lie solely with the British Government and no one else, and I have a hope that by degrees there will be the same bonds of friendship between you on the one part, and myself and the frontier officers of the British Government on the other part, which has existed between the said officers and other tribes who reside outside the limits of the boundaries of the Peshawar District.

'(8) The last request is that you should firmly believe, and on this point I will give you every assurance and satisfaction, that the Government of India has no intention of going beyond these limits, which form the present boundaries of the Indian Empire, and that it has no desire to mix itself in any way with the affairs of your country. Written on the 7th of Zu'l-hijjah 1311 H.=A.D. June 12, 1894.'

This proclamation, written in the Persian language and character and signed R. Udny, was distributed across the British border amongst the tribes concerned, and immediately the fact became known, the Sipah Salar issued orders and sent messengers to have all the copies secured and brought to him, and they were either destroyed or sent on to the Amir at Caubul. This information was conveyed from the Mohmand country, and it was hinted that the Amir and the Sipah Salar were very much offended at such a document having been circulated amongst the Amir's people at a time when a British mission was going as a guest of His Highness into his dominions, and was to be escorted by his troops and Commander-in-Chief over the country to be mutually demarcated. But, like all rumours coming from Afghanistan, no one had the means of proving this one to be altogether correct. Why should the Amir and his Commander-in-Chief have revealed such thoughts, if they ever entertained them, to the common public of Afghanistan?

At the commencement of July 1894 H.E. Lord Elgin's frontier tour was announced to the public. The Viceroy was to visit Peshawar in the month of November, go up the Khyber Pass, then proceed by rail to Quetta, and, returning to Lahore, hold a darbar there; but later on this tour was altered.

Two members of the Mohmand-Bajawar Boundary Commission, Mr. Udny and Surgeon-Captain Macnabb, arrived at Peshawar on August 12 and went on to have an interview with the Sipah Salar Gholam Hyder Khan, at Jelallabad, and on this meeting depended the future fate of the Boundary Commission.

Very little occurred during the next three months that requires particular mention. My assistant, Captain Minchin, who had joined the Khyber staff on April 15, 1893, was not satisfied with his position and status under the Panjab Government, and had made up his mind to return to his former appointment in the Political Department under the Government of India. I was sorry at this, but not surprised. Sorry, because I felt sure that once he left me (and I had begun to like him and the willing way he undertook any duty or work that was entrusted to him) it would take months, perhaps years, to get a successor to him sent to me. I might think myself lucky if any assistant like Captain Minchin were sent to replace him, but it was just possible that the Government at Lahore would alter this arrangement, which had been supported by one Lieut.-Governor, Sir James Lyall, and had received the sanction of the Secretary of State for India in Council. It made me jealous to look at the list of military officers lent by the Government of India to the Gilgit and Chitral Agencies, some twenty or more figuring in the Quarterly Panjab Civil List supplied from the Accountant-General's office at Lahore, and to find such difficulty in my getting even one man as a help to the Khyber staff. I was not surprised at Captain Minchin forsaking the Khyber and the Panjab Government, for his prospects under the Government of India were far better and more roseate.

On November 9, 1894, Mr. Curzon, now Lord Curzon of Kedleston, Viceroy and Governor-General of India, arrived at Peshawar, and I had the pleasure of meeting him the next day. He was then travelling for pleasure, a trip which had for its object a journey on horseback from Peshawar to Caubul, where he was to be the guest of Amir Abdur Rahman Khan; after that he might undertake a ride to

Candahar, then to Chaman, and take the railway to Quetta. Or, if he could induce His Highness to let him journey over the Hindu Kush during the winter season, he might go along the whole length of the new road made by Amir Abdur Rahman Khan over the Chatrar Dar and see for himself what chances there were of a European army going towards Caubul by the Hindu Kush route. Everything depended on the willingness of the Amir to help him in carrying out his own private wishes. On the morning of the 12th the future Viceroy, Colonel the Hon. M. Curzon, commanding the 3rd Battalion Rifle Brigade, and Lieutenant-Colonel Aslam Khan started with me for Jamrud, where a company of the Khyber Rifles was drawn up to receive the party. After a light breakfast at Ali Masjid, we reached Landi Kotal by 1.30 P.M., so there was the whole afternoon before us to arrange for Mr. Curzon's march to Caubul. The Amir had sent up baggage animals to carry the luggage, a horse for our guest, and two riding animals for his servants. We had a pleasant dinner, and next day, Tuesday, about 11 A.M., we wished Mr. Curzon good-bye and all prosperity and success on his solitary journey to the Court of the Amir. If he had come back by the same route, it was my intention to have asked him to stay three or four days in the Khyber Range, to see Tor-Sappar, and return to Peshawar by the Shilman route. But fortune did not favour my desire, and Mr. Curzon was able to carry out his original intention of riding from Caubul by Ghuzni, Kelat-i-Ghilzi to Candahar and Chaman, where he took the rail to Quetta. He is presumably the only Englishman who has had the rare fortune of doing this trip singly without any European companion. After bidding our illustrious traveller good-bye, Colonel the Hon. M. Curzon and I returned to Peshawar. The Zakha Khel children in the Khyber now regularly turned out to greet us whenever we journeyed up and down the Pass.

His Excellency Lord Elgin reached Peshawar on the morning of November 19, and two days later, with the Commander-in-Chief, the Lieutenant-Governor of the Panjab, and a large and brilliant following, proceeded up the Khyber Road as far as Ali Masjid and had lunch in the fort, a visit which was much enjoyed. I had now the extreme satisfaction of having taken three Viceroys of India in succession into the defiles of the historical Pass, and not one of these trips had been marred or spoilt by any hitch or accident. It is a great gratification to look back on this, and I was extremely thankful that such good fortune had attended my humble efforts and the work of the Khyber staff and Khyber Rifles, who laboured heart and soul to assist me. Whatever success was secured was entirely due to their exertions, and to them must be assigned all the credit.

In a previous chapter on Amin Khan, 1892, I have pointed out that circumstances of State had necessitated getting rid of my native assistant, who was an Orakzai gentleman of good family, but who could not keep aloof from intriguing with the representatives of the independent tribes, and he had been permitted to retire on a pension. I tried my utmost to get him replaced by a European extra assistant, because in my opinion it was better, safer, and wiser to have an honest Englishman to deal with the trans-border tribes than to seek the medium of a native middleman, who would most certainly bring us into complications in the end and cause Government a large expenditure in money in punishing some tribe for the faults of our own Agent. There was no extra expense to be incurred, and the advantages would be certain in adopting the recommendation submitted by me. But, as I have already stated, I received no answer to my many letters. The file seems to have been lost in the pigeon-holes of the office of the Commissioner of the Peshawar Division. Nearly four years after the retirement of this native assistant, his place was given, on my recommendation, to Abdul Kerim Khan, my head clerk, who had served well in the Khyber office for nearly fourteen years. If I had delayed much longer in waiting for the European assistant there was the danger of seeing this appointment struck off our list as being no longer required.

CHAPTER XVII

FINAL YEARS IN THE KHYBER

1895–1897

In the very centre of the Khyber, which belongs to the Zakha Khel Afridis, but about a mile due north of the Khyber Road, is a spring known to the residents as 'Slipola.' In a good season its water supply may have reached 3,000 gallons a day; in a season of drought the limit was reduced to about 1,200. The spring was high up the side of the mountain in a deep cliff, and by applying your ear to the rock a noise was heard of a larger volume of water dashing within than what trickled out into the open. Blasting the rock might have increased the volume of water, which was of such immense value to men and animals in this region, but the natives were averse to any such action, as they were afraid that it might dry up the spring entirely. During the period of our occupation by a large military force in 1879 the two Maliks and their people were quite averse to giving up this water for the use of travellers and others; however, in the end I persuaded them to adopt my scheme. A tank was made at the head of the spring, and covered to form a reservoir. The water was brought to the foot of the hill in exposed pipes, whilst from here to the Khyber Road they were laid underground, the land having been willingly given over by the owners without asking for any payment.

It was pleasant to see a large covered reservoir on the Khyber Road, full of clear water, and supplied with taps for turning on or stopping the precious liquid. The completion of this work was an immense boon to the Afridi women, who were saved from going eight to ten miles every day to fetch water when their own tanks, their sole supply, were dried up. But even here the two Maliks, Khwas and Walli Muhammad Khan, gave constant trouble by quarreling over their respective shares of water, and it was hard at times to keep the peace between the two.

The Mohmand Boundary Commission had at last commenced their work, and the political horizon looked fairly clear, when suddenly the Mehtar of Chitral was murdered by Amir-ul-Mulk, and Umra Khan of Barwa and Jandul, with Sher Afzal, threw themselves into the now stormy arena of Chitral affairs, and sealed their own destruction, for it brought the British power into the field, which brushed their obstruction and resistance aside. On this Chitral war breaking out, the work of the Boundary Commission was stayed for the moment, and we heard that its members were on the point of returning to the Panjab. We were also watching Caubul to ascertain which of the trio, H.H. Amir Abdur Rahman Khan, Sardar Habibulla Khan, or Sardar Nasrulla Khan, was likely to visit England. In the midst of this expectancy I received rather a peremptory message by express one night from one of the lady doctors who had journeyed up to Caubul, and had now arrived at Landi Kotal, desiring an immediate passage down the Pass, as she had been sent on to make arrangements for Sardar Nasrulla Khan's approaching visit to India and England. This lady seemed to have forgotten that, under arrangements made by the British Government with the tribes of the Khyber Range, the Pass was open to caravans on Tuesdays and Fridays in every week, for of this circumstance she had been made aware when going up to Caubul from Peshawar. Sardar Nasrulla Khan, and not his elder brother Sardar Habibulla, the presumed heir apparent to the throne of Afghanistan, had been selected to take up the coveted invitation, and I had again the troublesome duty of supplying the wants of the Afghan party, as I had to do in 1885, when H.H. Amir Abdur Rahman Khan journeyed down to the Rawal Pindi darbar.

We were first told that the Sardar would reach Peshawar on April 6, 1895; the second intimation was that he would be at Landi Kotal on the 11th, and reach Peshawar two days later with a retinue of seventy-nine persons. So Lieutenant-Colonel Aslam Khan and I travelled to Landi Kotal on the 9th, and were there joined by Lieutenant-Colonel Talbot and Surgeon-Major Leahy, who had come up to meet Sardar Nasrulla Khan and accompany him to England, on Friday, April 12. Day after day we waited; all the supplies of fruit brought up from Bombay and Peshawar became spoilt, and had to be thrown away. On the 15th for the first time we received reliable information that the Sardar would arrive on the 17th, and that his suite would consist, not of seventy-nine, but of 300 persons, 600 horses, mules, and ponies. So fresh arrangements had to be made, for nothing extra was obtainable nearer than Peshawar—thirty-one miles away. At last the morning of April 18 found us with a squadron of the 13th D.C.O. Bengal Lancers waiting at Tor Kham to receive Nasrulla, who with his suite arrived about 8.30. One man I knew well, and that was Sardar Muhammad Hassan Khan, the Governor of Jelallabad in 1879, whose career I have already fully described. Our stay at Landi Kotal and the halt at Jamrud the next day were periods of great anxiety, and the camp at the last place was surrounded by three circles of watchmen: (1) in the outer circle came posts of the Kuki Khel tribesmen; (2) then came sentries of the Khyber Rifles; (3) sentries from the regular regiments of Native cavalry and infantry; last of all came the Sardar's own guards, who kept to their own camp. Fortunately both nights were passed peacefully, and it was with extreme joy that we found ourselves within the Cantonments of Peshawar on the morning of April 20.

Captain Minchin, in accordance with his wishes, had gone back to his original department under the Government of India, and the Khyber was deprived of his services. What I had anticipated and feared actually occurred. His place was not filled up in all 1895, nor until October 1896. Why or wherefore this great delay occurred need not be entered into here, beyond stating that it was needless and positively wrong in principle. In the meanwhile the Chitral war progressed; Surgeon-Major Robertson had been released, and the gatherings of Sher Afzal and Umra Khan dispersed. But the Chitral problem remained to be grasped.

Peace and quiet reigned in the Khyber Hills during the whole of 1895, and the Civil Engineer, P.W.D., was busy at Landi Kotal improving the Tangi water supply scheme. So many trips had to be made up and down the Khyber that I had little time to make a careful inspection of the buildings, huge reservoir, and enormous tanks and troughs for watering animals which had been brought into existence by the energy of the Engineer Department.

The return of Amin Khan, and his reappointment as Malik of half the Kuki Khel Afridis by the Panjab Government, had caused much discontent amongst the party who had been on the side of the British Government during the period when this young man was viciously opposed to us and doing his best to ruin himself. I could see that there was an inclination to constitute him sole Malik, and turn out Kambar, the son of Malik Akbar Khan, deceased. However, the matter was not attempted with a strong hand just then, and it would have been a cause of deep, bitter regret had it succeeded at any time, more so during my incumbency of the Khyber arrangements. The party in Jam and Sarkai who belonged to Kambar's side were, however, guilty of a very serious and extremely foolish offence in the northern hornwork of Fort Jamrud, which offence they wished to place on the shoulders of Malik Amin Khan and his allies. For this the tribe were heavily fined, and it was explained to Malik Kambar that measures of this nature would only ruin his cause and eject him from the half Maliki he was now enjoying. In a measure Amin Khan was to blame for this himself. He had been warned by Mr. Hastings, and again repeatedly by myself, not to go to Jam on any account without first obtaining the sanction of the Political Officer of Khyber. He failed to obey these orders, which in the first instance came from the Government of the

Panjab during the period I was away on leave; and the Kuki Khel Afridis, knowing of this disobedience on his part, carried out their foolish programme, the burden of which fell on themselves in the end. But Justice overtook Amin Khan with a strong hand. He had arranged for the murder of a man named Khairai, whose fort lay at Dwa-Toe, where the Bara River and the stream from Bagh in the Maidan of Tirah meet, and which fort was occupied by Sir W. Lockhart and his head-quarter staff on November 22, 23, and 24, and December 7, 8, and 9, 1897. Khairai, who belonged to Rissaldar Kaddam Khan's and Malik Kambar's party, was assassinated in accordance with Amin Khan's wishes, who was under the impression that the secret of his complicity in the murder was unknown to the other side; but men who lived with their lives in their hands understood at once that except Amin Khan no one else could be the instigator. So, when he presented himself at the house of the murdered man to attend the funeral, and to assure the Kuki Khels of Rajgal of his entire innocence, the sons of the dead man met him with smiling faces. At the same time they arranged to give him a warm treatment at the time of his departure. As he was leaving, two Sniders, fired at close range, missed a vital part in his body, but both bullets crashing through the right shoulder made pulp of the bone down to the right elbow. His brother, Zaman Khan, bravely rushed forward and dragged him into a ditch, and there they lay hidden until sunset, whilst their friends, taking cover, opened fire on Khairai's fort, with the hope of saving the two brothers. By a wonder Amin Khan and Zaman Khan escaped the close fire brought to bear on them until their removal to a place of safety. But Amin Khan's days were numbered. He had lost his left eye some years before in trying to ram down a Snider bullet into a Martini-Henry rifle, and now his right arm was rendered completely useless. On August 17, 1897, he rushed into Jamrud, and warned Sir Richard Udny and the British authorities that an Afridi lashkar, 10,000 strong, with 1,500 Mullahs from Ningrahar, was moving to attack all the Khyber posts, from Landi Kotal downwards. When I came from Tirah by the Bara Valley, and was ordered by Sir William Lockhart to tackle the Afridi question at the commencement of January 1898, Amin Khan was worked with the other Afridi Maliks and jirgas part of that month and the whole of February and March, by the end of which time nearly the whole Afridi fine in rifles and cash had been paid up. Ill health forced me to leave Jamrud on April 5, 1898, and I never saw him again. He was murdered at Jam on December 6, 1898. No particulars reached me as to who did this act, but Amin Khan had waded knee-deep through blood and murder, and it seemed certain that vengeance would overtake him sooner or later. He could not have been more than thirty-four years old at the time of his death.

The month of August 1896 saw me once more at Landi Kotal, and Lieutenant-Colonel Aslam Khan made the journey with me at the commencement of the month. The hundreds of peach, mulberry, and almond trees planted in the serai were making splendid progress, but what was more gladdening was to go down towards Landi Khana for about 1,200 yards by the main road, and see the grand reservoir and the three immense open tanks all full to the brim with excellent water, whilst on the road were laid open troughs for watering all animals journeying up and down the Khyber Road, to or from Dakka. All this work, the labour of years, had been carried out with the friendly assistance and co-operation of the Shinwari tribesmen, without having caused a second's anxiety to Government and without invoking any outside aid. A splendid serai for kafilas and caravans had also been built, and now poor travellers could have the means of securing shelter and cover from the rain and storms of wind that often swept with great violence over the plateau. The reproach of lack of shelter for these poor travellers had at last been wiped away. Major and Mrs. Chesney came up to Landi Kotal for a couple of weeks. The former was our Engineer in Chief, and looked to all the repairs and requirements from Landi Khana to the caravan serai at Jamrud, where a splendid hospital had been built for the men of the Khyber Rifles, and a dispensary organised for the use of those men and women of the independent tribes and kafilas who cared to place themselves under the care of our worthy native doctor, Kazi Imran. The little folks, boys and girls, of the Landi Kotal plateau had their two or three treats, and then I went down to Peshawar, and my last summer stay in the Khyber Hills came to a close.

At the commencement of November 1896, Captain Barton, of the Corps of Guides, came to me as assistant, and he was to take up the command of the Khyber Rifles when Lieutenant-Colonel Aslam Khan retired on pension. This native gentleman would have been retired some three years previously under the age clause had I not recommended his further retention for the old man's sake, and further because no arrangements had been made until then to obtain a successor to him. Sir William Lockhart arrived at Peshawar on November 26, but his intended trip to Landi Kotal and Tor-Sappar was set aside on account of torrents of rain. The Lieutenant-Governor of the Panjab, Sir D. Fitzpatrick, who had been interviewing the Tarakzai, Halimzai, Burhan Khel, Isàkhel, Dawezai, and Utmanzai, the six clans of the Mohmands affected by the Durand boundary line, at a darbar held near Shabkaddar, also journeyed into Peshawar when the ceremony was over.

I was fortunate enough, at last, in being able to carry out a great wish of mine, which was to take General Sir W. Lockhart to see Tor-Sappar. Under arrangement, Sir William and Captain Haldane left Peshawar with me very early on the morning of February 22, and having spent a good hour at Tor-Sappar, we were back in Peshawar the same evening by 7 P.M., having done our seventy-eight miles since morning. On March 10 I took up Mr. (now Sir R.) Udny and two members of the Mohmand Boundary Commission to Landi Kotal, and the next morning they went to interview Sipah Salar Gholam Hyder Khan, Charkhi, at Landi Khana, and there was a conference extending over several hours. When they returned at 5.30 P.M. in the evening it seemed evident from what one could pick up that the Boundary Mission was doomed. I was compelled to go back to Peshawar on March 12, and a few days later these three gentlemen returned also, and in this way the Boundary Demarcation Mission came to an end. Three days later—i.e. on April 7—Major-General Sir E. Collen, Captains Dick and Barton,

Lieutenant-Colonel Aslam Khan, and I left at 7 A.M. for Landi Kotal, arriving there at 11 A.M.; at 1 P.M. we rode on to Tor-Sappar, where Sir E. Collen spent two hours in examining the Mohmand Hills, and then we returned to Landi Kotal for the night. The next day we were back in Peshawar, and Sir E. Collen with Captain Dick left by the 5 P.M. train for Simla.

The time was approaching rapidly and quickly when I was to bid adieu to the Khyber Hills and to my wild, savage friends, after an acquaintance commencing on August 1, 1879. The few days that remained were spent in paying up the tribesmen, and settling all claims and disputes for them and against them. My time of retirement was really July 11, 1897, but to escape the heat of the plains I had applied for three months' furlough from the forenoon of May 11, which would enable me to spend these months in a cool climate, and not necessitate my returning to Peshawar until actually compelled to meet the wishes of Government. What I had dreaded and feared, and had done my best to induce the authorities to avoid, was now about to happen. If I had received a European assistant in the days that I had earnestly pleaded for one, he would in the course of seven or eight years have learnt all that was required, have made friends with the Maliks and elders of all the tribes who had helped me so very greatly, and when the time came for my departure he could have stepped into my place, and Government should at once have given him another assistant to learn the work on the same principles and routine. The little extra money required for this purpose would, in the face of what occurred later on, have amply repaid Government in the end. But other people knew better, and now, when the day of my departure arrived, there was no European officer to take my place, and the Khyber charge was entrusted to Lieutenant-Colonel Aslam Khan, whose pension papers were already before the Panjab Government, the command of the Khyber corps being taken over by Captain Barton.

For days Peshawar swarmed with Afridis, who had come for their allowances and purchases before migrating to their summer quarters in Bara, Tirah, Rajgal, and the Bazàr Valley, for the hot weather was rapidly coming on. There was no single question troubling their minds seriously which was likely to induce them to take up arms against the British Government. The increase in the salt tax, however repugnant it might have been to them some years before, had now been almost forgotten. The Samana question even in 1891 and 1892 had no interest for them when they learnt that their own Afridi country was not to be invaded, provided they abstained from interfering with the troops operating against the Orakzai clans in the Miranzai campaign. With the affairs of Swat they had no concern, and I am convinced that the Khyber Rifles would have willingly shared in the Chitral-Swat campaign if they had been allowed to go. The Durand Boundary Line caused them no alarm, and its settlement was looked forward to by our Shinwaris, as they hoped to get back the hamlet of Derbend and some grazing lands then held by the Amir's people which they claimed. Regarding the restoration of their women, there were in some cases just cause of complaint against us; but since the number of females who were concerned was so few, say two or three in the year, the mass of the people did not care to trouble themselves much over it. When the husband or near relation of the woman worried a Malik or a jirga to plead his claim, they did so, as tribal custom forced them to do it. Having once made the appeal, these retired and left the subject alone for the future, until worried by the husband to make a second appeal. With the exception of this grievance, and a complaint of Peshawaris going sometimes into Afridi land and cutting wood and dwarf palm belonging to others, I can honestly affirm that I knew of no other grievance which the Afridis could have had against us. And on that afternoon of May 10, 1897, when some English friends came to bid me good-bye, there were hundreds of Afridis—Maliks, elders, and jirgas—crowding the railway platform to take a last look at one who had been associated with them, off and on, for nigh eighteen years. It was with a very sorrowful heart that I saw the last of them that evening, as the 5 P.M. train steamed out of the Peshawar Cantonment station towards Rawal Pindi. I little dreamt then that the 'Khyber *Débâcle*' of August 1897 would carry me through every quarter of Afridi land, in the toughest and hardest fought campaign I ever had the misfortune or honour of being associated with.

Two months were spent pleasantly at Murree, and then July 11, 1897, came round and my time of service in the Khyber expired, and Lieutenant-Colonel Aslam Khan was confirmed in the officiating post of Political Officer, Khyber Pass. The accompanying letter from the Government of the Panjab was forwarded to me by Sir R. Udny, Commissioner and Superintendent, Peshawar Division.

Copy of a Letter, No. 874, *dated Simla, July* 23, 1897, *from L. W. Dane, Esquire, Official Chief Secretary to the Government Panjab, to the Commissioner and Superintendent, Peshawar Division.*

In forwarding for communication to Colonel R. Warburton, C.S.I., the accompanying copy of Panjab Government Gazette, Notification No. 834 S of this date, replacing his services at the disposal of the Military Department, I am desired to convey the following remarks.

Colonel Warburton has been in charge of the Khyber almost ever since the British Government took over charge of the arrangements connected with the Pass in 1879, and practically continuously since 1882, and the credit for the success which has been obtained in carrying out the arrangements initiated by the late Colonel Hastings, and thereby securing the safety of the road and the establishment of fairly friendly relations with the Khyber Afridis, must largely be attributed to his efforts. These efforts have been recognised by the conferment on him, on January 1, 1890, of the C.S.I.; but as he is now leaving civil employ, the thanks of this Government are due to him for his services, which in the earlier days of our management of the Pass at any rate involved considerable personal risk and exposure. The task which Colonel Warburton and his able Assistant Colonel Mahommad Aslam Khan, C.I.E., had to perform was novel and of unusual difficulty, and the fact that the Khyber on a Kafila day is now as safe as a high road in India, and that the Khyber Rifles have been developed from a body of rude Jezailchies into a fine Corps, keen for active service under the British Government even out of their own tribal limits, will be a lasting memorial of the good work which Colonel Warburton has performed in the service of Government.

A copy of this letter should be furnished to Colonel Warburton.

Extract from the Panjab Government Gazette, Notification No. 834 *S, dated Simla, July* 23, 1897.

The services of Brevet-Colonel R. Warburton, C.S.I., Indian Staff Corps, Political Officer, Khyber, are placed at the disposal of the Government of India in the Military Department, with effect from July 12, 1897, under the operation of Articles 679 (*a*), and 689 (*a*) of the Civil Service Regulations.

No. 2434 P,

Commissioner's Office. Peshawar Division, Peshawar, dated July 26, 1897.

Copy of the foregoing forwarded to Colonel R. Warburton, C.S.I., Political Officer, Khyber Pass, for information.

(Signed) R. UDNY,
Commissioner and Superintendent.

CHAPTER XVIII

THE KHYBER DÉBÂCLE

1897

I HAVE already noted in the previous chapter that at the time of my leaving Peshawar on the afternoon of May 10, 1897, the horizon of Khyber politics was unclouded and bright. After years of patient work, and without any aid in force from Government, the roads, season after season, had been repaired, the military posts kept in excellent serviceable order, a large fortified serai, and a kafila one had been built up at Landi Kotal and the water supply in the Khyber and at Landi Kotal had been satisfactorily provided for. A reservoir had been made at Yakh-Chena, 14,000 to 20,000 gallons was the daily supply given out by this means in the exceedingly dry season of 1888, when measured by Lieutenant (now Lieutenant-Colonel) Macdonald, R.E. Malik Amin Khan's movement had been crushed in 1892, but he had been given another chance to do us mischief if the Sniders of his victims had not maimed him for ever. The Maliks who had helped in his ruin were themselves sufferers by the course of events. I knew that a British officer could have been taken to Chora, the Bazàr and Bara Valleys, and even up to Tirah, but the Commissioner of the Peshawar Division had written that neither I nor my subordinates were to go to either side of the Khyber Road without permission obtained from certain authorities. Anything that we wanted done on the Khyber Road or from ten to fifteen miles on the North towards the Caubul River could have been accomplished and carried out with as much ease as if in the Peshawar Valley. British and Indian life and property were as safe in the Khyber as in any part of the Panjab Province. When the Afridis and I parted on the railway platform that afternoon the salt tax, the Samana occupation, were matters unheard of. And it was a question which never troubled the Afridi mind once he had realised the fact that we held the Samana in order to prevent Orakzai thieves and raiders stealing and carrying away Bangash property, and not with the sinister object of invading and annexing his beloved Tirah. The complaint regarding their women still rankled in some minds, but the numbers were so few that pressure in this matter was by no means great. There were about 2,500 Afridis in the service of the British Government, distributed amongst the various regiments, corps, and police, who were permitted to enlist men of this class. I believe that in this lot the men of the Khyber Rifles who were Afridis were not included. Then there were several hundreds who enjoyed monthly pensions for long years of good and meritorious service, and last of all came the Khyber allowances. The reader may then ask, since the Afridis had been loaded with kindness and had no real grievance against the British and Indian Governments, how came it that they were induced to rise and attack the posts in the Khyber Pass, and by their own voluntary act bring on the unequal war which ended in the invasion of their lands, the destruction of their forts, and the ruin of their country's prestige? The Afridi boast that no conqueror had ever dared to force his way into Tirah cannot now be maintained. I give the cause of the revolt as I heard it and as it was communicated to me in writing, but whether it is correct and right in every detail I shall not discuss here.

The circumstances which had plunged Greece into a war against Turkey, and the abuse showered in England on the Sultan of Turkey, had caused deep annoyance and indignation in the heart of many Muhammadans, but this indignation was centred at Constantinople and in those cities where the Sunni faith was in the ascendant, and to which places news was conveyed rapidly as to what was said and done in certain capitals of Europe. The wild man of the independent hills on the Peshawar Border was ill-informed on such matters, and what was more he did not in the least care. His daily life was one of ceaseless labour to provide for the wants of his family and to save enough money to buy some day a Martini-Henry rifle; and this life he was perfectly satisfied with and content to live. The wise men of Constantinople, then smarting under the abuse heaped on the successor of the Prophet, looked round to see what countries they could turn against for this wrong, and whichever way they viewed the matter there were only three Governments that had Mussulman neighbours and subjects, and in this case the sole offender was that Power which has the greatest number of Muhammadan subjects. And so, at the end of May 1897, reports were circulated at Peshawar that an agent from Constantinople had reached Caubul, had interviewed the ruler of the 'God granted

Kingdom,' who had sent for all the noted Mullahs in his country, had introduced them to this agent, and after telling them to go to their homes and preach a religious war (*Ghazà*) to their people and secure one out of every eight males as reservists for his army, had permitted them to leave. The agent from Constantinople—possibly sent by the 'Ulema' alone without the Sultan's knowledge, and instructed by word of mouth, with no letter of introduction—may have reached Caubul early in May, as it takes news about fourteen days to reach Peshawar by kafilas, and it was at the end of May that this information reached those who were loyal enough to forward it to me. The ruler of Afghanistan had periodically for a series of years been constantly warning his people to prepare for a *Ghazà*, so that at this juncture, by preaching this religious cry, he was merely carrying out an old pastime of his which he had played twelve or thirteen years before without doing much damage.

It was about this period that Sipah Salar Gholam Hyder Khan, Charkhi, who had had his final interview with the Commissioner of the Peshawar Division (Sir R. Udny) at Landi Khana regarding the Mohmand-Bajawar demarcation, was encamped at Jelallabad. The *émeute* at Asmar between the two regiments had not yet taken place; this occurred later on, necessitating his hurried journey to Asmar. Sayad Akbar, Akhundzada of the Aka Khels, now turned up at Jelallabad, and Gholam Hyder Khan went with bare feet to the edge of his camp to meet him, and brought the Akhundzada with great respect and dignity into his own tent. There is nothing on record to show why Sayad Akbar went on this journey; whether he was invited by written or verbal invitation. All that he gave out was that he was bound on a pilgrimage to the ziarat of Mehtar Lam in the Laghman Valley, just two or three miles south of Tigrī. The Sipah Salar treated the Sayad for three days with great hospitality and kindness, and at the time of his departure presented him with 300 rupees. When Sayad Akbar, after doing his pilgrimage, returned to Jelallabad *en route* to his own country, he found that Gholam Hyder Khan had been forced to hurry away to Asmar on account of the fight between the two regiments of the Amir's army. So he journeyed back to the Bara Valley to his home in Warān, without having a second interview or meeting with the Sipah Salar. But there was nothing to prevent his being in daily or weekly communication with the Sipah Salar, the 'Mullah of Hadda,' or the 'Mad Fakir' of Swat, during the whole of June, July, and the greater part of August 1897. There were hundreds of 'Talibs' available, quite ready to go on this or any service under the orders of their head; the service might have been merely to carry a verbal message, and food and shelter were available for them at any place where there happened to be a mosque. In that quarter of the world messages of import are generally sent by word of mouth. A man will write to his dearest friend in words like these: 'I am sending this by hand of So-and-so, who will tell you verbally what I want you to do.' This sort of procedure leaves no evidence to grapple with once a great mischief has been produced. It is the system which has been adopted on all occasions by the Arbab and middleman of the Panjab N.W. Frontier.

It is impossible to note here on what grounds and by whom Sayad Akbar was selected for this special *rôle* of raising up the Afridis and Orakzais against the British Government. Of the three chief Mullahs amongst the Afridis he ranked lowest in every way in the estimation of the tribesmen. He was known to be grasping and fond of money, and had taken an active part in trying to unite the Aka Khel, so as to extract from the numerically weak Sipah Afridis a portion of their Khyber allowances, the Aka Khel themselves having no share in that arrangement. He had taken the side of Malik Sher Muhammad Sipah, who was trying to put into his own pocket the share which he should have given entirely to his fellow tribesmen. It was an open secret in the Bara Valley that he had committed these two acts, not for the sake of religion, but to grab good solid rupees. The building of a magnificent house for himself in Warān, which took three years in its completion, was another proof of his selfish nature. He only troubled himself with worldly matters, leaving the service of the Prophet and the progress of Islam to the other two spiritual leaders. These facts lost him a good deal of *status* amongst the 'grey beards,' the wiser portion of the jirgas, which constitute the strength of any tribe. At the weekly prayers held in the simple, unostentatious mosque at Bagh, situated in the Malikdin Khel quarter of the Maidan of Tirah, which was the meeting-place of seven tribes of the Afridis, representing an armed populace of some 20,000 fighting men, the man who commanded the greatest respect and whose voice secured the closest attention and obedience was the venerable Mullah (Mauzoon) of the Malikdin Khel Afridis. He was an old man, whose life had been spent in prayer and in telling the wild Afridi the way he should walk in this life, and this Mullah seldom or ever interfered in worldly matters. At the period that Amin Khan spent all his money in 1892 to win the Mullahs to his side and bribe them to get up an Afridi rising for Amin Khan's cause against the British, I was in communication with the old Malikdin Khel Mullah, and he wrote to me saying that he would never countenance Amin Khan's action in any way. Afterwards the old Mullah's son used to visit me at Peshawar, and we met for the last time just before my leaving on May 10, 1897. The family were interested in keeping up friendship with the 'Sarkar,' so far as a Mullah could be depended on for doing so. At all events, in case any real trouble was about to be hatched, they had promised to warn me of it in ample time. So little was Sayad Akbar liked and respected that at that period, in May 1897, and for some years before, it was never believed that he could secure a joint rising of Afridis and Orakzais. All that was recognised about him was that he was young in age, excessively fond of money and power, and that the Afridis called him behind his back a 'Loe Shaitan.'

It is not possible to say with any amount of certainty whether the preaching of the *Ghazà* was to be carried out at one and the same time in Waziristan, in Tirah, amongst the Mohmands, and by the 'Mad Fakir' in the Swat Valley, so that the rising should be simultaneous from Maizàr in the Tochi Valley to Chakdarra and Malakand. It is believed that the Wazir Mullah Pawindah, was at Caubul during May, but at the same time we knew for certain that the 'Hadda Mullah' would never venture into the capital of Afghanistan. This old gentleman—who lived a quiet, religious, God-fearing life at his native village Hadda, about five miles from Jelallabad, during the winter of 1879–80—in no way attempted to raise his hand against the soldiers of the British Government when I was there with General Sir R. Bright's force. But in 1883, when the Amir came to spend the winter in the Jelallabad District, the holy man, in mortal terror of his life, fled to Jarobi in the Mohmand country. He had evidently committed some act hostile to the ruler of Afghanistan which the public knew nothing about, but which the ruler had been apprised of, for the Mullah for fifteen years has persistently refused all overtures of a friendly nature to enter Afghan territory and place himself in the power of the Afghan officials. On the other hand, since 1883 he has been a persistent and vindictive enemy of a Government that never caused him directly or indirectly an iota of injury until the invasion of the Mohmand country by our forces subsequent to the events at Shabkaddar in August 1897. It was not difficult or impossible from Jelallabad and Asmar to be in touch with Sayad Akbar in Tirah, the 'Hadda Mullah' at Jarobi, and the 'Mad Fakir' in Swat; so that if a combined move in all three quarters was required, it might, under favourable circumstances, have been executed nearly simultaneously within a period of seven days. But the facts show that it was at least fourteen days after the 'Mad Mullah's' first advance against Malakand and Chakdarra that the Mohmand gathering, urged on by the 'Mullah of Hadda,' descended into the plains of the Peshawar Valley and made its attack on Shabkaddar on August 9. And it was on the 22nd, nearly fourteen days later, that the Afridi lashkar appeared at Lala Chena and commenced the attack on the posts of Shadi Bagiar, Jehangira, Fort Maud on the following day. When these posts had been secured and burnt then they moved westwards to concentrate their attention on Fort Ali Masjid. It may be accepted, therefore, that there is no proof of any attempt having been made to raise the border from Maizar round northwards to the Swat Valley in one combined movement against us. The 'Mad Mullah' made his attack, and when he found that he could not succeed he applied to the priest of Hadda for help, and that gentleman in his turn sent messengers to Sayad Akbar, asking him to co-operate and make a diversion with a joint lashkar of Afridis and Orakzais.

Whether Sayad Akbar was in unison with the Sipah Salar Gholam Hyder Khan, or with any other official of the Afghan Government, in bringing up this Afridi-Orakzai gathering there is no proof of a reliable sort beyond intelligence brought down by word of mouth; but news of this nature can never be trusted. Some may deny even his journey to the ziarat of Mehtar Lam in Laghman, and his meeting with Gholam Hyder Khan at Jelallabad during the month of May 1897. To this one answer might be given, which is that unless the 'Hadda Mullah' or some of his principal supporters had met and seen Sayad Akbar in Jelallabad, or had been previously acquainted with him in some way, there was no reason why an appeal should have been made to the least influential and weakest of the three noted Afridi Mullahs to preach a religious war amongst

Afridis and Orakzais, and induce them to combine against the powerful British Government.

I heard from friends who were in Peshawar during that month of August 1897 that it was not until after the Shabkaddar incident of August 9 that news came down from Tirah of agitation by Mullahs, urging the Afridis and Orakzais to commence war against the British Power. But even with this agitation, our men on leave were allowed to come and go freely to and from Tirah, and no visible pressure was brought on them for being in the service of our Government. On August 13 I had been invited to the house of General Sir G. Wolseley, K.C.B., Commanding the Forces, Panjab, who was anxious to learn news from the direction of the Khyber, and, returning home at sunset, I found an urgent State telegram from the Foreign Secretary to the Government of India worded thus: 'If Government proposed to re-employ you specially with reference to Afridi affairs, would you be willing?' My answer was: 'Ready for any Government service if required.' And to make sure that my reply should be sent off that very night, I despatched it by the hands of my orderly, and received his report on his return that my instructions had been carried out, and the receipt from the telegraph office delivered to me. But a week, or rather eight days, passed, and all endeavours to get news from Peshawar or Fort Jamrud ended in failure. At last came the fatal August 22, when the Afridi 'lashkar,' moving along the same route as the Afridi 'lashkars' of 1878 and 1892, appeared in the country to the south of Lala Chena. It was then that the impertinent message was sent asking that the British troops be cleared out of the Samana and the Malakand, the salt tax to be lowered, and their women to be restored; which conditions being carried out the Afridi gathering would return to their homes. I believe this message never came from the Afridis, but was sent by some rascally Mullah, and that the assembly were afraid to tell the truth about it.

I shall say nothing here that may help to re-open old sores and create fresh pangs. A certain policy has been carried out by the Supreme Government, and to that policy every servant of State must bow so long as he remains in the service of Government. But there can be no objection in writing what I am now doing. Before going to Tirah I had opportunities of seeing Afridi native officers at Rawal Pindi, at Kohat, and in Tirah itself, and when we came down to Jamrud all the negotiations with the Afridis, except those with the Akha Khels, were entirely in my hands from January 1 to April 5, 1898. I had therefore opportunities of conversing with and interviewing some thousands of men. Those that I questioned said, 'their lashkar had not come down to fight the Sarkar.' 'Then what made you come down?' 'The Mullahs brought us down.' 'Why did you obey the Mullahs, and why did you not turn them out of your country?' 'They were too powerful for us.' 'Had you any real grievance against the British Government to induce you to fight against it?' 'No, we had not.' 'Then why did you attack the posts?' 'The Mullahs forced us.' This may appear rank falsehood, but, knowing the power of the priestly class in a Muhammadan country, I look to the report brought down by Malik Amin Khan, Kuki Khel, on August 17, and it appears worded in Sir R. Udny's telegram to Government in this fashion: 'Malik has just reached Peshawar in person, but with no following, and reports that Afridi lashkar, said to be ten thousand strong, accompanied by fifteen hundred Mullahs from Ningrahar, started from Bagh, Tirah, yesterday morning to attack Khyber Road and posts from Landi Kotal downwards. This lashkar was to reach Bazàr Valley to-day and the Khyber to-morrow, and consists of all Afridi clans connected with Khyber Road, except Kuki Khel, who are holding entirely aloof.' If the above report was true and not exaggerated, regarding the fifteen hundred Mullahs from Ningrahar, or if Sayad Akbar was assisted by only three hundred of this priestly class, then no Afridi could have dared to object openly joining with this lashkar and coming down with it on to the Khyber Road. What they expected us to do, or what they hoped might be done, to avert the catastrophe that followed, and to save them from a war with a Power whose might they know only too well, must be left to the regions of imagination. We were in for what I had laboured all my years and by every means in my power to avert—a great Afridi war.

The 'Khyber *Débâcle*' and the burning down of our forts and posts was followed by the Orakzais attacking their quarter of the Kohat District, and by the 15th of the following month the aspect of affairs had been changed into an Afridi-Orakzai war.

By this time General Sir William Lockhart was on his way from England to take command of the forces that had been told off for the punishment of the Orakzai and Afridi tribes. Thanks to his powerful and strenuous representations, I was fortunate enough to be appointed to his political staff in the Tirah expedition. I am convinced that without his intervention on my behalf I should not have shared in that campaign. This telegram reached me: 'Simla, September 29, from Foreign, 3697 F. General Sir William Lockhart has asked that you be appointed to his political staff in the Tirah Expedition, on which Sir Richard Udny is chief political officer. If you are willing to serve, please let Sir William Lockhart and me know, and arrange directly with Sir William as to joining him. I shall then settle the question of pay and of your re-employment.' Sir William Lockhart and his Chief of the Staff, General W. G. Nicholson, had arrived a couple of days before at Murree from Simla, so I hastened to Sir William at once to thank him for his goodness and to await his orders. I also replied to the Foreign Department accepting the position. I journeyed to Kohat, which was reached on October 7, and I was at Kahi on the 18th of that month, when the first attack on Dargai took place. We reached Shenawari on the 19th, and the next day, field-glass in hand, I witnessed the whole panorama of fight, which meant the second attack on Dargai. It was 10 A.M. as the first gun on our side opened fire, and five minutes to 3 P.M. when the bayonets of our men on the heights of Dargai told of the capture of that place after a stubborn fight of five hours. The combatants looked so near at hand that, with a good powerful glass, the different attacks could be plainly and easily discerned. My attention was often drawn to the left of the enemy's position near 'Narikh Sukka' (to our right as we looked in that direction), where a figure in white was seen standing on the ridge and waving his 'lungi' at intervals. My own opinion was that this figure in white was a Mullah, who had placed himself in a prominent position to watch our advance and give warning when the rushes were made. He was seen in the same position for a very long time by myself and others, although he was not visible to the batteries firing from the plateau. What became of him eventually none of us could tell. His behaviour, however, was admirable and brave to a degree.

The Sampaga Pass was stormed on October 29, and the Arhanga captured two days later, and on the last day of October 1897 three brigades of the Tirah Expeditionary Force were encamped in the Maidan of Tirah. As we expected to remain for a few days, we did what we could to make ourselves comfortable by digging down a foot or so inside our tents to shelter ourselves from the wind, and to secure a place where it was possible to eat our meals under tolerable cover. The days were certainly fairly warm and sunshiny, but the nights and mornings were intensely cold. The thermometer showed twenty-one degrees of frost on some nights, and water in the washing basins outside the tent was frozen to a thickness of two and a half inches during the night. If I who lived in very tolerable comfort, with a small tent over me and sufficiency of clothing at night, felt the intense cold, what must have been the condition of the officer, soldier, European or native, who was out on night duty, whether in camp or on the heights surrounding us, or the feeling of the camp followers from Central and Eastern India who had never before felt such weather? Luckily rain, which meant snow in those high regions, kept away, and during our residence at Maidan and Bagh we hardly had a cloudy day, the forerunner of wet weather on the North-Western Frontier of India. For a few days the camp was annoyed by prowlers firing indiscriminately into it. On the 9th about thirty-one representatives from the Afridis came in to interview us, and I went across the ravine to a large building which had been set apart for their accommodation. One old man of about seventy, who at one period of his existence had been in the ranks of some regiment of our native army, was kind enough to say to me, 'With the exception of your field-guns, which we have not, man to man we are as good as any of you.' But there was no exaltation in the minds and appearance of any Afridis that it was my luck to interview and converse with during the campaign. In the first batch that came in were four to five of our old pensioners, each man with three or four medals pinned on to his left shoulder or slung round his neck, records of twenty to twenty-five years of devotion and service to the *Sarkar* in all parts of the world—Egypt, Tel-el-Kebir, Suakim. Were these the men who wanted to bring on an Afridi war against England? Their small pensions were the stand-by of their homes in their old age, to secure which they journeyed twice a year to Peshawar, and every Afridi envied these old veterans. Their faces showed pain and sorrow, for they and the whole nation were about to suffer for the fault and mischief of a rascally Mullah.

On November 13 General Kempster's brigade was sent into Warān Tirah, and I was directed to proceed with it, and did so, taking five of the Aka Khel Afridi jirga. Our route lay by the foot of the southern spur from the Saràn-Sar Range, which was well covered with fir trees, through the Tseri-Kandao (*tseri*, oak; *kandao*, pass) or Oak Pass, belonging to the Zya-ud-din Zakha Khels. Why it is called the Oak Pass I cannot understand, for there is but one solitary tree of that species, cut across at a height of some fifteen feet, giving the trunk enormous umbrageous branches. There was one very lofty stone-built tower here, visible from the furthest parts of Maidan, belonging to Mir Osman, a man who acted as one of our informers for over a dozen years, and who was one of the first to be shot down by the Khyber Rifles when Landi Kotal was attacked on August 24. Below the dip, on the left-hand side of the goat's track leading to Warān, lay the sixty or seventy huts of that most thieving community the Zya-ud-din Zakha Khels. The next day I had the pleasure of being introduced to Sayad Akbar's palatial house, which had taken three years to build. Alongside of it was an enormous mosque. As I looked at it a wicked thought came to mind, and I asked myself, 'Why was there not someone to shoot this man down before he had caused so much mischief?' Our hospital assistant, who was secured by the Afridis after the fall of Landi Kotal, told me at Jamrud that at one period of the attack Sayad Akbar came close to the wall to make some address during a lull, when a young Zakha Khel in the Khyber Rifles, turning to his chief's rascally son, said, 'Here is Sayad Akbar; let me shoot him and end this business for good and ever.' Malik Khwas Khan's son abused and struck the soldier, calling out, 'Would you destroy the light of Islam?'

November 16 saw us returning to Maidan, and by

midday I was at Tseri-Kandao, and heard Colonel Abbott, commanding the 15th Sikhs, talking with General Kempster. When I joined the last-named officer at the spot where the Zakha Khel hamlets commenced due south of the gun-tree position on the Saràn-Sar ascent, we felt assured that the Afridis meant business. At intervals of fifteen yards or so, never together, man after man was seen coming down wearing the flat skull cap, the pyjamas knotted at the knee, and the rifle carried in the usual way, and all disappearing behind a projecting hillock far up on the ascent.

November 19 saw the Headquarter Camp moved to Bagh, and two days later, at 6 P.M., intimation was conveyed to me that I was to proceed on the morrow with Sir William and part of the Headquarter Staff, and Fourth Brigade, to Dwa-Toe. About 8 A.M. on November 22 Sir William with his staff started down this defile, and a very raw cold evening was setting in when, after wading some seventy times through icy-cold water, we at length reached the tower on the right bank of the Bara stream which marks and gives the name (*dwa*, two; *toe*, streams) to the junction of the Bara and the overflow from Bagh. We soon found our camp, but our kit did not arrive till 3 P.M. the next day. A good Samaritan in that grand regiment, the King's Own Scottish Borderers, dragged me over to his mess and gave me a cup of cocoa and some food. The guard of the 3rd Sikhs cooked some bread, and from their slender stock brought what they could for the wants of the officers of the Headquarter Staff. All that night, with the thermometer something like 20° below freezing-point, Annesley and I lay to the leeward of a roaring fire, trying to warm ourselves from the icy-cold wind blowing hard from the snow-clad Safed-Koh. There was no rest for any of us that night, and gradually one by one all came and sat round the fire, and waited there till daybreak.

The officers of the K.O.S.B. gave me some breakfast, and by 3 P.M. our things were in and we had a good lunch. But by evening time the enemy got possession of a peak, from which they plumped three bullets into our fire, which then had to be put out. However, the night of the 23rd passed under better circumstances than the previous one. On the 24th we journeyed back to Bagh, a strong wind blowing down this detestable, diabolical defile; and so cold was it that the rushing water froze on my pony's feet and flanks wherever it touched the animal. It was with some difficulty that I could induce him to face the water. If a strong hardy animal smarted under this cold, what must have been the feelings of the dooley-bearers and the drivers, who had lived all their lives in a warm climate? I myself was compelled to get off, and for warmth's sake take to the path which went up the hill on the right-hand side, but the country and the path were on a par. Just before leaving Dwa-Toe that morning Lord Methuen had kindly given me four or five small biscuits, and told me to put them into my pocket as they might be of use on the journey back. Walking up that bad road I came upon two or three men of the K.O.S.B. who were on baggage guard, and offered the biscuits to one who seemed to be in charge of the party. Breaking each into four small portions, he gave one bit (hardly a bite) to each of the escort, calling up the rest who were in front to share. It was a generous, unselfish act on his part, for he might have put the lot into his pocket, no one being a bit the wiser. The road was, as I have said, very bad, but when I was in difficulties over a nasty bit of ground these men came back a hundred yards to give me a helping hand.

Sir W. Lockhart returned to Bagh on December 6 from his trip to the Champ Kanni country, and orders were issued for the Second Division to march to Dwa-Toe again on the 7th and remain there on December 8 and 9. This time there was no opposition until Dwa-Toe was reached, and for three days and two nights not a shot was fired in the defile. The Kuki Khel, who had promised to meet us at Dwa-Toe with their jirga and hand over as much of their fine in rifles and cash as they possibly could, were led astray at the last moment by emissaries from the Sangu Khel Shinwari country. So they met us as enemies instead of as friends, and suffered for it severely in consequence.

December 10 saw us marching down the Bara Valley, the Fourth Brigade in advance, whilst the third took up the *rôle* of rear guard, and our halt was at Sandana in Sipah Afridi-Bara. Clouds had gathered round, concealing the mountain tops, and slight rain fell during the night, making it extremely unpleasant for those who had no shelter. The morning of the 11th, sunless and chilly, saw us marching through the Zakha Khel country to Sher Khel Killi in the limits of the Aka Khel, and here we halted for the 11th and 12th to enable the brigade to come up. My native assistant, Sayad Secunder Shah, had a very narrow escape on the 10th, and I was very anxious about him, as he was the son of a man who had done a lot of good work for Cavagnari and other Deputy Commissioners of Kohat, as well as for myself. During a halt one Lee-Metford bullet wounded two men in a group near where we were, a second removed the button from the helmet of a Gordon signaller, and a third, fired by the same marksman, hit Secunder Shah, as he was talking to me, on the right side, and passed out at his back, a quarter of an inch from the spine. It was a miraculous escape, and, fortunately for him, it was an old bullet and not the new 'Dum-Dum' pattern. We were at the time under the cover of a high bank, and had no conception from where the bullets came or from what quarter the Afridi marksman fired his rifle. This is one of the advantages of your rifle with the smokeless powder falling into the hands of Jack Afridi, to be used against you in his own highlands. You are made to feel the bullet long before you hear the crack of the rifle. That night of the 11th, and the swamp in front of and close to our camp to the north side, will long be remembered by those who shared in the march down the Bara River.

The Third Brigade now took the lead, followed by the Fourth, and after crossing and recrossing the river time after time, we turned up the left bank, and encamped in a waterless region known as Narkandai: this was on December 13. The Fourth Brigade were engaged in a stubborn fight until sunset, and it was here that Sergeant Walker, of the R.S. Fusiliers, fell into the hands of the Afridis. The next day we again marched down to the river, and, crossing it twice, passed through General Hammond's brigade encamped at Sewikot, and pitched our own tents a mile further on and nearer to Peshawar. The enemy clung to the rearguard until it was clear of the hills. Here we remained resting on December 14, 15, and 16, and on the morning of the 17th I suffered the first loss of property during my eighteen years' experience in the Khyber—my baggage pony, a charger belonging to Colonel Barrow, a pony of Captain Swanstone's, and some mules ridden by signallers, having been appropriated by some clever Afridi thieves. On the 17th we moved to Bara, and after a few days' grace the First Division was concentrated at Ali Masjid on December 24. I had there the pleasure of being introduced to General Sir H. Havelock Allan, who arrived at Lala Chena that evening. Sir W. Lockhart was going with his staff and General Gaselee's brigade to Chora, whilst General Symons and General Hart, V.C., with the First Brigade, were to proceed by Ilacha, and spend Christmas Day at Karamna. At the last moment I was directed to proceed with the Karamna column. The journey to Karamna was a trying one, as the road was very bad, and it was late in the evening when we reached our goal. General Hart with the rearguard, however, did not come in till midday on the 26th. Luckily the march to Barg, down a difficult defile, was not more than three miles, and by sunset of the 26th the whole brigade was united. Our encamping ground was a beautiful spot with a clear stream of running water, and well covered hills to the east and south, just the place suitable for Afridi sharpshooters, but happily we were not much troubled by them. We remained at Barg till the morning of the 28th, when we retraced our steps to Karamna, and I passed an exceedingly trying day with fever and ague on me. The rain, too, kept pouring down till the time of our departure for Ali Masjid, which was reached about 1 P.M. on the 29th. The enemy was as active as ever, and followed up our rearguard to within 2,000 yards of the camp. The usual Ali Masjid wind was blowing a tornado down the Pass, and the flapping of the tents made our rest unpleasant; but the next morning repaid us, for with a clear sky overhead and no wind to trouble anyone we marched to Jamrud and took up our quarters there until the Afridis complied with the orders of Government. Those who could and were permitted to depart, bade farewell to the regions of the Khyber Range. I went into Peshawar about midday on December 31, but had been barely there two hours when an urgent State telegram was handed to me informing me that Sir Havelock Allan was missing, and that I was to proceed at once to Ali Masjid to make inquiries as to what had become of him, and if found alive to bring him back. However, before my tonga had passed the limits of Peshawar Cantonments *en route* to Jamrud I met another tonga, under a cavalry escort, carrying in the dead body of the unfortunate General. I continued my journey to Jamrud, whence in due time I reported for the information of Sir William Lockhart all that I could learn regarding the death of the gallant officer.

I had done the whole of the Tirah campaign on foot (except about three miles through water on horseback) and the result was that I enjoyed most excellent health whilst we were on the move. Now my duties at Jamrud confined me to a small room and the Afridi jirgas. There was no rest from 6 A.M. till 12 midnight. I did my utmost to prevent a spring campaign, for I knew that if one was necessary it would last to the following November, costing millions in money and many lives. My whole thoughts and energies were therefore devoted to the establishment of a permanent peace. All the native Afridi officers from the various regiments, who had come up to Jamrud to assist me, especially Subadar Major Yasin Khan, all the headmen and jirgas of the various Afridi tribes, Captain Barton, my native assistant, Secunder Shah, all worked might and main to give me a helping hand towards this object. General Symons, commanding the First Division Tirah Expeditionary Force, and Generals Gaselee and Hart, commanding the Second and First Brigades, rendered every support. What with threats on the one hand and honest earnest exertions of the elders of the tribe on the other, the wished for result ensued on April 2, 1898, the Afridi fine in rifles and cash was paid up, and the spring campaign prevented just in the nick of time. It was the exertions of others which produced this happy result. Without such exertions my work would have been in vain.

I have no desire to write a word on the military portion of the Tirah campaign, for that is a subject I do not pretend to criticise. But para. 2 of the Special Order, dated Camp Peshawar, April 4, 1898, puts the matter admirably.

From the beginning of October to the middle of January the Force was engaged in active operations, and seldom have troops been called upon to undergo greater fatigue, or to meet a more vigilant and enterprising enemy. After long marches in cold and wet, harassed by distant rifle-fire and by assaults at close quarters, the columns bivouacked in positions which had to be protected by numerous strong picquets posted on commanding heights, and those picquets were always liable to determined attacks,

SIR ROBERT WARBURTON, LIEUT.-COL. ASLAM KHAN, OFFICERS AND SOWARS KHYBER RIFLES.

and to molestation in withdrawal. There was, in fact, little or no rest for the Force, the most careful chosen camping ground being generally open to long range fire from scattered individual marksmen, armed with the most accurate weapons.

The Tirah campaign brought out the finest qualities of the British officer and British soldier, and of their companions of the Native Army and Imperial Troops. And this campaign made me respect the Afridi greatly, not only as enemies but as friends also. I had good reason to do so. From the first week in October 1897 to April 5, 1898, I had with me four Afridi orderlies from the Khyber Rifles who acted also as guides or scouts, and were continually being requisitioned for that purpose. All proved faithful and loyal, although working against their own countrymen. One of them broke down from pneumonia, but the others continued to do the trying and perilous duties required of them. They would often go out of their own accord to gather information, and frequently returned with their clothes riddled with bullet holes, proofs of the wonderful escapes they had had. When it is remembered that they were literally carrying their lives hourly in their hands, and knew the cruel certain fate which awaited them if they were taken prisoners, I do not think that I exaggerate in saying that such loyalty to the Sarkar deserved recognition, and that no men better earned the Victoria Cross or the Military Order of Merit than these. But they got nothing.

The true political history of the campaign could only be written by one man—Sir William Lockhart, who commanded the Tirah Expeditionary Force. Without his express sanction I would not venture to trespass on such ground. I have had the privilege of knowing my chief for thirty-one years, since we first met in Abyssinia in 1868. However much I respected and honoured him as a soldier and as a General, this campaign of 1897–1898 has in my mind doubly endeared him to all who had the privilege of closely watching and knowing what he did and what he had to go through. With sincere thanks to him, to General Sir W. G. Nicholson, Colonel Barrow, Captain Haldane, and all the Headquarter Staff who so helped me in my labours, I close my contribution to the 'Khyber *Débâcle*' and its consequences.

CHAPTER XIX

FRONTIER POLICY

1898

It is surely time to look back, and ask whether the present Panjab policy as regards Hazara, Peshawar, Kohat, Bannu, Dera Ismail Khan, and Dera Ghazi Khan, excluding the Cis-Indus portions of Bannu and Dera Ismail Khan, and which is the same policy with little alteration which was introduced when these districts came into our hands on the fall of the great Sikh power, has answered the purpose intended and should continue to be maintained? Or has it been a failure for years? A third question might be put also: Has the Panjab policy, or the so-called Forward policy, been the cause of our numerous, costly, and exhausting wars on the North-Western Frontier?

When the Sikh power advanced into Hazara and crossed the Indus, it came into contact with a race of men belonging to the Muhammadan faith, who at one time regarded themselves as conquerors, and who despised and loathed the now powerful Khalsa community. The Sikh, in return for this antipathy was not the sort of individual who willingly offered his cheek to the Afghan or Pathan smiter, and he returned a blow by one somewhat harder, or by an act of revenge—one generally of stern retribution. What the Sikhs did in the city and district of Peshawar during the period of their rule, under men like General Avitabili and others, is known only to the very few survivors of those days, but the effect of their harsh rule was to bring into the field against them men like Syad Ahmad Shah, the head and founder of the Hindustani Fanatics, and to fill the independent hills in certain localities with enemies—men of influence and position—around whom rallied all the Mullahs and disaffected rascals in the district. The Sikhs on their part, later on, were compelled to employ Arbabs or middlemen as go-betweens and farmers of revenue. The last measure often saved them from having to move out a force when the harvests were being gathered in, in order to secure the quota of revenue due from some distant powerful and recalcitrant village close to the independent borderland. Of this Arbab class was Mir Babu of Chargullai, a leading man of the Sudum Valley, bordering on the powerful Buner country—the father of Ajab Khan, whose career and ultimate fate has already been described in a previous chapter.

When we broke the Sikh power, and took from them the districts which constitute Hazara and those across the Indus, we took also upon our shoulders, for the time being, all the heritage of antipathy and hatred which Syad Ahmad Shah's descendants, the Mullah leaders, and refugee notables had for the cruel Sikh. We were on trial, and the Afghan war of 1839–42 was not forgotten, but hung in the balance against our record.

Fortunately for the Panjab and the North-Western Frontier—by which name I always mean here Hazara, Peshawar, Kohat, Bannu, and the Trans-Indus portions of Bannu and Dera Ismail

Khan, also Dera Ghazi Khan—there happened to be at that time alive and in considerable power a great and good man, known as Sir Henry Lawrence. Not only was he personally and privately good, and officially a great man, but he had the marvellous instinct of selecting for positions of trust and importance the most able and capable men as subordinates; and having made his selection, he gave such officers his very greatest confidence, and advanced their interests with might and main whenever and whereever he had an opportunity of doing so. No success, however great, on the part of a junior officer created any pang of jealousy in the heart of this singularly pure-minded gentleman. The greater the success or repute, the more did the heart of Sir Henry Lawrence rejoice.

It was to this wise instinct of selection that Frederick Mackeson, Herbert Edwardes, James Abbott, George Lawrence, John Nicholson, Harry Lumsden, and others, were placed on duty on the frontier at a time when great men were wanted there in order to meet and to overcome difficulties with a tight and yet a kindly hand. Mackeson's reputation had been made during the first Afghan war, and he was in fame perhaps the greatest Englishman who ever served on that frontier. I go by native evidence and opinion, which is always a good standard to judge by, and the name and character of Mackeson are at this moment as fresh on the Peshawar Border and the Khyber Range as if he had passed away but yesterday. Yet Frederick Mackeson died over forty-five years ago, and his history has not been written either by one of his own countrymen or by an Asiatic, to recall what he did, and how he acted, and how he made himself loved and respected by the robber clans and tribesmen of the Khyber. James Abbott was another modest, good, great man. His control of the Hazara District at a period when the Sikh power was up in arms against the authority of John Company is well known. In 1857 the tribesmen of the Black Mountain, at the request of Colonel Beecher, turned on the Sepoy mutineers, who, escaping from Mardan before the furious attack of General John Nicholson, had taken shelter in Swat, in Bunnu, and had crossed the river Indus to the left bank. These Sepoys were either killed, or driven back across the river, or handed over as prisoners to the British authorities. James Abbott's influence over the Hazara mountaineers caused them to attack our enemies and treat them in this fashion. Let anyone now go and ask whether the procedure and rule of the later Panjab school of Deputy Commissioners in Hazara could produce a similar result amongst the tribes of the Black Mountain.

In 1897, after the fall of the Khyber Pass into the hands of the Mullah Afridi 'lashkar,' and the burning and destruction of all our posts, forts, serais, &c., I happened to be walking one morning from Kuldanna to the post office at Murree. Two very old men were walking ahead of me, and hearing the name Abbott repeated time after time, curiosity induced me to join in their conversation, and ask of whom they were talking and who they themselves were. They were both residents of the Hazara District, and one had been in the police at the time when James Abbott was Deputy Commissioner, and the second man had also been in the service in some other capacity. To my inquiries they both said, 'Abbott Sahib was loved in the district, and the old people reverence his memory even now.' The elder of the Hazaras then spoke of his own accord: 'Abbott Sahib's heart was like a fakir's; he was always thinking of and for his people.' Then besides Sir Herbert Edwardes, John Nicholson, Sir Harry Lumsden, there were others whose names I have omitted, who formed a body of officers selected for service on that newly conquered and lately annexed frontier, which could not have been produced by any other country in the wide, wide world.

In those days of rough and ready justice, before an extremely elaborate code and hair-splitting technicalities of law had been introduced into the Panjab, it was possible for a district officer to do his work, and in a way amalgamate with the people he was placed in charge over, and to learn what their wants and wishes were. If the residents of his district, or on his independent border, happened to belong to the Baluch race, who generally paid implicit obedience to their chiefs or Tumandars, then his work was comparatively easy; for all that he had to do was to win over the Tumandar, and his people would follow him, as a dog his master. But should the residents of his district be Pathans—and the independent hills are full of men of the turbulent race—the difficulties of his charge and position were enormously increased. He had then to win every man over, or a number of the ablest men, in every section of every tribe, and this was a matter which required enormous patience, good judgment, and time to accomplish. But in the olden days our splendid band of selected officers, having more command of time and power than falls to the lot of the district officer of later times, and being assisted in their trans-border work by Arbabs and middlemen whom they could supervise effectually, worked wonders in checking crime and bringing under proper control their troublesome districts. The harsh rule of the Sikh had been replaced by the kind, just, and firm government of John Company, carried out under the management of most capable officers, and one of the best signs of the change was seen in some eleven hundred men of the Malikdin Khel Afridis marching in to help one of our district officers against a common enemy. The same good sign was noticed at the commencement of our troubles in the great Indian Mutiny of 1857.

But from its first institution the Arbab or middleman system between the district officer and the trans-border tribesmen, was a mistake and should never have been continued. It might have answered for a period when the European official knew his work thoroughly and had time and power to control his agent, but this was not always possible. From its very origin it was an error to have allowed it, and as I go on I shall try and prove in a few words that from Agror round the border to the southernmost parts of the Kohat District, the middleman has been the cause of nearly every disagreement and of much of the bloodshed between the British Government and the savages of the Independent Hills.

In the first years of our rule on the North-West Frontier of the Panjab our district officers do not appear to have complained of overwork and want of time to mix with the people and learn their customs and ways. The system of procedure in those days was exceedingly simple and brief, and the work was done quickly, satisfactorily to the people, and without those endless appeals which the natives regard as an evil in these times. Then came the Mutiny, which unhinged for years the civil system of the province. When that catastrophe was tided over, and more peaceful times came in, then the lawyers commenced to pour in codes, enactments, procedure rules, &c., to torment the heart and mind of the frontier official; and then came the first growl from one of our ablest men (there may have been complaints before, but I have had no opportunity of seeing them), the late Major James, Commissioner of Peshawar about 1861–1864, which is given in para. 62 of the Reorganisation of the Frontier Minute by the late Lord Lytton, then Viceroy of India. It is dated April 22, 1877, and I give it here in full:

In the first place, then, I think it should be our aim to cultivate more direct and frequent intercourse than at present exists between ourselves and the tribes on our borders. I have already had occasion to observe more than once, what I cannot too often repeat in reference to this subject, that it is to the effect of the straightforward, upright, and disinterested action of English gentlemen, and to the influence which higher mental power and culture never fail to exert over those who are brought much in contact with them, rather than to superiority in fighting power and appliances, that I attribute British supremacy in India, as well as the exceptional success of British rule in all quarters of the globe. If personal character and influence be the powerful engines I believe them to be, it is desirable that their force should be exercised as constantly and directly as possible. For this among other reasons, I propose the appointment of a Chief Commissioner at Peshawar, invested with exceptionally high powers, who can represent to the native mind more directly and personally than either the Lieutenant-Governor at Lahore, or the still more distant Viceroy at Calcutta, the embodied power and dignity of the British

Government. For this reason, also, I propose to increase the administrative staff of divisions and districts, so that the Commissioners and Deputy Commissioners, relieved of much purely routine work, may have more time for visiting and becoming personally acquainted with their troublesome, but not hopelessly unmanageable, neighbours. I have before me now a minute by Major James, formerly Commissioner of Peshawar, in which, as the result of thirteen years' frontier experience, he expresses himself most strongly as to the absolute impossibility of combining a proper intercourse with the border tribes with the execution of his ordinary civil duties. The then Lieutenant-Governor and Lord Lawrence hinted, indeed, that this incompatibility of functions was Major James's own fault, yet from all quarters I hear Major James spoken of as one of the ablest and most active administrators the frontier has known, and one who, but for his untimely death, had a brilliant career before him.

Here we notice for the first time a complaint made by an exceedingly able man, a most competent and capable writer, the gentleman who carried out the first summary Revenue settlement of the Peshawar Valley, and wrote a history of its residents and neighbours which will always be a standard work of reference. Major James, Commissioner of the Peshawar Division at a very trying period, solemnly asserts that he could not carry on his ordinary civil duties and keep up a proper intercourse with the border tribes.

He wrote this evidently between 1860 and 1864. In those years the Chief Court of the Panjab had not been established at Lahore. The Civil and Criminal Procedure Codes, the Jail Manual and Prisons Act, Municipal Laws and Regulations, Revenue Act and Rules pertaining to the same, and the thousand and one other Acts, Regulations, and Rules, which now cling to the district officer with the tentacles of an octopus, had not been thrown into the Panjab. My experience of the Panjab dates prior to even 1862, the year in which I landed at Calcutta an officer in H.M. service, but I had no knowledge of civil and district work until I joined the Panjab Commission at Peshawar in July 1870. I presume that after Major James's death, which occurred in 1864, the work of the civil officer increased largely. That it has in no wise decreased since I can answer from my own experience. My whole time was fully taken up in learning my duties, carrying out my office work, and preparing for my examination. As to having any time to see and converse with the people of the district, or to have any intercourse with the independent tribes of the border, managed through our Peshawar Arbabs and middlemen, that was impossible. The short time I spent in Hazara—that splendid district created especially for Englishmen to journey about both in winter and summer—was fully occupied at head-quarters looking after the treasury and settling the petty claims of banniahs. When I was re-transferred to Peshawar, heavy murder files had to be tackled, and my position was no better. In the Yusufzai charge, which I held off and on for seven years, the Assistant Commissioner was hemmed in by heavy work and immense difficulties. The Gaduns and Khudu Khels were managed by a member of the Zaida family, and until he was turned out those men were not allowed to come near the Assistant Commissioner without the Khan's permission. Chamla and the Buner country were under the shelter of old Ajab Khan of Chargullai, and until he was hanged in 1878 I was only permitted to see men whom he chose to produce before me. Affairs pertaining to Swat were in the charge of a young Khan, who managed them so well that in 1877, thanks to his exertions, the Ottoman representatives who went to see the Akhund at Saidu were turned back and stoned, and taunted with being spies of the British Government. Later on, when we were on the verge of war with the late Amir Sher Ali Khan, a letter was written by this young reprobate to Sherdil Khan of Aladand, asking the Swatis to create a disturbance in their quarter. This letter was secured, and taken to the late Major Sir L. Cavagnari in 1878. The same middleman agency was employed in working the Utman Khels and the Mohmands. The Khalil Arbab had political charge of the Mullagoris, Afridi, and Shinwari tribes of the Khyber Range. The Mohmand chief looked after the Aka and Adam Khel Afridis. Bahadur Sher Khan, Bangash, had the Kohat Pass. The Khans of Hangu paid special attention to the Orakzai clans on the Miranzai Valley Border. This system was evidently at the zenith of its power when Lord Lytton wrote the minute to which I have already drawn attention, for para. 63 of the same despatch is thus worded:

> Again, for the reasons given above, I think that the employment of Arbabs, or middlemen, should be discontinued as much as possible. I do not myself believe that it strengthens our hold even upon the small class we thus employ. For every man gratified by employment a host of jealousies are raised against him and ourselves. There is some reason to fear that these personages are not altogether incapable of provoking or promoting difficulties on the frontier in the hope of increasing their own importance; and the police authorities at Peshawar have now ascertained that one of the Arbabs most trusted by the Panjab Govern-

ment on that frontier was carrying on a few months ago a treasonable correspondence with persons in Caubul, which nothing but the man's death enabled us to detect. I admit, however, that there are many occasions on which the services of Arbabs have been, and may again be, most valuable to us, especially in opening communication with frontier tribes; but I think that whenever their services can be dispensed with, and direct communication opened or maintained by our own authorities, this should be done. Even if we could always depend on the absolute loyalty of Arbabs, these men cannot convey to the native the same clear idea of our views and character that he would gain by personal intercourse with British officers.

I have used the words 'hemmed in by heavy work and immense difficulties,' and it is no exaggeration to write so. When your work is of a nature that keeps you occupied from 10 A.M. to nearly 7 P.M., and often up to midnight, there is little time left to interview and mix with the people under your charge or to associate yourself with their feelings. When out in camp in the district, the chances of seeing the headmen of villages and landowners were increased, but what prospect had the civil officer of learning the characters of these men? The time at his disposal was limited. His daily routine work had to be carried out *nolens volens*, whether he interviewed people or not; and by the time he began to know something of the district and its people, ten to one that he found himself transferred to some other charge.

The same remarks will apply to interviewing the jirgas (council of elders) of the independent countries and hills adjoining your charge. If the special tribe concerned had committed some outrage, necessitating their council being summoned to your headquarters, this work had to be carried out through the Khan who had political management of that border. He selected and brought in those men whom it pleased him to produce before you. They were generally individuals who were tied to his fortunes in some way. I can answer for myself that time after time at Hoti-Mardan the presence of these hill men was obnoxious to me; they took up my time, and, in spite of my command of the Persian and Pashtu languages, I felt that I could do no good with them. The change after Ajab Khan's disappearance improved matters, for then I got acquainted with and was permitted to know the leading men in Buner, and in October 1878 they made overtures to help us against the then Amir of Afghanistan. With all my desire to mix with the trans-border men, however, the opportunity—and, what is more, the time—to do so was wanting. It fact, it was an impossibility.

Between the years 1870 and 1879, when I joined the Khyber appointment, I noticed no attempt made to do away with the middleman agency. Taking over the Khyber Range and the tribes concerned in its management, and placing them directly under a British officer, coupled with the death of Arbab Majid Khan and his son, Arbab Futeh Muhammad Khan, at this juncture deprived the Khyber of all Khalil interference in its affairs, and up to July 11, 1897, no Khalil middleman was permitted to have any voice in my work. The drowning of Arbab Sarfaraz Khan in 1886–87 took the Aka and Adam Khel Afridis out of the hands of the Mohmand chiefs, and the death of Bahadur Sher Khan, Bangash, removed another obstacle from the Kohat Pass. Then came the deportation of Muzaffar Khan of Hangu and his son, Bazgul Khan, to Lahore in the year 1891. In the Agror Valley, Ata Muhammad Khan was removed in 1868, and brought back on the representations of the Settlement Officer of the district. Twenty years later his son had to be deported from Agror to Haripur.

Whatever little relief has been given to the Deputy Commissioners and the civil officers of the frontier districts to enable them to mix with their troublesome trans-border neighbours, the agony has been piled on and the work increased in other ways. Those who pass by the Deputy Commissioner's House and Civil Buildings at Peshawar every evening, and notice the crowd collected there until sunset (even in 1898), can bear witness to the manner in which those officers are tied down to their desks by their ordinary civil duties. After discharging these, what time or leisure has the Deputy Commissioner to attend to his trans-border work? It may be said that he has the Assistant Commissioner at Mardan and the Commandant of Border Military Police to assist him. This may be so, but the final orders have to be given by him. Then the last-named official is often changed. In 1883–1885 it was the late Major Nixon. The command was then transferred to Ibrahim Khan, but later on a new Deputy Commissioner put him aside and replaced him by Syad Muhammad Amir. The advent of another Deputy Commissioner in 1892 induced Syad Muhammad Amir to retire on a pension to his free grant lands, some two hours' railway journey from Lahore. A British officer was then appointed, but when the Chitral campaign commenced he was sent away as Political Assistant, and his command for the time being was handed over to the Subadar Major, a Khalil Arbab. Mr. Donald did excellent work in Kohat as Commandant of Border Police after he had become acquainted with the people and after many years' residence there, but just when his stay would have been still more useful to Government he was transferred to the Khyber. The same changes, transfers, &c., occurred in other places, but to dwell more on this subject would be to unduly lengthen this chapter, and render it more tedious to the English reader.

The Panjab policy, then, from 1870 to the time of my departure from Peshawar on April 15, 1898, is in principle the same policy which worked well enough on the North-West Frontier, when selected men were appointed to the Hazara and the Trans-Indian districts. It worked excellently so long as the men were *selected*, and had time to carry on their ordinary civil duties and some leisure to cultivate more direct and frequent intercourse with British subjects under their charge and with the independent tribesmen across the border. But a time came when selection —entire selection—was set aside, and the enormous growth of civil work tied the district officer to his desk all day, and barred his chance of becoming acquainted with the first and prevented all intercourse with the second. Lord Lytton, as Viceroy and Governor-General of India, had made up his mind to apply the knife to this malady, and had fully determined to separate Hazara, Peshawar, Kohat, Bannu, Dera Ismail Khan, Dera Ghazi Khan, with the exception of the Cis-Indus portions of Bannu and Dera Ismail Khan, from the Panjab Province. Everything was ready prepared when the wretched Afghan campaign of 1878-1880 took place, ruined all chances of progress, and sent Lord Lytton back to England. Since then no ruler of India has attempted to re-open this very important question.

The old Panjab policy began to totter in the Sixties, and a fitting landmark would be the year which saw the introduction of the Chief Court into the province. A year or so on this side or that of the period need not be taken into much account. The weakness was discovered and pointed out by a very able Frontier Commissioner, but the subject was pooh-poohed, set aside, and the Panjab officials had little opportunity of learning Major Hugh James's opinions on this important subject. Another difficulty began gradually to make its appearance, and this was that two masters had now to be considered in the land of the five rivers. The Chief Court insisted on its judicial work being done promptly, in accordance with the strict lines of procedure and rules laid down by it; whilst the peace of the frontier required the services of a good, strong administrator, who knew the people and their ways, and a man of this calibre was of far higher value to Government than the frontier lawyer. Moreover, it was not always possible to secure the attainments of a good lawyer and a good frontier officer being combined in one and the same person. But both requirements had to be considered, and this added a fresh link of weakness to the chain, and as this weakness increased year by year, so did the necessity for a change come more prominently into view. And H.E. Lord Lytton was very near the mark when he wanted this frontier change to be carried out in the year 1877 or 1878. I would even prefer placing the year as 1879—i.e. after the signature of the Treaty of Gandamak—for then the Beluchistan Agency was secured. The Khyber had been tacked on to the Panjab charge under circumstances already related, and the fate of Kurram, taken away from Afghanistan, had to be disposed of. There was thus the certainty of a large increase of responsibility and work on the already heavily burdened Panjab Province, and then was the proper time to have carried out the Frontier Separation Scheme.

I am a great opponent of the native Arbab or middleman agency in dealing with our trans-border neighbours. I have the greatest regard for our Asiatic brethren as soldiers, and in any capacity that it pleases Government to employ them except this one, which I would prefer seeing in the hands of Englishmen alone, wherever they could be usefully and safely employed. An Englishman will never intrigue with the trans-border tribesmen against his own Government, and my experience of the Asiatic is that he is certain to do so if he can better himself or injure an enemy or a rival by so doing. The procedure in this is very easy to carry out, and extremely difficult to detect and punish; therefore, the safer side is to avoid all risk, and employ an Englishman alone, keeping the native, the man usually worked in such dilemmas, far in the background. If an English officer had been appointed to do solely political work in the districts of Hazara, Peshawar, Kohat, &c., many years ago, what a number of frontier complications and wars, and consequent expenditure of blood and money, might have been avoided!

I speak in the same language of the middleman who, as chief or Malik of the tribe, is accepted by us as the go-between with his people and the Indian

Government. My experience in the Khyber may be put down in a very few words on this important subject. Let the tribe concerned select one man from each section, or even two men, to receive their allowances and represent their tribal interests. Let them then appoint their Maliks to receive their chiefs' allowances. Pay each separately yourself. If you hand both to the Malik, he robs his tribesmen, gets rich himself, intrigues against Government, and brings on grave difficulties. So the wiser course is not to give him the opportunity of getting dangerous. Giving a Malik power means giving him wealth to injure us, and does not win over his tribesmen, for across the border, in a Pathan community, all men are equal. Amin Khan's case is a good example of a dangerous policy which should never be carried out. The aim of a Government official should be to win over the twenty, thirty, or forty elders from the many sections which form the strength of the tribe concerned. When I explained these matters to the people in authority over me, they turned and said: 'But it is not everyone who can understand these details.' I replied: 'Select your officer, give him time to learn up the people, and these details are exceedingly simple.' In fact, the Malik system, selected to save trouble, causes in the end the gravest inconveniences. The middleman, therefore—whether he be one selected from our own subjects to deal with the trans-border tribesmen, or whether he be one of their own chiefs—has caused the greatest amount of misery and trouble on the Panjab Frontier for the past thirty-five years. And the evils of the system are even now being continued, in spite of every assertion to the contrary, as was witnessed at

Maizar in 1897, and, later on, in the Afridi and Orakzai countries previous to the operations which led to an advance into the heart of Tirah.

There are officers in the Panjab Government, or serving under it, who may say that the employment of English officers to do all the political work on the frontier is objectionable on two grounds: (1) expense; (2) their incompatibility to mix with the trans-border man and understand his ways. There is no very great difficulty in answering these questions. First, as regards expense; this may be greater than in employing solely the Arbab and middleman agency, but if war and bloodshed can be avoided by utilising the services of selected English gentlemen, whatever expenditure is incurred is certainly well spent. What has been the aggregate cost of the wars on that Panjab Frontier? Twenty millions, thirty millions sterling? Who can tell the full amount, and total up the interest alone on the full capital of cost in order to strike a profit and loss account? But let me try a rough guess-work average from the late Afridi, Orakzai, and Mohmand war to show what our losses in one direction have been. The cost of keeping the Khyber Pass open, deducting the gain in octroi in the good years, before H.H. the Amir damaged the trade of Afghanistan, was nearly 150,000 rupees—put it at 200,000 for argument's sake. If the war cost one million sterling only, the interest on this at three per cent. comes to £30,000 = 450,000 rupees = two and a quarter times the cost of keeping the Khyber open. If the war expenditure was increased to two or three millions sterling, the interest would be augmented to £60,000 = 900,000 rupees + £90,000 = 1,350,000 rupees, and this would enable the Panjab Government to maintain four and a half or six and three-fourths Khyber Passes open along their frontier on the interest alone of the money spent on such war. But sometimes acts are carried out which seem unaccountable. My native assistant, whose sanctioned pay was 500 rupees a month, had to be sent away in 1892 for constant intriguing with Maliks, after Malik Amin Khan's escapade had damaged him for good. But all my attempts to get him replaced by a European, although his employment did not cause a pennyworth's increase in the sanctioned expenditure, met with the greatest opposition. I wrote for nearly a year, and, never getting a reply, I determined to do without the native assistant for the time being. I believe my papers never passed Peshawar towards Lahore. Similar remarks will apply to the military officer whose appointment was approved of and submitted by the Panjab Government either at the close of 1891 or the commencement of 1892, and which received the sanction of the Government of India and the Secretary of State for India in Council. He was to have learnt his work, and taken my place when I retired in July 1897. But where was he when this period arrived?

I now come to the question of 'the incompatibility of the English officer mixing with the trans-border man and understanding his ways.' I think this subject is not understood by the officials, who believe in that theory. Mixing with the untrained savage of the hills does not mean that you are to live with the man, or share the same house with him, or partake of food from the one platter. All that the Englishman need do is to encamp in his own tent, with his own staff of servants, wherever he can do so with perfect safety. If he has quarters or a house to reside in, so much the better. In the early mornings, before office work has commenced, or in the evenings when the day's work is over, let him walk out, or sit outside his quarters, and allow any and every savage to come and sit down in the assembly and join freely in the conversation that may be going on. The same thing can be done at Peshawar or any frontier Cantonment station; but I have found it to answer best in the country of the independent hillman in his own home. When some confidence has been assured, these men will speak of their customs, their feuds or friendships, and of what is going on amongst them—information which is not only extremely interesting, but of great service for the future to the Englishman who listens. The germs of confidence once established amidst these people always bear fruit and increase, as I have found out, and the English official is treated with far greater deference and respect than by the British native subject of Peshawar, Rawal Pindi, or of any other part of India. After twenty-nine years' experience of Peshawar, the British native subject would have stolen the last coat off my back if he had seen a chance of doing it with safety. In the Khyber Hills, at Landi Kotal, Tor-Sappar, Shilman valleys, &c., wherever my camp happened to be, it was a point of honour with the independent hillman that nothing was ever removed from it. And the same security was assured to and secured to every visitor, European or native.

I admit that there is another side to this picture, which is not quite so roseate. To go and live in those hills for any length of time means to the average Englishman: considerable personal danger and risk, until a certain period has passed and his reputation has been assured; privations in the way of food, and increased expenditure in securing the ordinary comforts of life; deprivation of English papers, society of English friends, of club, mess, polo, and all amusements. But all these difficulties can be overcome by selecting good officers, who must be good linguists in Persian and Pashtu, for without command of these two languages the English official is utterly useless. But it is also most important that such officers should be treated in a proper spirit. The political appointments on the frontier should be given to the very best men that can be got, and once they have been secured, they should be well paid and retained on that frontier all their time of service, having assistants under them, who will learn their work on the same lines, and take up the duties of their seniors when the time comes for them to do so.

Anything and everything, compatible with sound sense and honour, should be done to put a stop to these frontier wars. Scenes that were enacted during the summer, autumn, and winter of 1897 and the first month of 1898 will not easily be forgotten. Where a family residence, house, or fortress has been destroyed, and some of the male members killed in protecting their lives and property, or where their wives and children have been brought to death by exposure to cold, frost, and snow, feelings of revenge will be cherished, and be remembered when the time comes for paying off the Power who has been the cause of these wrongs. I am certain that the remedy is in our hands, and that it will be found to be a very simple one if the Government of India will only take the frontier management into its own hands. The Panjab system has failed, after a trial of nearly half a century.

It is a matter for some wise expert to decide when the term 'Forward Policy' first came into fashion, and what it really means. Does it cover the period when the British power first went across the Indus in its tide of annexation and conquest after the fall of the Sikhs? Did it come into use between the years 1885 and April 1893, when Lord Roberts was Commander-in-Chief of the army in India? Can it be put down to the date when Colonel Algy Durand was sent to re-open the Gilgit Agency? Or was it first made use of after Sir M. Durand had made his agreement with H.H. Amir Abdur Rahman Khan demarcating the Afghan and British spheres of influence in November 1893? If the question were put to the British public as to what the 'Forward Policy' is, and who inaugurated it, I doubt whether one man out of a thousand could answer the question. It is easy now to lay the blame of the Chitral misadventure on the events of 1895, but it must be recollected that during the years 1873 and 1874 British policy was exceedingly active and energetic in Yarkand, on the Pamirs, and constituted the first Gilgit Agency. Ten years later there was another political mission in the direction of Chitral, Gilgit, Hunza, Mastey, and the Oxus. And, lastly, Sir G. Robertson was hovering about Kafiristan and Chitral between 1890 and 1893, two years previous to his being besieged in Chitral during March and April 1895. I shall therefore try and point out the wars which, in my opinion, can be put down to the 'Panjab Policy,' separating them from those for which the 'Forward School' may be considered answerable.

Let me begin with Hazara. Here there has been no attempt to seize and secure the lands of its independent neighbours, and therefore the 'expedition to Kagan, November 1852,' the 'expedition against the Hasanzais on the Black Mountain, 1853-54,' 'expedition against the Black Mountain tribes, 1868,' 'expedition against the Black Mountain tribes, 1888,' 'expedition against the Black Mountain tribes, 1891,' and the 'Baio expedition, 1892,' cannot be placed to the credit or discredit of the Forward school.

But take the following expeditions: 'The affair with the Hindustani fanatics in January 1854,' 'the affairs at Sheikh Jana and Narinji in 1857,' 'the expedition to Sittana under Major-General Sir S. Cotton, K.C.B., April 1858,' 'the Ambeyla campaign, 1863,' 'the coercion of the Jaduns and Utmanzais, 1864,' 'operations in Baizai, 1847,' 'operations in the Lund Khwar Valley, 1849,' 'expedition against the Ranizais in March 1852,' 'punishment of the Utman Khel in May 1852,' 'second operation in the Ranizai Valley, May 1852,' 'the three small expeditions against Iskhàkot and Sapri, 1878,' 'operations against the Mohmands, 1850,' 'affair at Panjpao, April 1852,' 'against the Michni Mohmands in 1854,' 'affairs with the Mohmands, December and January 1863-64,' and 'the Shabkaddar event of 1897, which brought on the invasion of Mohmand country,' 'the Khyber *débâcle* of 1897, and the invasion of Tirah, 1897-98.' Besides these, there were of lesser note the 'expedition against the Kohat Pass Afridis, 1850,' 'expedition against the Bori Afridis, November 1853,' 'against the Aka Khel Afridis, 1854-55,' 'demonstration against the Hassan Khel section of the Adam Khel Afridis, 1867,' 'closing of the Kohat Pass, 1875–76,' 'Jawaki campaign, 1877–78.' If we turn our attention to the Miranzai Valley, there was 'the expedition under Captain J. Coke, 1851,' a 'second expedition under Brigadier Chamberlain, 1855,' 'expedition into the Kuram Valley, 1856,' 'punishment of the Orakzai tribe in the autumn of 1855 by a force under Brigadier Chamberlain,' 'affair with the Bazotis at the Ublan Pass, 1868,' and the 'two Miranzai expeditions in 1891 and 1892.' We now go further south to the Waziris, and note first of all the 'expedition against the Umarzai section of the Ahmadzais, December 1852,' 'against the Caubul Khel section of the Utmanzais, under Brigadier Chamberlain, December 1859,' 'demonstration against the Caubul Khel Waziris, 1869,' 'expedition against the Mahsud Waziris, April 1860,' 'expedition into the Dawar Valley, 1872,' 'the Shirani expedition, 1853,' 'against the Kasrani tribe, April 1853,' and 'the Bozdar expedition, 1857.'

I need not go further south amongst the Beluch tribes to compile a heavier list of expeditions. For all of these the 'Panjab Policy' is solely answerable. I know that the ordinary English reader will hate wading through a long list of tedious campaigns and expeditions; but it is right that truth, even if tedious, should be revealed, so that the people in England may know that the 'Forward Policy' is not to blame for all the wars, bloodshed, expenditure, and ill-feeling which have taken place on the North-Western Frontier of the Panjab. The 'Forward Policy,' on the other hand, is certainly answerable for the events in Chitral and Malakand, and northwards of the same, since

March 1895, and for the expeditions against the Waziris subsequent to the Durand Demarcation Treaty of 1893.

The greatproblem for the Government in England, for the Secretary of State for India and his Council, and for the Viceroy and Governor-General of India to decide is how the peace of the North-Western Frontier of the Panjab is to be always assured; and in what way, and by what means, the independent tribesmen can be turned into friends instead of being kept enemies of the English Sarkar. That it can be done I am firmly convinced. In the remote past, as history shows, the Seljuk, the Tartar, the Moghul, the Persian Shia, and the Afghan Durani have been able to win the aid and friendship of particular portions of these mountaineers in the invasion of India. History may repeat itself some day once more if ever a Power rises in the future, energetic and strong enough, capable of taking in hand such an undertaking. It may be very difficult, extremely hard, but it is not impossible. If the 'Panjab system,' now under trial for so many years, has ended in complete failure, why not change it for another that may succeed?

The Panjab (or, as its admirers named it at one time, the 'Model' province) is not now the same land of 'the five rivers' which it was when it was turned into a Lieutenant-Governorship. Nor is it by any means the same province which it was when in 1877 Lord Lytton wished to separate the North-West Frontier districts from it. There was the greatest opposition in creating a separate Beluchistan, in severing Kashmir, the Panjab Frontier Force, and the frontier districts from the embraces of the Lahore Government; but Lord Lytton knew that the Panjab was quite large enough to require the entire capabilities of the ablest Governor who could be got in the land, and he had determined on taking a step which he knew would be beneficial first to the Panjab, and, secondly, advantageous to Beluchistan, to Kashmir, to the Panjab Frontier Force, and to the Panjab Frontier districts in getting them away from the Lahore control. Unfortunately, the Afghan war of 1878 broke out, and the frontier districts were left to their fate.

Since 1860 enormous changes have taken place in the Panjab. A railway now runs from Delhi to Peshawar, from Lahore to Karachi, from Lalla Musa towards the Indus, and down its left bank to Multan. The Chief Court has been introduced, and numerous Acts and Rules relating to matters civil, criminal, educational, municipal, police, revenue, and to other subjects have been enacted. Therefore, taking these matters alone, the work of the Lieutenant-Governor has been now doubled, if not trebled. Although the Malakand and Swat have been under the Foreign Office of India since 1895, the Panjab charge has been increased by having the difficult Khyber and Kurram added to it, and since the settlement of the Durand boundary there has been a further increase of difficulties to the westward of the 'Durand line.' The Panjab has an area of 110,667 square miles, or 10,448 square miles less than the total area of the United Kingdom. Its population in 1891 was 20,866,847, a larger population than that of Portugal and Spain together. Besides the territory under British administration, which is as large as Italy, there is an area of one-third that size belonging to thirty-four feudatory native States, with a population of more than four and a quarter millions, of whom the Lieutenant-Governor of the Panjab may be considered the chief. Surely this is an enormous charge for one man to bear the heat and burden of in these days, and it is impossible that one individual can grasp adequately one half of the questions which have to come up to him for decision. But there is still a third and even more difficult charge which he is called upon to understand and grapple with, viz. the frontier tribes across his Panjab Border, split up into numerous clans with divergent interests and with a fighting strength estimated at 200,000 armed men.

How can one man, however able and competent, understand all the various problems which arise from so difficult a charge? Many frontier questions require an expert hand and speedy action to save future complications. They often necessitate an immediate visit to the locality, which the Lieutenant-Governor cannot always undertake, and a knowledge of the Pashtu language, which no Lieutenant-Governor that I know of has yet acquired. I may be in error, but to the best of my belief no Governor of the Panjab has ever been able to converse with the border people in both Persian and Pashtu, and without this colloquial knowledge no man should be allowed to remain permanently in the Trans-Indus districts or be chief over them. An official in those parts does not want to see the Arbabs and Darbaris and city magnates only, who come to him and talk fluent Hindustani. He ought to see the landowner in his own village, and to have the time and be able for himself to ascertain how the revenue, the alienation of land, the cost of litigation, and various other matters affect each village community.

The Panjab Province is increasing in importance every day with new canals, growth of trade, and a development of wealth all over, especially in its capital Lahore. It can with ease and credit carry out a political 'Hari Kari,' and sever its future connection with its trans-frontier districts. This may be very painful at first, but in the end the province will rejoice over the act, and the frontier will be glad. The only way to prevent future wars on the frontier and to create a friendly impression on the wild man of the independent hills, is to alter the system which has proved useless for thirty-five years. Replace it by the scheme which His Excellency Lord Lytton intended carrying out when he was Viceroy of India, and which met with the approval of the Marquis of Salisbury and the Government then in power. Let there be a Chief Commissioner or officer on special duty (no matter what name he may be called by), one well up in Persian and Pashtu, and able to visit every spot wherever his presence is required. Let him be supplied with a sufficient staff to carry on the higher civil, criminal, and revenue details, so as to give him sufficient leisure for his border work. Let Deputy Commissioners, Assistant Commissioners, &c., do purely and solely the civil work of their districts. And, lastly, have political and police officers to undertake the trans-border police duties. Let all these be selected officers, with fair pay and promotion, passing their entire service on that frontier, with no danger of transfer to a Cis-Indus charge. Give this scheme, which has thus been briefly noticed, a fair trial, and there is every certainty of a vast improvement in the relations between the Indian Government and the independent hillmen quickly following.

CHAPTER XX

THE TRIBES OF THE KHYBER

It is necessary to say a few parting words of the people, with whom I have lived and been associated continuously for so many years. The tribes of the Khyber Pass consist of six sections of the Afridi and the Shinwaris of Landi Kotal, making in all seven. I give their names, and their tribal limits on the Jamrud-Khyber-Dakka road: (1) Kuki Khel from Jamrud to where Mackeson's road begins; (2) from there to Shagai come the Sipah Afridis; (3) the Kamrai hold from Shagai to Sultan Tarra; (4) Kambar Khel from Sultan Tarra to the white Mosque of Ali Masjid just below the Fort; (5) from the Mosque to Gurgurra is the limit of the Malikdin Khel; (6) Gurgurra to the Kandar ravine near Garhi Lala Beg belongs to the Zakha Khel; (7) westwards to Tor Kham the responsibility rests with the Shinwaris of Landi Kotal. Three other sections (Kam and Loi Shilmanis and Mullagoris) on the North, who own and hold the Tartarra route, complete the ten tribes of the whole Khyber political charge. And what manner of men are these, who now inhabit the historical entrance into the plains of India—an entrance which has seen Persian, and Greek, Seljuk, Tartar, Mongol, and Durani conquerors, with the hosts of Alexander, Mahmud of Ghuzni, Genghis

Khan, Timur-i-Lang, Baber, Nadir Shah, Ahmad Shah, and numerous other warrior chiefs pass and repass through its famous rocky defiles during a period of 2,000 years?

Mackeson, writing of them, says: 'The Afridis are a most avaricious race, desperately fond of money. Their fidelity is measured by the length of the purse of the seducer, and they transfer their obedience and support from one party to another of their own clansmen, according to the comparative liberality of the donation.' Another authority says: 'Ruthless, cowardly robbery, cold blooded, treacherous murder are to an Afridi the salt of life. Brought up from his earliest childhood amid scenes of appalling treachery and merciless revenge, nothing can ever change him; as he has lived—a shameless, cruel savage—so he dies.' One more authority: 'On the whole,' says Elphinstone, 'they are the greatest robbers among the Afghans, and I imagine have no faith or sense of honour; for I never heard of anybody hiring an escort of Khyberis to secure his passage through their country—a step which always ensures a traveller's safety in the lands of any other tribe.'

To this let me add my little experience of nearly eighteen years, secured after a longer insight of Afridi character inside and outside their country than generally falls to the lot of any English official. The Afridi lad from his earliest childhood is taught by the circumstances of his existence and life to distrust all mankind, and very often his near relations, heirs to his small plot of land by right of inheritance, are his deadliest enemies. Distrust of all mankind, and readiness to strike the first blow for the safety of his own life, have therefore become the maxims of the

KHYBER RIFLES AND AFRIDIS

Afridi. If you can overcome this mistrust, and be kind in words to him, he will repay you by great devotion, and he will put up with any punishment you like to give him except abuse. It took me years to get through this thick crust of mistrust, but what was the after-result? For upwards of fifteen years I went about unarmed amongst these people. My camp, wherever it happened to be pitched, was always guarded and protected by them. The deadliest enemies of the Khyber Range, with a long record of blood-feuds, dropped those feuds for the time being when in my camp. Property was always safe, and the only record of anything being ever removed was the gear belonging to a trooper of the Khyber Rifles taken away from the serai at Landi Kotal, which was a case of enmity, but every item was brought back and placed at Malik Walli Muhammad Khan's gateway in the Khyber. The only loss ever incurred by me was that I have already related, when my pony, Colonel Barrow's charger, Captain Swanstone's pony and some ten mules were carried off from the camp of the Second Division Tirah Field Force at Suvikot on December 17, 1897. Time after time have the Afridi elders and jirgas supported me even against their own Maliks. Lastly, when at Bagh in the maidan of Tirah during November, December 1897, with war, and burning houses and desolation surrounding them, when I told the old men of the Afridis in reply to their cry, that it was out of my power to help them then, the jirga with tears in their eyes replied: 'Never mind, Sahib, whatever happens we are earnestly praying that you may not be injured in this campaign.' These old men were witnessing the destruction of everything that was dear and sweet to them in life—

the burning of their homes, built up with enormous labour, and after several years of work, for in Tirah, forts are not built by contract. And yet in that supreme hour of their distress they had a thought for the safety of the Kafir who had done nothing for them, except to try to be their friend.

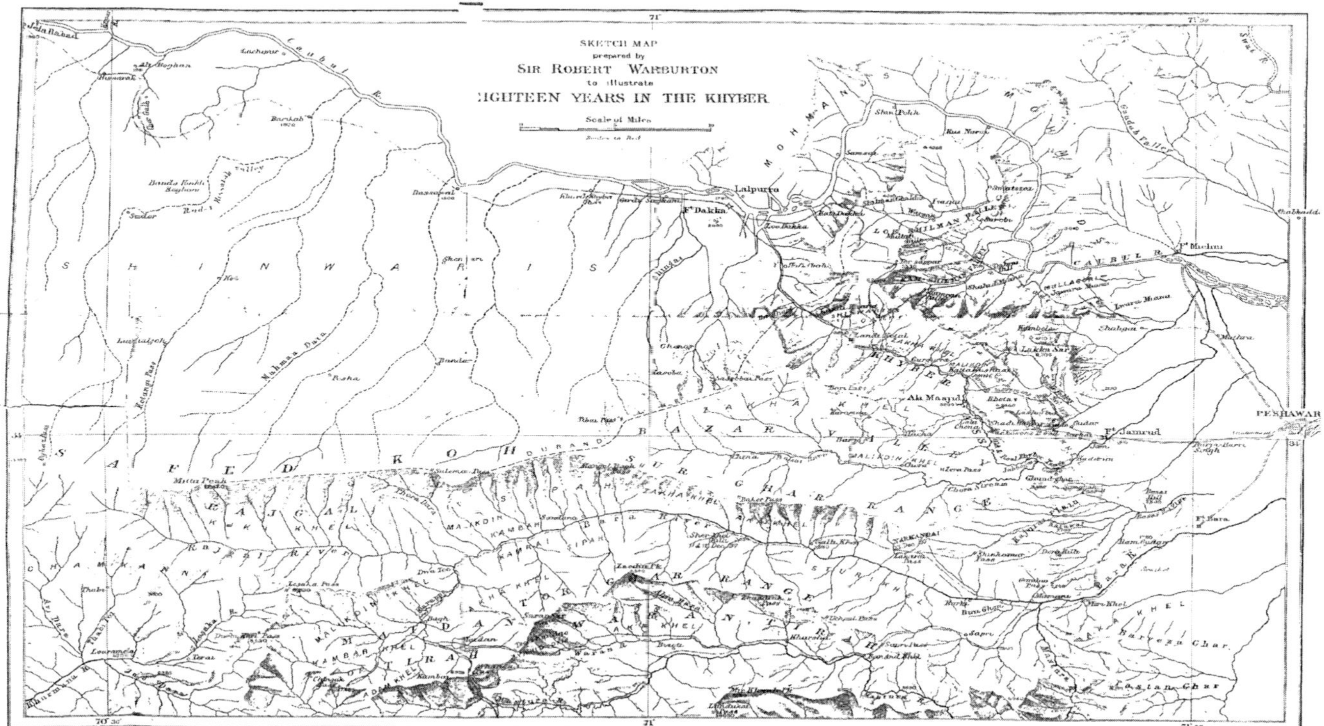

London: John Murray

Stanford's Geog! Estab! London.

INDEX

PRINTED BY
SPOTTISWOODE AND CO., NEW-STREET SQUARE
LONDON